Praise for

# After the Fall

"In a fast-moving, richly researched volume that breaks new ground, Kasey S. Pipes describes that most improbable of political journeys, the post-presidential return of Richard Nixon, this time to the private role of advising Presidents Reagan, Bush, and Clinton on foreign policy. Drawing on private Nixon family records, letters, and memos, Pipes shows the former president was far more active in helping shape America's grand global strategy—and more successful—than previously realized, even as he suffered political exile. The story is a must for anyone wanting to understand Nixon's life after Watergate."

—**Karl C. Rove,** deputy chief of staff in the George W. Bush administration and author of *The Triumph of William McKinley: Why the Election of 1896 Still Matters*

"Kasey S. Pipes's *After the Fall* is a book worth reading; it is also a book worth thinking about in deeply reflective ways. At one level it is an insightful chronicle of Richard Nixon's return to grace as he deftly uses his foreign policy expertise as the vehicle to establish new relationships with policy makers, politicians, and the public. Pipes's depiction of the eulogies for Nixon by Senator Dole and President Clinton reads as an evocative exclamation point for this groundbreaking story of Nixon's successful twenty-year return journey. Yet at another, more reflective level it is a study in the power of resilience, determination, and character in shaping a life—Nixon's, to be sure, but more broadly perhaps, our own as well."

—**Larry Taylor,** U.S. Ambassador to Estonia, 1995–97

"Three and a half years after departing the White House in disgrace, on the occasion of his sixty-fifth birthday, Richard Nixon contemplated the future. 'I had to decide,' he wrote, 'what to do with the rest of my life.' The road less traveled in Nixon scholarship is the twenty-year span following his presidency. In *After the Fall*, Kasey Pipes fills in the missing parts of this journey. Its apt subtitle is *The Remarkable Comeback of Richard Nixon*. Nixon's regeneration was remarkable. So is this book."

—**Carl Cannon,** Washington Bureau Chief, RealClearPolitics

"Based on his exclusive access to Nixon's post-presidential papers, Kasey Pipes has written a fascinating account of Richard M. Nixon's last and greatest personal crisis: rebuilding his credibility after Watergate. Pipes has mastered and carefully weighed the facts, and he tells the story well."

—**Bruce Buchanan,** professor emeritus, Department of Government, the University of Texas at Austin

# After the Fall

# After the Fall

## The Remarkable Comeback of Richard Nixon

## Kasey S. Pipes

REGNERY
HISTORY

Regnery History™ is a trademark of Salem Communications Holding Corporation
Regnery® is a registered trademark of Salem Communications Holding Corporation

Cataloging-in-Publication data on file with the Library of Congress

ISBN 978-1-62157-284-8
ebook ISBN 978-1-62157-560-3

Published in the United States by
Regnery History
An imprint of Regnery Publishing
A Division of Salem Media Group
300 New Jersey Ave NW
Washington, DC 20001
www.RegneryHistory.com

Manufactured in the United States of America

10 9 8 7 6 5 4 3 2 1

Books are available in quantity for promotional or premium use. For information on discounts and terms, please visit our website: www.Regnery.com.

*For Lacie, Lincoln, Crosby, and Betsy*
*and*
*In Memory of Brett Foster*

# Contents

*When they kept on questioning him,*
*he straightened up and said to them,*
*"Let any one of you who is without sin*
*be the first to throw a stone."*
*—John 8:7*

"Failure," Truman Capote wrote, "is the condiment that gives success its flavor." In every life and in every story the fruits of victory are planted with the seeds of defeat. Every setback teaches lessons; the question is, will the defeated listen and learn?

What follows is the story of the final years of the great political tragedy of American history. Richard Nixon's fall from power was Shakespearean. So was the man himself. In some ways, he symbolized the American story: born to a family of little means, finding his way in the world through his own hard work and intellect, and reaching the top of the greasy pole in Washington, D.C. But then at the height of his power, he lost it all.

Entire libraries' worth of books have been written about Watergate. But comparatively little has been written about what happened after Nixon left the White House.

This book is not a book about power; it is a book about the *loss* of power. What does the most powerful man in the world do once he is forced into exile? What happens when the flame turns to ash? Like Napoleon Bonaparte at Elba, Nixon was a restless soul. But he didn't dream of military takeovers; he dreamed of relevance. He wanted to redeem himself and be able once again to use his greatest gift—his mind. He envisioned not a rehabilitation of his career, but a redefining of his life. He not only wanted to be accepted again, but he also wanted to help shape foreign policy for years to come. How Nixon achieved both of those goals is told in this book. And in many ways the achievement of those goals represented the greatest triumph of all for Nixon—overcoming Watergate.

It should also be noted that this book doesn't deal with the specifics of Watergate. The entire ordeal predates the period of time covered in this book. Watergate is mentioned in these pages only when Nixon wrestles with the aftermath of the scandal. In these pages, we see Nixon unconfined and unbound by the trappings of presidential power.

Few books have been written about Nixon's post-Watergate years. Robert Sam Anson's *Exile*, Stephen Ambrose's *Ruin and Recovery*, and Monica Crowley's two books about her time with Nixon largely represent the canon on Nixon's post-presidency. And none of them covers the entire twenty years from Watergate until his death in 1994. This is the first book ever to do so.

The chief reason why this rich quarry had not been mined previously is because the Nixon post-presidential papers are privately owned by the Nixon family. Although they reside at the Richard Nixon Presidential Library and Museum in Yorba Linda, California, under a deposit agreement, they are not accessible to researchers unless researchers are granted access by the family.

In 2008 I was fortunate to secure special permission from both Tricia Nixon Cox and Julie Nixon Eisenhower to use the post-presidential papers in writing this book. That access allowed me to become the first researcher to pore through the final twenty years of Nixon's papers—including his memos, letters, and notes from meetings.

Those papers revealed a man who was singed by the fire of Watergate, yes. But Nixon ultimately was strengthened by a lifetime in the fire. He was determined to make the most of the time left to him on this earth.

The story in the pages that follow is the story of resilience, of resolve, and yes, of redemption. As Charles Krauthammer—a columnist Nixon enjoyed reading—once wrote, everyone experiences challenges: "The catastrophe that awaits everyone from a single false move, wrong turn, fatal encounter. Every life has such a moment. What distinguishes us is whether—and how—we ever come back."

This is the story of how Nixon faced the aftermath of his catastrophe—Watergate—and of his remarkable efforts at a comeback.

# A Note from the Author

I had thought writing a book about Nixon's post-presidency would be difficult. I was wrong; it was almost impossible.

But as I tried to navigate through the mist of the darkest period in Nixon's life as best I could, I had one constant to serve as my compass and guide—Nixon's post-presidential papers. These papers, housed at the Nixon Library in Yorba Linda, are not open to researchers. They are owned by the family and had never before been shared with a historian. For the first time ever, the family granted access to a researcher. Once I obtained the family's blessing to use these records, I made the strategic decision to focus mostly on them in the research and writing of this book.

This proved to be the right decision, which became clearer when I began doing interviews for the book. Some of Nixon's associates declined to talk to me. Several others did, and they are quoted throughout the book. But from start to finish, the papers guided the book. I used the interviews mainly to find out more about what I had found in the papers. While people's memories can falter,

The Richard Nixon Research Library houses Nixon's post-presidential papers, but they are owned by the Nixon family and are not accessible to researchers without the family's permission. (Jeremy Thompson)

documents—though they too must be carefully studied for context, intent, and motive—tend to be the most reliable resources.

The research I conducted at the Nixon Library, as well as the interviews that I conducted, enabled me to make numerous discoveries about the final twenty years of Nixon's life—a remarkably active period for the former president.

I was able to examine Tricia Cox's personal account in her diary of her father's resignation and its immediate aftermath. Cox writes in a very vivid manner and her firsthand account of these events is replete with great attention to detail and fascinating vignettes. Her story of the exchange with George H. W. Bush has never been published before; it demonstrates how difficult Watergate was for the people who were living through it.

I was also able to review Nixon's own post-resignation diary entries about his failing health and near-death experience in the hospital. These entries showed how frightened the man was and how close he believed he was to death. Though much has been written about Nixon's surgery, Nixon's own thoughts at the time are new territory.

Former Nixon staffer Ken Khachigian has granted very few interviews since his time with Nixon. He moved to San Clemente to work
with Nixon during the early days following his resignation and was
able to paint a portrait of what the former president looked and
sounded like following the traumatic resignation.

I was able again to rely on Nixon's own diary as he described his
return to health and the beginnings of his career as an author.

And I was able to interview key Nixon associates for new material
on the Frost-Nixon interviews. Khachigian gave me the never-before-
reported story of how Nixon's on-air "confession"—which the Frost
movie portrayed as an accident on Nixon's part—actually came
about. This is all new territory.

I discovered from Nixon's letters and memos that he was far more
involved in advising Ronald Reagan's campaign than had previously
been known. The ex-president sent the campaign ideas and even
made successful appointment recommendations once Reagan won
the election.

Nixon's private papers reveal that he continued to be a powerful
influence on the Reagan White House. He cultivated relationships
with key Reagan advisors like Mike Deaver. The idea of the Saturday
morning radio address was actually Nixon's idea. More importantly,
he worked through aides like National Security Advisor Bud McFarlane to shape Reagan's negotiations with Mikhail Gorbachev. Until
now, we haven't fully appreciated Nixon's role in advising Reagan on
how to use the Strategic Defense Initiative (SDI) in those negotiations
and how those negotiations shaped the course of U.S.-Soviet relations
and changed history. Again, these are all new discoveries.

He continued as an outside counselor to President Bush and later
President Clinton. But Nixon's pace did begin to slow in the 1990s.

Although trying to influence policymakers remained a large part
of his post-presidential work, Nixon also worked with friends to help
refurbish his own legacy. I discovered that he was more deeply
involved in the writing of a biography of himself and in its sale to a

publisher than has ever before been reported, and that Nixon actually provided questions for an interview of himself on CBS. And he made peace with old enemies. Hubert Humphrey and George McGovern both went out of their way to help their former adversary as he climbed his way out of exile.

In addition, I uncovered numerous personal writings in which Nixon reflected on his life, his fall from grace, and his attempts to get back up again.

The papers showed a Nixon insistent on forging ahead. "Remember Lot's wife," he would sometimes remind friends, of the Old Testament story, saying, "don't look back." He was determined to look ahead. Did he have nefarious ulterior motives, as his critics claim? I'll leave it to others to read and decide for themselves. But I imagine anyone in his position would try and stage some kind of a comeback. In that sense, his motives were simply human.

What I discovered in working through Nixon's letters and documents from 1974 to 1994 was a man with a restless mind who never stopped working. Indeed, he never stopped working as a way to keep his restless mind sharp. This twenty-year period was the most prolific part of Nixon's life in terms of his own writing. He wrote eight books—not including his memoirs—and his books, while touching virtually every public policy issue, mostly focused on foreign policy. As this book demonstrates, many of these ideas had a direct impact on national policy.

The papers I spent so much time with ultimately showed a man who never stopped thinking, writing, and influencing from the dawn of his exile to the dusk of his life.

Kasey S. Pipes
January 10, 2019
Washington, D.C.

# Chapter One

# The Beginning of the End

*"That's enough."*

"Hey, you're better looking than I am, why don't you stay here?"[1]

A forced smile creased the man's face as he spoke to the young aide who had been sitting in the leather chair behind the oak desk and working with the television crew as it tested the lights and sound. It was a few minutes before nine o'clock in the evening (EDT).

"Blondes, they say, photograph better than brunettes," the man said, settling gently into the leather chair. He sat at the oak desk, nervously fingering a stack of papers as he looked around the room. As the technicians found the right camera angle and artists touched up his makeup, the man rested his face on his left hand and continued his banter with the young aide.

"You are a blonde, aren't you? A redhead?" The man's view was obstructed by the glare of the television lights.

"Brunette, sir."

1

Richard Nixon becomes the first president of the United States to resign from office. At this point, he has not had time to think much about what he will do as an ex-president. (Courtesy of the Richard Nixon Presidential Library and Museum)

"Well, we're the same." Dressed smartly in a dark blue suit and tie with a small American flag pin on his left lapel, the man looked down at the stack of papers that he held with both hands. Then he looked straight ahead.

"Do you have an extra camera in case the lights go out?" he asked, squinting his eyes.

The man continued to banter with the group of aides. Mild anger appeared only once when photographer Ollie Atkins took too many pictures.

"That's enough," he said curtly. "My friend Ollie always wants to take a lot of pictures." The coerced smile returned to his face. He began to practice reading from the text in his hands.

"Good evening, this is the thirty-seventh time I have spoken to you from this office where so many decisions have been made that shaped the history of our nation." The man behind the desk stopped and waited for feedback from the television crew, who assured him that he looked and sounded fine. It was almost time.

He turned his attention back to his photographer, a stern tone coursing through his voice: "Ollie, only the CBS crew will be allowed in here.... No, there will be no picture." He waved his hand from left to right for emphasis. "Did you take one just now? That's it."

Then the man turned his attention to another group of people: "Now, all Secret Service...are there Secret Service in the room?" He waited for an answer and performed another wave of the hand: "Out." With most of the room now cleared of staff members, a few more moments of banter with the television crew ensued. The red light went on, the camera rolled, and Richard Nixon announced to the world that he was resigning from the presidency.

It was 9:01 p.m. on August 8, 1974.[2]

Chapter Two

# In Exile

*"It's only a beginning."*

O ne of the last people to leave the White House the next day
had been one of the first to know the end was coming.
Nixon's elder daughter, Tricia Cox, had visited her father
in July at "La Casa Pacifica," his home in San Clemente, California.
The large Spanish-style Mission Revival mansion was perched on
a cliff overlooking the Pacific Ocean. For years, a small seven-hole
golf course on the property had been managed by Republican Party
volunteers. No more. That July, Tricia and her husband, Ed, walked
to the course and found it "wasted, neglected, ugly, dead." She
remembered, "Ed and I came upon it on our first stroll around the
grounds, and its quality of finality, of hopelessness smote us with
an almost physical intensity. Ed tried to overcome this feeling with
nervous levity. He said, 'Looks like someone forgot to water the
golf course.'"[1]

The symbolism was not lost on Tricia: if Nixon's friends
couldn't take care of his house in San Clemente, there was little
hope that his friends could save his presidency in Washington.

Now just one month later, she prepared to join her father as he entered his exile. After delivering his resignation speech on the night of August 8, Nixon left the Oval Office and walked past the Rose Garden and into the residence where his wife, Pat, along with Tricia and Ed and his younger daughter, Julie, and her husband, David, embraced him.

"As I patted him on the back, I could feel the perspiration that had drenched his coat," Tricia said.[2] Later on as the family made its way down a hallway, they could hear a crowd outside. Initially the family thought it was a group of supporters. But when they moved closer to the window to listen to what the crowd was chanting, they heard jarring shouts from Pennsylvania Avenue: "Jail to the Chief!"

The next morning—Nixon's last day in office—Edward and Tricia decided to walk through the grounds of the Rose Garden, where they had been married just three years before.

Their stroll would not provide the solace they were seeking.

A fierce sun beat down on the couple as they entered the garden first created by Woodrow Wilson's wife, Edith. As guests began walking to the East Room for the president's farewell to the White House staffers, many of them came through the Rose Garden. A procession line of sorts developed as staff members and other attendees spotted Ed and Tricia and sought to comfort them. Republican National Committee (RNC) Chairman George H. W. Bush extended his hand and recalled "what a lovely wedding" the couple had had in the Rose Garden.

Tricia was appalled. These well-intentioned comments struck her as "inappropriate," given the context of her father's political demise. She found herself in no mood for pleasant memories or funeral-like condolences.[3]

Beyond the White House, political leaders—past and future—were celebrating the demise of the president. Nixon's resignation, Senator Hubert Humphrey told reporters, represented "a personal tragedy for the president and a new hope for the nation." Nixon's opponent in the 1972 election, George McGovern, told reporters that what "was wrong with Watergate was not just that the president's associates got caught, but what they did."

And a Senate lawyer who had been investigating Watergate expressed her shock at what she had heard on the Watergate tapes. "He justified and rationalized what he had previously said in order to deny or minimize his involvement in ongoing White House efforts to defy the laws and the Constitution," lawyer Hillary Clinton claimed to her friends.

Now the time had come for Nixon to say his farewell to his staff. As the ceremony itself began, the two daughters and their two husbands joined Pat Nixon and stood behind the president. He struggled to fight back tears as he spoke: "It's only a beginning, always. The young must know it. The old must know it. It must always sustain us because the greatness comes not when things go always good for you, but the greatness comes and you are really tested when you take some knocks, some disappointments, when sadness comes, because only if you have been in the deepest valley can you ever know how magnificent it is to be on the highest mountain...."

Nixon also talked at length about his mother, calling her a "saint." But he could not bring himself to mention the other women in his life. With his wife and two daughters standing there, the president feared that talking about them would be too much. "I wasn't about to mention her or Tricia or Julie and have them break down in front of all the people in the country," he would later explain to a friend.[4]

In fact, the Nixon women had been holding Nixon up during the last few days. Pat, especially, had always been strong. She had always had to be that way. Born Thelma Catherine Ryan, her father nicknamed her "Pat" because she had been born on the day before

St. Patrick's Day. Throughout her life, she had grown accustomed to traveling down a hard road. As a child, she lost first her mother and then her father to illness. As a result, she grew up in a hurry. A stoic façade would cover her the rest of her life. But beyond it, she could be warm and loving with her family. She had been a rock of strength for her husband during those last few days. She remained defiant to the end, not wanting her her husband to resign.

"Dick has done so much for the country," she said to a friend, asking, "Why is this happening?"

With the brief farewell ceremony over, the Nixons left the East Room and made their way down the stairs and through the hallway to the Diplomatic Reception Room. The Fords awaited them there. Handshakes and good wishes ensued.

"Drop us a line if you get the chance," Ford told Nixon awkwardly. "Let us know how you are doing." Then the Nixons exited the door to the South Lawn where Marine One waited.[5]

Ed and Tricia boarded the helicopter while David and Julie stayed behind and stood by President and Mrs. Ford on the South Lawn. As

Nixon says farewell to Vice President Gerald Ford before he boards Marine One. Ford would soon be faced with a monumental choice about Nixon's legal fate. (Oliver F. Atkins)

he reached the top of the stairs to the helicopter, Nixon defiantly raised his arms in his trademark "V for Victory" salute. Then he turned and entered the helicopter.

On board, the family looked for the name cards designating their assigned seats. As the helicopter rose and hovered over the White House, a housekeeper in the Lincoln Bedroom window waved a farewell with a white handkerchief.

There was an attempt at small talk. Ed tried to lift Nixon's spirits by saying that he had left at the height of his career with "the nation at peace and the economy strong." Nixon said nothing. Then Ed spoke of the future. The "reconciliation period would take ten years," he said. Nixon agreed.[6]

At Andrews Air Force Base, the presidential party exited the helicopter and boarded Air Force One for the last time. At noon during

Nixon defiantly makes his trademark V for Victory sign as he boards Marine One to leave the White House after his resignation. On the helicopter, Nixon's son-in-law told him it might take ten years for the public to accept him again. (Oliver F. Atkins)

the flight, some of the passengers aboard the plane gathered to watch a televised broadcast of Gerald Ford as he was sworn in to office. Nixon remained ensconced in the back cabin. Those who watched the ceremony were given headphones to hear the audio more clearly. Ford made no mention of his predecessor, a fact not lost on the Nixon party. "A shallow, selfish speech from a little man," Tricia privately fumed. As the plane flew over Missouri and Ford became the thirty-eighth president of the United States, its call signal changed from Air Force One to SAM 27000.

Later in the flight, Nixon emerged and attempted to lighten the mood. "I think I'd like a martini," the now-former president announced. The crew did its part to maintain a presidential ambience. A fancy lunch was served: prime rib accompanied by potatoes and tossed salad and topped off with cheesecake.[7]

No one did more to encourage the passengers than Nixon. "Is everybody enjoying the trip?" he asked as he made his way down the aisle. No one answered.

Pilot Ralph Albertazzie emerged from the cockpit to speak to the ex-president.

"Ralph," Nixon said to his longtime pilot, "you know that before we went to China, I told you that when we got back, I'd make you a general. I really meant to do that. But like so many other things I meant to do...." Nixon couldn't finish the thought. Even in making small talk, he couldn't help but stumble against the fact that he no longer served as president.

Nixon soon composed himself and continued his greetings. When he came upon staffers Frank Gannon and Diane Sawyer, he said to Gannon, "I see you remembered to bring along the good-looking girls."[8]

As the plane began its descent into Southern California, the passengers prepared to land. As the plane got closer to the ground, Tricia looked out the window and noticed that a mass of people had assembled at El Toro Marine Corps Air Station. She could make out American flags and homemade signs. The passengers grew excited at the prospect of a welcoming crowd.

"Down there is the first spontaneous demonstration for Richard Nixon that was never planned," Frank Gannon joked.[9]

Nixon wondered if he should say something to the crowd. Ed and Tricia told him he should. After the plane landed on Runway 43, it taxied to a stop. Now the crowd of about five thousand people could be seen as they cheered and sang "God Bless America."

The scene moved Nixon. Again he asked if he should say something. "Yes," Tricia answered, saying, "it would mean a good deal to them." She knew it would mean even more to him.[10]

As Nixon stepped onto the jetway, he thrust his arms out one more time in the familiar "V for Victory" sign. The crowd roared its approval. He then made his way to a bouquet of microphones set up on the tarmac just in front of the crowd.

"With all the time that I have which could be useful," he said, "I'm going to continue to work for opportunity and understanding among the people in America. I am going to continue—we are all going to continue—to be proud of the fact that we, too, are Californians and we're home again." The crowd cheered its approval.[11]

Then, as he had so many times before, he turned and began walking to the helicopter that would take him to La Casa Pacifica. Only this time Marine One would not be waiting for him; it would be a small Marine Huey.

"Oh, no," Tricia sighed when she saw the helicopter representing the loss of presidential power.

"This is best," Ed responded, adding, "let the change be gradual."[12]

Before boarding the helicopter, the former president took one last picture with Albertazzie.

"I'm sorry it's ending this way," the president said emotion, creeping into his voice.

"I am, too, Mr. President," the pilot responded.[13]

When the helicopter landed a few minutes later in San Clemente, the Nixon family was surprised at how good the grounds at La Casa Pacifica looked. The overgrowth that Tricia had seen in July had been tended to by neighbors. Motivated by sympathy for their neighbor, local residents had worked on the yard so that Richard Nixon would at least see a beautiful lawn and garden when he arrived. Tears filled Nixon's eyes as he walked onto the patio and heard the gentle cascade of water from the pyramid-shaped fountain with a statue of Cupid at the top. He was home.

Later that night, the family gathered in the living room before dinner. This was the largest room in the house and it included Nixon's baby grand piano and a Spanish-tiled fireplace. Exhausted and emotional, Nixon slumped on the couch, again spoke of his mother, and again referred to her as a saint. He also spoke of his policy goals that would remain unfinished and how he had tried to create peace in the world. And once more he spoke of disappointing his family.

"I hope I haven't let you down," he said. Then he turned away and began crying.

# Chapter Three

# The Pardon

*"Tell me what prison is like."*

R esigning the presidency proved to be the beginning of Nixon's troubles—not the end. Within days of his arrival in San Clemente, the former president began to see the size and scope of what he was facing. Lawsuits began to be filed by political opponents and concerned citizens who felt that the former president should be held accountable for Watergate. Reporters surrounded his home and the prospect of a criminal trial loomed over him.

Nixon responded to the chaos by seeking refuge in an organized routine. Thanks to a two hundred thousand dollar transition fund, he could pay a staff with government money for a few months. Colonel Jack Brennan, a tough marine who connected well with Nixon, now effectively served as his chief of staff. But as is often the case when someone is recovering from shock, an element of denial permeated the air. The post-presidency staff meetings bordered on the surreal.

"I've called you here to discuss an important topic," he said at one such meeting, "and that is, what are we going to do about the economy this year?"[1]

He made time for visitors. Long an introvert, Nixon seemed to be willing—and even eager—to see old friends. They were typically shocked by his appearance and demeanor. His always slender frame now appeared even thinner. Dark bags hung under his eyes. He slumped in his chair. One who saw him early in his exile was Egil "Bud" Krogh Jr., who had served time in jail for his role as a member of the Plumbers, a group of political operatives who had broken the law while attempting to find and punish Nixon staffers who leaked information to the media. In their meeting, the former president got right to the point.

"Tell me what prison is like," Nixon pressed Krogh. After Krogh talked about his experience in jail, the conversation turned to the burglary of Daniel Ellsberg's psychiatrist's office. Nixon shocked Krogh by asking if he as president had known about the break-in. Krugh told him no.

"Do you think I should plead guilty?" Nixon persisted.

"Do you feel guilty?" Krogh responded.

"No, I don't," he answered. "I just don't."

"Then you can't, you can't do that," Krogh told him.[2]

Nixon spent most of his days inside a prefabricated office building next to La Casa Pacifica. Each morning around seven o'clock, he would get into a golf cart and ride the few yards to the office. Invariably dressed in a dark suit and tie, he would meet with staff, make phone calls, and talk about his future with guests and aides.

He was aging: the dark hair was seasoned by a tinge of gray, the ski-jump nose looked more pronounced, and the loose jowls looked even looser. His voice often broke and his eyes sometimes moistened as he spoke.[3]

Visitors encouraged him to occupy his mind with a project. Ron Ziegler, who had been his press aide, urged him to get busy writing his memoirs. But before he could begin that process, emissaries from the White House contacted him to discuss his legal fate. President Gerald Ford was more and more convinced that a pardon might save the country from years of Watergate turmoil.

Back in Washington at a meeting in the Oval Office, Ford contemplated the implications of a pardon. The president, Ford's transition team head Phil Buchen, White House Chief of Staff Al Haig, and Robert Hartman, who had been Ford's chief of staff as vice president, discussed Ford's options. The presence of both Haig and Hartman demonstrated the inner conflict that plagued the Ford White House from the beginning. To ensure continuity, Ford had kept Haig on after Nixon left. But because he wanted his own team, he had promoted Hartman to the role of counselor to the president. The two men saw things very differently, and many in the White House suspected that Haig was still loyal to Nixon.

But even if his staff wasn't getting along, Ford very much looked and acted like a president just days into the job. A fit and trim man, he still looked like the former football star that he had been in his younger days at the University of Michigan. Dressed in a dark suit and puffing on his pipe, he talked over his options with his senior staffers.

Just a few days earlier, President Ford had spoken to the country for the first time as its chief executive. In the same speech that the Nixon family watched him deliver from Air Force One as they traveled to California, the new president tried to reassure the country. Ford had long been widely respected on the Hill; indeed, his character was one of the virtues that made him the perfect replacement when Spiro Agnew left the vice presidency in shame. Yet few in

America had ever heard Ford speak until that fateful day in August 1974.

He did not disappoint. What some in the Nixon family found offensive, millions of Americans found reassuring.

"Our Constitution works," he told the country. "Our great Republic is a government of laws and not of men. Here the people rule." But the speech's most powerful and memorable moment came when he directly addressed Watergate: "Our long national nightmare is over."

The speech had been a success. The country seemed eager to give the new president a chance and even more eager to be done with Watergate. Now as Ford sat behind the Wilson Desk that Nixon had used in the Oval Office, he thought of his promise to the country that Watergate was over. That promise meant he would have to deal head-on with the issue of Nixon's criminal liability.

Ford thought through all the reasons for why pardoning Nixon would make sense. It would save the country the drama of watching a former president go through a criminal trial. It would keep Watergate from dragging on for months, if not years. And it would get the inevitable pardon—which any president would almost certainly feel constrained to confer on the ex-president if he were convicted and about to be sent to prison—done and out of the way. In short, it would mark the true end of the long national nightmare.

To the simple man from Grand Rapids, it was a simple question. "If eventually, why not now?" he asked the men in the Oval Office. No one disputed his logic. But Buchen tried to stall. The head of the president's transition team may have been anticipating the backlash Ford would feel from the country.

"Is this the right time?" he asked.

Ford remained unconvinced. "Will there ever be a right time?"

Haig excused himself to make a phone call. In his absence, Hartman made one last attempt to stop the pardon. And he tried to use Ford's own words to convince him.

A few days earlier, Ford, while addressing reporters at the White House, had been asked by Helen Thomas of United Press International (UPI) if he would pardon Nixon. Hartman had the transcript with him and quoted it back to the president, saying that "until any legal process has been undertaken, I think it is unwise and untimely for me to make any commitment."

Ford pushed back. "You didn't read the part about my not ruling it out," he said defiantly. "I refused to make a commitment one way or the other." Like countless politicians before him and since, Ford hid behind his own mixed message.

"That isn't what I heard or what most people heard," Hartman persisted. He told Ford that if he pardoned Nixon now he would experience "a firestorm of protest that will make the Saturday Night Massacre seem mild." (The counselor to the president was referring to the events of October 20, 1973, when Nixon had accepted the resignations of two successive attorney generals who refused to dismiss special prosecutor Archibald Cox at the president's behest before Robert Bork fired him.)

The president didn't disagree with that assessment, but he was still unpersuaded. In fact, he seemed impatient with Hartman. He told his old aide and friend that he wasn't going to let majority opinion tell him what was the right thing to do.

Hartman was devastated. He left the Oval Office knowing that Ford was headed toward a pardon. Now the only question was how to execute it in a way that the country might accept. And Hartman, a master wordsmith, did not relish the prospect of finding the words to explain the decision to the country.

Meanwhile, to handle the task of the actual pardon, the president met with Benton Becker, a young lawyer on his staff who was handling the Nixon papers and tapes. With Haig joining them, Ford told Becker that he wanted him to travel to California to meet with Nixon. He authorized the lawyer to discuss a pardon, but he wanted him to tell the former president that contrition was the price.

"You'll never get it," interjected Haig, who had maintained communication with Nixon in exile.

But Ford held his ground. He insisted that Becker push for the apology. "Be very firm out there," he said, "and tell me what you see." Becker agreed and soon made plans to travel to San Clemente.[4]

When Becker arrived in San Clemente, he was told by Nixon's staffers that no apology would be issued. How did they know he would ask for one? Becker assumed Haig had tipped them off. Still, he persisted in working out an arrangement.

The Nixon team desperately wanted the pardon. They had been de facto lobbying for it, sending a memo to President Ford documenting Nixon's poor health. David Eisenhower had even called the president from San Clemente and ominously warned that his father-in-law "might go off the deep end."

Yet as much as the Nixon team wanted the pardon, they wanted it on their terms, not Ford's. During the negotiations in San Clemente, Herbert Miller, representing the Nixon team, drew a line in the sand on Nixon's records. Nixon wanted them—all of them. Eventually they reached an agreement. The Nixon records would be stored at a federal facility in Southern California. The federal government and the former president would both claim ownership of the material. Written records could be subpoenaed for three to five years. After that, Nixon would control his papers the way other presidents controlled theirs. Meanwhile, the tapes were a separate matter. Since the tapes had helped seal Nixon's fate as president, Ford's negotiators weren't as lenient on them as they were with the papers. The agreement reached was that the tapes would held by the General Services Administration and could not be destroyed. If Nixon wanted to consult them for the writing of his memoirs, he could do so. And after ten years he could seek to destroy the tapes.

As with any agreement, there was plenty in it for everyone to dislike. Democrats wouldn't like that Nixon could eventually destroy his tapes; Nixon wouldn't like that he didn't have an absolute claim to his papers like other presidents had.

This was a major concession for the former president. Historical precedent dictated that a president kept his papers. And he didn't know how he could write his memoirs without them.

Once the two legal teams agreed on the tapes and the papers, the negotiations turned to the statement of contrition. Buchen told Miller bluntly what Ford wanted: "I hope you would persuade your client to develop something that would tell the world, 'Yes, he did it, and he's accepting the pardon because he's guilty.'" Miller made no promise in response, other than to talk to the former president.

Miller had reason not to raise Ford's hope about Nixon's contrition. When the former president discussed with his lawyer how the talks were going, he seemed ambivalent about the pardon. "I'd just as soon go through the agony of a trial, so we can scrape away at least all the false charges," Nixon said, "and fight it out on those where there may be a doubt."

But for all his bravado, Nixon knew he could not face a trial. His health was not good. And his emotional state was even weaker. And so the negotiations continued.

A few days into the talks, former White House spokesman Ron Ziegler entered the scene. Ziegler had become well known to Americans as the face and voice of the Nixon White House. Before the word "spin" became part of the Washington vernacular, he had mastered it. He once famously said that Nixon had enjoyed a great year except for Watergate. Still boyish-looking at thirty-five, Ziegler remained fiercely loyal to his boss. And he brought his gift of spin into the negotiations.

Behind the scenes, Nixon enjoyed a secret weapon. He stayed in close contact with Haig, and Haig almost certainly had told him that Ford wanted to grant the pardon and be done with it. Armed with this knowledge, Nixon had Ziegler renegotiate the terms of the agreement that had apparently been settled. He wanted control of the tapes sooner. Becker, perhaps knowing that the hardest part of the negotiation—securing the apology—was yet to come, gave in and agreed to let Nixon have the tapes in five years instead of ten.

Even this concession didn't satisfy the former president. But his team urged him to take the deal. "I'll sign it," Nixon finally conceded before adding, "I'm not sure it's the right thing to do...."[5]

Now discussion over the apology began in earnest. Ziegler offered an initial version of a statement from Nixon that Becker rejected immediately. When Becker insisted that the statement include some sort of sorrow, Ziegler responded tersely, "Contrition is bullshit."

Becker didn't care. He told Ziegler the statement must include an apology. At one point, he went further than his boss probably wanted him to and threatened to withdraw the pardon offer.

Finally on the fourth draft, Ziegler produced a type-written document that he showed to Becker:

> I have been informed that President Ford has granted me a full and absolute pardon for any charges which might be brought against me for actions taken during the time I was president of the United States. In accepting this pardon, I hope that his compassionate act will contribute to lifting the burden of Watergate from our country.

Here in California, my perspective on Watergate is quite different than what it was while I was embattled in the midst of the controversy and while I was still subject to the unrelenting daily demands of the presidency itself.

As he read those first two paragraphs, Becker didn't see what he was looking for. But to his surprise, the statement then addressed Nixon's role in Watergate:

Looking back on what is still in my mind a complex and confusing maze of events, decisions, pressures, and personalities, one thing I can see more clearly now is that I was wrong in not acting more decisively and forthrightly in dealing with Watergate, particularly when it reached the state of judicial proceedings and grew from a political scandal into a national tragedy.

The statement was getting better. But still no remorse. Then Becker read this:

No words can describe the depth of my regret and pain at the anguish my mistakes over Watergate have caused the nation and the presidency—a nation I so deeply love and an institution I so greatly respect.

I know that many fair-minded people believe that motivations and actions in the Watergate affair were intentionally self-serving and illegal. I now understand how my own mistakes and misjudgments have contributed to that belief and seemed to support it. This burden is the heaviest of all to bear.

As the statement neared the end, Becker read one last sentence:

That the way I tried to deal with Watergate was the wrong
way is a burden I shall bear for every day of the life that is
left to me.

Becker was stunned. Although this was not quite full contrition,
here was the former president saying that he had handled Watergate
"the wrong way" and that it was a burden he would have to bear for
the rest of his life. It was good enough to meet Ford's demands.

Still, Becker wanted to talk to Nixon in person before returning
home. Maybe Ziegler had written the statement and the former president had never seen it.

If Becker had been stunned by the statement, he was even more
stunned by the president. Becker would later say that Nixon "appeared
to have aged and shrunken in the month since his resignation. His
jowls were loose and flabby, and his shirt seemed to be too big for his
neck." He found the former president completely disengaged.

"Where do you live?" he asked. "How are the Redskins going to
do this year?"

Becker sidestepped Nixon's small talk and explained that by
accepting a pardon he was essentially admitting his guilt. Nixon
seemed uninterested. Finally, Becker lost patience and ended the meeting. As he waited for his car, Ziegler asked him to come back inside
and talk to Nixon one more time.

"You're a fine young man," the president said. "I want to give you
something. But look around the office." There was only his desk, his
reading chair and ottoman, and two flags. He reached into his desk
and opened two boxes of presidential souvenirs. "I asked Pat to get
these for me. She got these out of my own jewelry box. There aren't
any more in the whole world," he said, offering the young lawyer a
pair of presidential cuff links and a presidential tie pin. "I want you
to have them."

As Becker accepted the gifts, Nixon's commentary on his plight continued, saying, "I used to have an aide who would stand by and hand me these things. I'm sorry, but this is the best I have now."[6]

Becker left the office shaken by Nixon's performance. Upon returning to Washington, he told Ford that "I really have serious questions in my mind whether that man is going to be alive at the time of the next election."

Ford said he thought Nixon would recover by 1976.

"I mean 1974," Becker answered. Ford was shocked that Becker thought Nixon might not be alive in just two months when the congressional elections would take place. Still, Ford had what he wanted and what he believed the country needed—an apology from Nixon—and a clear path to a pardon.

On Sunday morning, September 8, 1974, Gerald Ford announced a "full, free and absolute pardon" for the ex-president. The next day Gallup recorded the largest ever drop in presidential approval ratings. Americans were appalled by Ford's action. The roots of this rage came from the very design of the American government. The Founding Fathers had created a republic in which citizens elected leaders and trusted them to make decisions. For the most part the system had worked. But in Watergate, some Americans thought they saw the limits of the Founders' vision. No longer could the American people be certain that their leaders would do the right thing. But if not, they at least trusted that the court system would hold political leaders accountable. Now with the pardon, Americans were enraged that Nixon would never have to answer for Watergate. This began a long decline in trust between the American people and the government that continues today.

By the time the pardon was announced, Nixon had left La Casa Pacifica for Sunnylands, Walter Annenberg's palatial 220-acre estate in the California desert with its own golf course and a 25,000-square-foot ranch house. The former president stayed indoors to avoid the

110-degree heat. In fact, he didn't leave the estate at all during his entire stay. On one occasion his valet, Manolo Sanchez, was accosted by a reporter at a supermarket. Sanchez declined to be interviewed but did tell the reporter that "the pardon was a big relief to us."[7]

But if Nixon felt relief, he wasn't showing it. He was outraged by the public outrage at Ford's gesture. Within a few days of the announcement, he called the president to offer to reject the pardon. Ford declined the offer and ended the conversation abruptly.

But perhaps no one was angrier than Pat. She had not been told that the pardon was coming. "Pardon for what?" she asked defiantly.[8]

Though it offered him little solace, Nixon's biggest legal problems—the threat of a criminal proceeding and time in jail—had been averted. But his troubles were only just beginning. As he sipped cocktails at the Annenburg Estate, he couldn't have known that things would get much worse before they got better.

# Chapter Four

# A Near-Death Experience

*"I don't think I'm going to
get out of here alive."*

The old marine's face was creased with worry. On the battle-field, Colonel Jack Brennan had seen a lot of men in bad shape. But this was different. Three days after the pardon had been extended, he saw a man who was dying.

Colonel Brennan served as Nixon's military aide. And he essentially ran the office at San Clemente. He had joined Nixon on the trip to Sunnylands. And now on September 11, he could see that Nixon's health was fading.

Nixon's physical well-being had always been a concern. Ford had been warned that Nixon might not make it to the end of the year. But now the ex-president's health was declining dramatically. So as chief of staff, Brennan decided to take action. He placed a call from Sunnylands to the office of Dr. John C. Lungren, who had served as Nixon's personal physician since 1952.

"Doctor, I know it's late," he said once Lungren got on the phone. "But could you possibly come out to Ambassador Annenberg's tonight and see the president? I am very concerned. The boss really needs you as he never did." [1]

"I'll come right away," Lungren answered. "I'll leave for Palm Desert as soon as I finish seeing my patients." Lungren arrived around ten thirty that night and was met by a Secret Service agent who escorted him into the estate. The doctor was a handsome fifty-seven-year-old whose face was bordered by still-brown hair and accented by horn-rimmed glasses. Before seeing his famous patient, Lungren was asked to speak on the phone with Admiral William Lukash at the White House, who had treated Nixon while he was president. The issue at hand, Lukash proceeded to tell Lungren, was a leg that had been giving the president trouble for several months.

"We have been quite concerned since just before President Nixon left for the Middle East to see [Anwar] Sadat," Lukash said, referring to a trip the former president had made earlier that summer on Air Force One. "That's when the leg really started to get worse. The president hid it from us until we were well on our way to Cairo. He told me in Salzburg of the leg's rapid swelling. I examined him immediately and diagnosed it as acute phlebitis in the lower left leg."

Lungren inquired about whether the long plane ride had had an impact on the leg. Lukash confirmed that it had.

"The president refused to sit down and rest his leg," Lukash said, of the trip to the Middle East. "The longer he stood, the more intense the pain grew. He suffered an acute flare-up in the leg and I placed him on anti-inflammatory drugs."[2]

Lungren ran through in his mind the implications of a leg riddled with phlebitis. He asked if the president knew how serious the situation could become.

"The president is aware that the condition is potentially fatal," Lukash answered. "I told him that a blood clot could break loose, travel through the veins from the infected leg to the lungs, triggering a deadly pulmonary embolus."

Lungren hung up the phone and braced himself. He would have to evaluate Nixon in a few moments. But more importantly, he would have to be brutally honest with him about what lay ahead. There were no easy options.

The doctor went to see the president in a guest bungalow. Lungren entered the living room, where he found Nixon leaning back in a chair with his left leg propped up on an ottoman.

As Lungren would later recall, "Nixon looked exhausted; he was pale and had obviously lost considerable weight. Drawn and tense, he was dressed in blue pajamas, a blue robe, and black slippers. Despite his apparent exhaustion, however, his voice was a strong as ever. While his penetrating intellect seemed intact, there was also fear and anguish that I had never seen in him before."[3]

Perhaps sensing that Lungren was shocked by his appearance, Nixon tried small talk.

"Jack, how are you?" he asked. "Glad to see you."

"The important thing is how are you?" Lungren answered.

The doctor sat down beside his patient and began asking him questions about the leg. After just a few minutes, Lungren was convinced that the president's condition required immediate action. He told Nixon he needed to go to the hospital right away. Nixon refused.

"If I do go to the hospital, I'll never come out alive," he said.

If Lungren couldn't force Nixon to go for medical treatment, then he would try to get the medical treatment to Nixon. He prescribed an anticoagulant and an anti-inflammatory drug and promised to take another look at the leg when the president returned to San Clemente.

After spending two hours with Nixon, Lungren began the drive back to Long Beach. As he did, he thought of the irony that the Ford pardon—intended to save Nixon legally—could do nothing to save Nixon physically. As he drove into the Southern California night, he worried about Nixon and the "progressive worsening of his physical condition, psychological exile, and social banishment."[4]

Lungren knew the road to recovery would be a long one—especially for an unwilling traveler. Even so, Lungren could not have foreseen how that road would become so difficult so soon.

———

Two days after Lungren's house call, Nixon's condition became worse. Pat worried that the swelling in her husband's leg had increased. She called Dr. Walter Tkach, one of the White House doctors who had treated Nixon, and he agreed to fly to California to evaluate the former president at La Casa de Pacifica when Nixon returned from his stay at Sunnylands.

Tkach looked at Nixon and echoed Lungren: "You have got to go to the hospital." Again, Nixon refused.

After leaving his patient, Tkach returned to Washington and gave a series of interviews to reporters eager for news on Nixon. The former president was a "ravaged man," Tkach said, who had "lost the will to fight." He told one reporter, "It will require a miracle for him to recover."[5]

In an effort to control the narrative, Nixon family members began talking to the press. But their messages were mixed.

President Nixon was "in good spirits," according to Julie Eisenhower, while her brother-in-law, Edward Cox, said he was "very depressed."

In reality, Edward's words painted the more accurate portrait of Nixon's state. Back in his office at San Clemente with his swollen leg propped up, the ex-president met with his former communications director, Kenneth Clawson, who was now working for the Ford administration.

"What's going on?" he asked. "What's happening to you, the others? How are the new people?" Clawson said a purge was in effect to get rid of the Nixon staff. Nixon sought to cheer him up. "I know you're feeling bitter," he said. "So am I. But we can't let it show, not now, possibly not ever...."

When the conversation turned to Nixon's legacy, the former president was less upbeat.

"We're out now, so they try to stomp us...kick us when we're down," he lamented. "They'll never give us credit. They never let up, never, because we were the first real threat to them in years. And, by God, we would have changed it, changed it so they couldn't have changed it back in a hundred years, if only...."

With that, Nixon's voice abruptly stopped. Clawson looked up to see his former boss looking through the window at the Pacific Ocean.

Then, after a moment of reflection, he spoke again.

"What starts the process, really, are the laughs and snubs and slights you get when you are a kid.... You were a good athlete but I was not and that was the very reason I tried and tried and tried."[6]

Then he spoke again of Watergate. "Now some people we both know think that you go stand in the middle of the bullring and cry, 'mea culpa, mea culpa,' while the crowd is hissing and booing and spitting on you. But a man doesn't cry."[7]

Clawson, perhaps made uncomfortable by the introspective direction the conversation had had taken, tried to change the subject and inquired about Nixon's leg.

"They say it's very bad," he said. "But I've already told them to go to hell. I've told them I wasn't setting foot outside the wall around my property no matter what. They can cut off the damn leg...I don't care."

At that point, Nixon took another introspective turn.

"You've got to be tough," he said. "You can't break, my boy, even when there is nothing left. You can't admit, even to yourself, that it is gone."[8]

Clawson left Nixon worried about his former boss's physical condition. He wasn't alone. Many of those who saw Nixon in the first few weeks since the resignation noticed his deteriorating health. His mind wandered, his words trailed off, and his spirit seemed broken. "Bob, a lot has happened, but I've realized something," he told his longtime friend Robert Finch. Then after a long pause, he said quietly, "You don't realize until too late who your real friends are." Many of those friends now worried whether Nixon would live through the year.

None more so than John Lungren, who returned on September 16 to examine Nixon again. Nixon valet Manolo Sanchez met the doctor at the gate and led him to the swimming pool area where Nixon was casually dressed and seated in a lounge chair next to Pat.

"I believe the damn leg is worse," the ex-president complained, with "more pain and swelling." Lungren pushed his hands against the leg, and the pressure caused Nixon pain. Still, the doctor knew it wouldn't be easy to get Nixon to do what was needed and go to the hospital. Julie Eisenhower was in town and Lungren enlisted her support.

Nixon finally grew too ill and too weak to resist any longer. "How can I not say yes?" he asked. "Go ahead and call."[9]

Nixon was scheduled to be admitted to Long Beach Memorial on Monday, September 23. When he arrived, Lungren met him at the loading dock in the back of the hospital. The hospital, located on Atlantic Avenue, was widely regarded as one of the best in Southern California. The khaki-colored building had been around since 1937. Nixon had visited the hospital before and the Secret Service agents had decided that it was best to take him inside the back entrance.

"Jack," Nixon said to his doctor as he got out of the car, "the leg is even worse. The pain and swelling have traveled up to my thigh." After riding up the elevator to the sixth floor, Nixon was placed in a wheelchair and pushed down the hall into a private room. There, Lungren performed an examination on the president and found the left leg "to be enlarged from the toes to the hip." Still, Lungren hoped this could be treated with an anti-clogging drug called Heparin.

After Lungren met with the family and told them about the exam and the medication he was prescribing, Ron Ziegler asked him to meet with reporters. The doctor made a brief statement in which he confirmed publicly for the first time that Nixon suffered from "chronic phlebitis" and talked about the treatment plan going forward.

Once he left the press conference, Lungren made one more stop by his patient's room.

"I'm miserable," Nixon told the doctor. "If I ever get out of this hospital, I'll never enter one again."[10]

Lungren scheduled some standard testing. He specifically asked for the medical staff to perform a chest film and a lung scan. The next day as he looked over the results, Lungren noticed a blood clot in the right lung. Yet the doctor still believed the medication and the rest at the hospital were what Nixon needed.

Not only did Lungren have to deal with Nixon's health problems, but he also had to deal with the press. Nixon still made news around the country and reporters camped out at the hospital hoping for updates. Lungren routinely kept them updated, but he was becoming increasingly frustrated with some of the reporting—in particular, with speculation about a possible medical "hoax" that might keep Nixon from flying to Washington to take part in a trial. Even though Nixon had been granted a pardon, his former aides had not. Prosecutors were eager to put the former president on the stand as a witness.

If they couldn't prosecute him, they could at least persecute him with endless courtroom examinations.

Lungren was enraged at the insinuation that he was taking part in a coverup. When Lungren again met with reporters on September 30, the event was billed as off the record—meaning that the reporters couldn't quote anything said at the event but could gain a better understanding of what was going on with the president's health. After opening with a statement in which he chided reporters and called the "hoax" talk a "despicable remark," Rick Davis of CBS News asked Lungren if Nixon would be able to travel in the near future and testify.

"Now you're getting political," the doctor angrily replied, "politically oriented. I don't want to be that way. I want to give you my professional opinion."

Lungren was shocked at how "relentless" the reporters were in pursuing the idea of a "hoax" cooked up to keep Nixon from testifying.[11]

The ex-president's doctor retreated from press conferences and began focusing exclusively on his patient. On October 4, Nixon's health had improved so much that Lungren discharged him and allowed him to return to San Clemente. Yet Nixon's condition remained serious enough that Lungren notified Judge John Sirica (who was presiding over the Watergate-related trials in Washington) that Nixon's phlebitis was life-threatening.

Lungren remained bewildered at the politics that had now invaded his medical practice. And he was outraged at what had happened to his patient, who was also his friend. On October 13, Lungren joined the Nixons at La Casa de Pacifica for dinner. Nixon appeared in a dark suit and tie for the event that was supposed to be a casual affair. Yet before long the conversation turned serious.

"Pat and I would both like to know what did we do wrong?" Nixon asked, clearly referring to Watergate and not his recent health scare. He then blamed the "double standard" of the press. After Lungren reflected on his own unhappy recent experiences with the media, Pat Nixon spoke up.

"I would have destroyed the tapes, but Dick's legal honesty prevailed," she said.

Lungren thought he had come for a casual dinner on a Sunday night, and instead he was hearing Richard and Pat Nixon talk openly about their feelings on Watergate.[12]

"My excesses were never greater than any of my predecessors'," Nixon continued with sadness tinging his voice. "Yet I attempted to protect my closest friends and in the process let my country down."

Lungren left the dinner worried not only about the physical health of his patient, but about his mental health, as well. Richard Nixon remained a deeply discouraged, depressed man.

Lungren had scheduled a lung scan and venogram for October 23. Nixon arrived again at Long Beach Memorial Hospital and was taken to the sixth floor for the tests. Although the test results revealed no new clots, blood-vessel blockage now existed in the femoral vein of his upper left thigh. The danger was that additional blood clots could develop and potentially cause a massive and fatal embolism.

Lungren immediately went to Nixon's room to give him the bad news.

"You're going to have to spend the night," he told his patient. After consulting with another surgeon, Dr. Wiley Barker from UCLA, Lungren knew that only one option remained, and he and Barker met with the former president to discuss his options.

"So it's surgery then?" the patient asked.

"If you want to go on living, it is," Barker answered.

"I can assure you about that," Nixon responded. "I've got too many things to do to go on being sick. Let's just get it out of the way."

He then turned to Lungren.

"Jack, I am glad you're here," he said. "Let's go and get it over with."

Later that day, Lungren again met with the media to break the news. He read a statement that said the "presence of a large clot extending to the left external iliac artery" required that "urgent surgery should be scheduled."[13]

The primary challenge facing the doctors was that Nixon's clotting now blocked more than 99 percent of his blood flow. And if the clot traveled to the lung, the result would be death.

So Lungren decided to insert a "Miles Clamp" that essentially would allow for circulation of the blood flow and stop the clot from moving upstream.

On October 30, 1974, at five o'clock in the morning, Nixon was wheeled into the surgery area. With Secret Service agents wearing scrubs, Lungren was joined by Dr. Eldon Hickman, a specialist in thoracic and cardiac surgery, and several other doctors. At five thirty, they began the operation.

The Miles Clamp was successfully inserted, and by 6:50 a.m. they were able to take Nixon out of the surgery room and into a recovery room.

Lungren went to tell Pat the news.

"I think Dick is sufficiently stabilized for you to see him," he told her.

"Is he going to make it?" she responded.

"I think so," he said, "but the next forty-eight hours will be the critical period."

Then, suddenly, Nixon took a turn for the worse. Lungren had returned to his office, but early that afternoon he received a call from the hospital. Nixon's blood pressure had dropped dramatically.

When Lungren got back to the hospital, he found his patient in "vascular shock." He was suffering from internal bleeding. Blood was storming into his vital organs. Lungren knew he had only about an hour to save the former president.

As medical staff urgently began administering intravenous fluids and blood transfusions, Nixon continued to drift away. At one point, he fainted and began falling out of the bed toward the floor. Two medical personnel grabbed him and pushed him back onto the bed. One of them, a female nurse, instinctively slapped his face.

"Richard, wake up!" she said. "Richard, wake up!" she repeated, and she continued to smack the former president across the face.[14] Amazingly, Nixon began to wake up.

He would recall those first few moments of consciousness: "My first recollection was of a nurse slapping my face and calling me. 'Richard, wake up,' she said. I knew it was not Pat or Lungren. In fact, only my mother called me Richard. When I woke up again, Lungren was taking my pulse."

Nixon remembered talking to Pat as she kept vigil by his bedside. "Pat and I have seldom revealed our physical disabilities to each other," he said. "This time I couldn't help it. I said I didn't think I was going to make it. She gripped my hand and said almost fiercely, 'Dick, you can't talk that way. You have got to make it. You must not give up.'"

On another occasion, Nixon awoke to see his old friend and longtime valet at his bedside.

"Manolo," he said, "I don't think I'm going to get out of here alive."[15]

Though Nixon was now awake, he still hovered near death. At one point, he said he wanted to record some final thoughts. Pat began writing as he talked. Later, Ron Ziegler took her place before Frank Gannon took his.

"Nixon looked utterly helpless with tubes up his nose and drips going into his veins," Gannon said. "He said he knew he might not live through the night." Nixon mainly spoke of his achievements and of what might have been. "It was a moving and rather terrifying experience," Gannon remembered.

For the next two days, Nixon improved slowly. Closely monitored by Lungren and his team of doctors and nurses, the former president's blood pressure stabilized. More importantly, the clot showed signs of dissolving.

The patient was improving, but the road ahead remained a difficult one.

———————————

The current president had been keeping up with his predecessor's condition. And in late October, President Ford, who was campaigning around the country for Republican candidates in the upcoming midterm elections, found himself in Southern California. Always a thoughtful man, Ford suggested that he would go see Nixon. His staff was appalled. With just a few days to go before the election, why put Nixon back in the news?

Ford insisted. "If there's no place in politics for human compassion there's something wrong with politics," he said. He did add that he would "leave it to Pat" as to whether Nixon wanted a visit from Ford.

On October 31, he called the former first lady to ask if she thought it "would help" if he came to see his old boss.

"I can't think of anything that would help Dick more," came the response from Pat.

On November 1, Nixon was sleeping when the loud sound of a hammer pounded into his dreams. He awoke to see hospital workers breaking through the door of his room, which had somehow become jammed. As it was pushed aside, in strode President Gerald Ford.

"Hi, Jerry," Nixon gamely offered as he lay half asleep with an air tube in his nose.

"Oh, Mr. President," Ford responded, shocked at Nixon's appearance. They talked for several minutes about the upcoming election. Ford put a brave face on the likely Republican defeat.

"We're going to do fine," he said. Nixon wasn't fooled. He knew the Republicans would lose seats. But he wanted Ford to stay the course—especially with his new vice president. He urged him to "hang in there with Rockefeller...."

As Ford got ready to make his exit, he thanked Nixon for "all you did for me."

Nixon responded by thanking Ford for coming: "I'm not feeling too well, but I'm going to make it." And no doubt thinking of the tremendous political risk that Ford had taken in coming to see him, Nixon thanked him and said he was "deeply grateful."

As Ford made his way to the motorcade outside the hospital, he stopped momentarily to brief reporters about the visit.

"He's obviously a very, very sick man," Ford said, "but I think he's coming along."[16]

Ford's quote made headlines around the nation, but his words did little to quiet the demands of Democrats who still viewed Nixon's illness as an excuse to escape from testifying in the Watergate trials in Washington. Judge John Sirica, presiding over the trial of former Nixon top aide John Ehrlichman, sent a team of doctors to examine Nixon. They unanimously agreed with Lungren and Ford: Nixon was indeed a very, very sick man.

On November 14, a few days after Ford's hopes of a strong election for the Republicans were met by a Democratic landslide in the midterm elections, Nixon was released from the hospital. Wearing a navy blue bathrobe, the former president was wheeled back to the elevator and then out to a waiting car. The three weeks in the hospital had taken a toll on Nixon and he had lost fifteen pounds. But he was alive. And that was no small feat. Lungren had worked magic.

But at home in San Clemente, Nixon soon realized how far he had to go in his recovery. The ex-president took the Republican Party losses in the congressional elections personally. "Watergate is a terrible burden for all of our people...." he lamented. He was especially pained by the defeat of four former prisoners of war in Vietnam who had run for Congress. "Just think, it was only a year ago in 1973 that we had that magnificent party for them and that the whole nation was at their feet.[17]

But the bad news extended beyond the election. Nixon also learned that he owed nearly three hundred thousand dollars in legal fees. And since he no longer had health insurance as a government employee, he would have to pay the entire bill for his hospital stay. In fact, Nixon's bills were enormous. He owed Long Beach Memorial Hospital twenty-three thousand dollars for his surgery, he owed a projected three hundred thousand dollars in legal bills, he owed $148,081 in back taxes for improper tax deductions he had claimed, he owed seventy-five thousand dollars in California state income taxes, and he owed thirty-seven thousand dollars a year in property taxes on La Casa Pacifica.

But those were battles for another day. For now, he focused on his health. Pain still consumed his body. He took codeine for it, but hated the side effects. "I would wake up at night and the room would be upside down," he wrote in his diary. So he began weaning himself off the painkillers.

But the mental pain proved to be a bigger enemy than the physical pain. Though it was never diagnosed, Nixon was almost certainly experiencing depression during this time. As he wrote in his diary: "I have a rather depressed feeling again. I have simply got to get over this because we just can't continue to exist with nothing but depression or bad news coming in."[18]

Later he would write that he and Pat would "see it through" and that the entire ordeal they were going through was a "test of character and we must not fail the test."

In his farewell speech to the White House staff in the East Room, Nixon had spoken about being in the "deepest valley." Now he began to set his sights on the road that would lead him out of the valley.

As he wrote in December, he knew he would have to "fight over the papers" and the "trial" and start thinking about writing "a book—maybe one, maybe more—and to follow it with speeches, television where possible, which will maybe put some things in perspective."

Here was the first glimpse of the roadmap that Nixon would use in guiding himself out of the valley of disgrace and despair. He would fight the government over his presidential papers, stand his ground in court, and start writing books and doing appearances as soon as the public was ready to hear from him again. He would try to escape his private turmoil by returning to the public square in some form. Nixon, ever the intellectual, had always been miscast as a politician. Now, at last, he could be what he had been created to be: a thinker and a scholar. In those dark days of late 1974, Nixon could see a shimmering light ahead. He could finally see a way forward.

This roadmap for his journey back would be useful for Nixon in the coming months and years. But he could not have foreseen how it would take him through some painful stretches in the road.

Chapter Five

# The Memoirs

*"Always look to the future."*

The office looked the same: the oak desk with the phone perched on top of it, the five flags representing the military services guarding the desk, the wooden walls accented by the large windows. But the feel in the room was different. No longer did the office at 4100 Calle Isabella serve as the second office for the president as he labored over decisions of state; now it merely served a former president as a reminder of what had been. And the issues now confronting him were personal.

Throughout history, men who have fallen from power have experienced battles with what Churchill called the "Black Dog." Nixon's proved to be a very strong breed. So his friends continued to worry about him. But they also knew that he needed to hear the truth about the challenges facing him.

Around Thanksgiving of 1974, Nixon was visited by two old friends—Bebe Rebozo and Bob Abplanalp. Rebozo was a Florida banker and longtime friend of Nixon's. Abplanalp was the inventor of the aerosol valve and also a personal friend of Nixon's going back many years. The two men came to check on their old friend; but they also came to talk business. They were concerned about Nixon's financial health and recommended some strong medicine. Nixon, they told him, needed to sell his Key Biscayne properties. To help out, the two men would orchestrate the purchase themselves. They proposed to pay Nixon more than one million dollars for those properties.[1]

Still, the overriding tone of the meeting was grim. As Abplanalp would later tell a reporter, "We're not talking about a welfare case; we're simply talking about shrinking his holdings, making it easier for him to make ends meet."

One of the primary sources of potential income discussed during the meeting was getting a book deal. Nixon liked the idea and was eager to get started on writing.

In spite of his physical and mental state, Nixon knew the cure would be to find some meaningful work. Like other leaders in history who have entered exile, Nixon was beginning think about his legacy and how he could shape it. The ex-president liked to quote Winston Churchill's answer to the question of how history would regard him. It would treat him kindly, Churchill explained, because, "I intend to write it." He did, and now Nixon would do the same.

Having survived the resignation and the surgery, the former president sat in his office in late 1974 and began to think seriously about the book he wanted to write. Nixon hoped to make some money from it; more importantly, he hoped to use it to begin his campaign to win back what he saw as his historical legacy.

Still, the former president feared that writing his memoirs would prove to be a difficult task. Ron Ziegler was urging him to get moving on the project. "I think Ziegler underestimates what it really takes to write a good book," he said. "We've got anecdotes and stories and great events and philosophical thoughts that would fill volumes, but to put it in readable organizational form is the trick." In a previous period of defeat in his life, Nixon had written *Six Crises*, a critically acclaimed book that helped him heal his intellectual wounds after losing the 1960 presidential election to John F. Kennedy.[2] But this would be a far more difficult challenge. Now he would have to write a book that covered his entire career—including Watergate.

As Nixon pondered his past, he couldn't help but think about the future. San Clemente had served as his home for years. But the real action was on the East Coast. And so in the fall of 1974, he first broached the topic with his two daughters. He mentioned the "possibility of moving to New York," and they both encouraged the idea. Julie lived in Philadelphia and Tricia lived in New York. They welcomed the possibility that their father would move closer to them.[3]

But Nixon was just thinking out loud. A move to the East lay far in the future. For now, he needed to focus on the task at hand.

As Christmas 1974 approached, sadness filled the air in San Clemente. Julie would remember it as the "lowest point in my father's life."

And the New Year brought more bad news. Watching the Rose Bowl at home, Nixon learned that a verdict had been reached in the trials of the three political aides who had been closest to him. H. R. Haldeman, John Mitchell, and John Ehrlichman had all been found guilty. Though Nixon had avoided having to testify in person in the case because of his bad health, his words from the White House tapes were crucial in the convictions. Nixon took the news hard. He remained discouraged for days.

Nixon was trying to regain his health. With the aid of Colonel Jack Brennan, his chief of staff, he began visiting the office and trying to maintain a normal schedule. Each day the boss would send for his staff and want to talk shop. He loved talking politics and still maintained a vast intelligence operation in Washington. His friends in Washington would give him the latest gossip on legislation, politics, and polling, and Nixon would send for a staffer and begin discussing the latest D.C. intrigue. One of these was Ken Khachigian, a young lawyer who had first met Nixon during the 1962 gubernatorial campaign when Nixon stopped by the San Marcos High School in Santa Barbara, California, where the young Khachigian was a student. Khachigian introduced himself to Nixon after his speech, saying that he was a member of the high school's debate team.

"I was in debate in high school, too," Nixon responded. "In my day you had to learn to be an orator. Nowadays you have to learn to be a conversationalist."[4]

After college and law school, Khachigian found his way onto the 1968 Nixon campaign staff and later worked as a junior staffer in the White House.

His skills as a researcher and speechwriter had not gone unnoticed by the president. In the fall of 1974, he was summoned to see the deposed leader at San Clemente. "He was down," Khachigian remembered. "Less so about the resignation than about the financial difficulty he faced." By 1975, Khachigian was working full-time for Nixon in San Clemente.[5]

Loie Gaunt was also there every morning. She had come on board to manage the office. Gaunt had met Nixon for the first time in 1951 and had been one of his best secretaries. Now she would help him try to rebuild his financial health. It would not be easy. The money he was getting from the government totaled only sixty thousand dollars—hardly enough to cover all of his expenses.[6]

And his early efforts at maintaining an office schedule weren't doing much to improve Nixon's physical or mental health. To cheer him up, Pat decided to celebrate his sixty-second birthday on January

9. She invited many of his old friends, including Rebozo and Abplanalp. She also insisted that they keep it quiet; she wanted the party to be a surprise.

That afternoon she met all the guests out in front of the house and them took them over to the office. Nixon was shocked when he saw his old friends there to celebrate. After everyone presented Nixon with gifts, they gathered in the living room. Nixon served drinks and urged everyone to eat some of the caviar being served on a silver plate that had been given to him by the Shah of Iran. "The Shah won't like it if you don't," he joked.

It was the happiest day since he had left Washington. Nixon told his guests that several people had called him to wish him a happy birthday earlier in the day, including Governor Reagan and President Ford. Later during dinner, the ex-president raised his glass to make a toast. He spoke of the importance of friendship. Then with tears in his eyes, he added, "Never dwell on the past. Always look to the future."

But after the party ended and the guests returned home, Nixon was left with the still-complicated realities of his life. Later in January, Barry Goldwater came to check on the former president. Nixon appreciated the gesture and enjoyed talking shop with Goldwater. Yet he was enraged the next day when he learned from the paper that Goldwater had revealed the meeting and apparently embellished the conversation, telling reporters that Nixon had said he might want to be the ambassador to China someday.

"I never told Goldwater a goddamn thing about wanting to be an ambassador," Nixon fumed. Then he quickly turned his anger toward the media. "They might have taken whatever Goldwater did say out of context—that's what the bastards do constantly."[7]

It was a reminder that any attempt Nixon made to reenter the public square would be greeted with more negative press coverage.

But a few days later on February 9, 1975, reporters were the least of Nixon's concerns. On that day, the six-month transition period after the resignation officially concluded. This meant that the support staff being paid for by the government had to be terminated. And not only did they leave, but they also dismissed the office staffers that they had been using and shipped all of the equipment back to Washington. The impact must have deepened Nixon's sadness. The last trappings of power were now gone.

And the news coming from Washington only added to his worries. Nixon had hoped that his deal with Ford would ensure access to his presidential papers. But many in D.C. were outraged by the deal and wanted the government to keep all the papers and the tapes. Not long after the pardon was announced, Congress took action, instructing the General Services Administration to seize the Nixon files. Now Nixon learned that a federal court in Washington had upheld the actions of Congress, which Nixon viewed as stealing his property. But he knew it would be a long fight to get his papers back.

One of the main reasons he wanted the papers was to help him in his new project: writing the memoirs. Whether he was ready to endure the physically and mentally grueling task of writing his life story was beside the point; Nixon needed the money from a book deal. His friend Swifty Lazar had served as his literary agent and inked a deal with Warner Paperback Library. The publisher would pay $2.5 million in advance royalties for the manuscript. Nixon's former White House aides Frank Gannon and Diane Sawyer would help research and write it.[8]

Later in February, Nixon felt well enough to attempt a round of golf while staying at Sunnylands, but he only made it through the first two holes and then had to stop. Afterward, he joined old friends at the Sunnylands main house for a party of sorts. Governor Ronald Reagan and his wife, Nancy, were there along with Bob Hope, Frank Sinatra, and others. At the end of the event, Nixon offered a toast. "When you are on top," he said gesturing at the luxurious home they were gathered in, "it is filled with all your friends. Afterward, you don't need a house so large."

Back at San Clemente the next day, Nixon tried to find solace in routine. He would ride a golf cart over to the office building at the Coast Guard's Navigational Aid Station where his office was housed. Dressed in a dark suit and tie, as always, he found himself surrounded by fewer people. Now that the transition period had ended, most of the staff had left except for Colonel Brennan, who would soon resign his commission to stay on as chief of staff. Brennan was an inspired choice for that job. He brought military organization and a keen insight into how to schedule Nixon's time.

"Don't make mistakes," Brennan said to himself on a regular basis. "Don't let him get hurt." He wanted to get Nixon active again but didn't want to expose him to unnecessary risks. He worried about how the public would treat the former president and feared unpleasant encounters. "When the opposite happened and people kept coming over to him to shake his hand, he was boosted right up," Brennan would say. "That taught me something and set a pattern." At one event, Brennan and Nixon's barber, Ken Allan, had arranged for a group of friends to celebrate Nixon at a home in Corona Del Mar. Among those who gathered to salute the former president was Hollywood icon John Wayne. The actor gave Nixon a Boehm sculpture of a horse. Nixon took the gift and held it in his hands as the famous actor began to speak.

"You know, Mr. President," Wayne said in his familiar cadence, "it's kind of ironic I'm giving this horse to you, especially after that rough ride you've had in Washington the past couple of years."

Nixon didn't hesitate to respond. "You never know," he told the crowd, "one day this horse may gallop again."[9]

Brennan and Ron Ziegler still hovered, but the time had come for Ziegler to leave. There simply was no money to pay him. And frankly, he wasn't needed. Ziegler's spin often rubbed reporters the wrong way. Still, Nixon disliked confrontation, so when the moment came to inform Ziegler, the former president left it to his chief of staff: "Ron, Jack has something to tell you."

With the staff now gone, Nixon and Brennan began to confront the financial challenges facing the former president. And Nixon was more convinced than ever before that the best way to earn money and salvage his reputation would be his memoirs. In early February, the former president began to think seriously about how to go about writing them.

For that task, Nixon would convene a team to provide research and written drafts for different subjects and chapters comprised of three writers, all of them former staffers. Each of them brought a unique set of talents to the task. Frank Gannon and Diane Sawyer preferred to work from their apartments lest they be consumed in conversation with Nixon. Ken Khachigian worked at Nixon's office and often found himself consumed in those conversations.

The organization of the work was largely based on the Randolph Churchill model. Gannon had actually worked on Randolph Churchill's research staff when the younger Churchill was writing a biography for his father, Winston Churchill. The Churchill model involved setting up "chronological files for every significant day of the subject's life" and providing "background papers on individual issues."

Each day Nixon would sit in his ottoman chair and dictate, sometimes for ten hours at a time. Occasionally the former president would express doubts about the project, and at other times his mind would wander.[10] "We're not making enough progress on the book," the ex-president would moan from the chair in his office. Then in the next breath he would add, "Do you think Reagan will run in '76?"[11]

Nixon established the writing process: he would call for his writers to join him in the office while he discussed his recollections about his life. They wrote as he talked. He also assigned each of the writers certain topics to research and sometimes requested that drafts of sections or chapters of the story be written.

Topic by topic, issue by issue, the president and his scribes worked their way through the Nixon story: from his early childhood, to college at Whittier College, to serving in the navy in World War II, to running for Congress, to serving as Ike's running mate, to the fiasco of the 1960 election, and to redemption in 1968.

But while the writing process may have provided an escape for Nixon, reality was never far away.

The prosecutors in Washington continued to investigate Watergate, turning their attention toward Nixon's close friend Bebe Rebozo. In 1970, Rebozo had received one hundred thousand dollars from Richard Danner, a staffer for Howard Hughes. Ostensibly the money was a campaign contribution, but Rebozo had kept it in his own bank account. He later returned the money to Danner.

If the money didn't go to the campaign, then what was the purpose of the donation? Federal investigators believed the money might have been part of a slush fund during Watergate. Could this have been the money Nixon referred to on the Watergate Tapes when he told John Dean he knew he "could get a million dollars...."?

To connect the dots, prosecutors wanted to interrogate Nixon. Negotiations began that spring of 1975 between Nixon's lawyers and Henry Ruth, who was now the chief Watergate prosecutor. The agreement reached allowed Nixon to testify at home in California with his lawyer present. Plus, the interrogation would be secret. The testimony was set for June 23.

When the prosecutors arrived, Nixon greeted them at one of the conference rooms inside the coast guard station. He was nine months removed from the health crisis that had almost killed him. And he was stronger and feeling better than he had since the hospitalization. This was a chance for him to mix it up with the men who had put his friends in jail, and it was a chance to defend Bebe. For the next day and a half, Nixon answered questions for eleven hours. And he didn't give an inch.

"I told you I didn't listen to the recording," he said defiantly, when asked about the missing 18.5 minutes on the tapes. "If you want to ask again, we can go all day on it." He denied any knowledge of any slush fund and defended Bebe. Above all, he handled the questions in a way that gave the prosecutors almost nothing they could use.[12]

On the final morning of the interrogation, Nixon sensed that he had endured his first test since leaving office and aced it. Never one to run from a fight, the former president seemed to relish the chance finally to have his say on Watergate and to push back against what he saw as unfair accusations.

He told the interrogators, "You probably have been somewhat, perhaps, disappointed that some of my answers have been, well, to put it mildly, rather testy which is not my usual way of trying to answer questions in a legal forum."[13]

Nixon not only had performed well under pressure, but he also had done so well that he had effectively ended the legal threat against his friend. Later that year, the Watergate Special Prosecution Force declined to indict Bebe Rebozo.

Nixon's handling of the prosecutors showed that he was capable of sparring successfully with his opponents and prevailing—in private. But before he entered the public square, he needed to finish his book.

Nixon soon returned to his memoirs. The section on Watergate proved to be the hardest challenge. Diane Sawyer was given the task of preparing this part of the book. She created folders with all the material she had found in her research. And she met with Nixon for hours as he worked his way through the Watergate section. The sessions took a toll on her.

"She would come back from them looking harrowed and sick," Frank Gannon remembered. "But she always recognized that Nixon had to do it his way, which was to talk himself through each phase of Watergate before dictating. He hated having to think and write about it, not least because there were a lot of things he simply didn't know about, but in the end he faced up and did it."[14]

As Nixon was working on the memoirs, he also began to make his first public appearances. That, too, proved to be a difficult task. "I don't like for people to come up and say they are sorry and I also don't want to run into unpleasant situations where people come up and snarl around." But he knew that if he wanted to reestablish his legacy, he would have to engage the public again. Writing the book served as one way to do that, but he also needed to meet people face to face.

"That is perhaps what we were made for," he said, "to be able to take punishment beyond what anybody in this office has ever had before—particularly after leaving office. This is a test of character and we must not fail the test."[15]

Nixon began making unannounced appearances at Dodgers and Angels games. And he ate at his favorite Tex-Mex restaurant, El Adobe, in San Juan Capistrano. But these were modest steps compared to the leap he took in early 1976 when he relived his greatest moment as president by traveling to China, where a large contingent of reporters watched him retrace the steps of his famous 1972 visit.[16]

To Nixon, it made perfect sense. He was still regarded as a master strategist on the foreign stage. His opening of the door to China continued to impress four years after it had occurred. And the Chinese were eager to welcome the former president back.

The road back to China began in November 1975 when David and Julie Eisenhower made their own trip and met with Chairman Mao Zedong. At that time, the chairman extended an invitation for Julie's father to visit. "When your father comes," he said, "I will be waiting for him."[17]

But Nixon had to tread carefully. It would be his first big step back into the public eye. And he had to be especially cautious with President Ford facing stiff opposition in the upcoming Republican presidential primaries. Governor Ronald Reagan had formally announced he would challenge Ford for the Republican nomination, and the Ford White House was rightly concerned. Still, Nixon believed that with Ford having already gone to China in November, he could now justify going himself. He wasn't interfering with the president and he wasn't going ahead of him. He knew, though, that the Ford White House would likely not be wild about the idea of his visit.

As a result, Nixon played coy. Privately, he made arrangements to fly out on February 20. Publicly, he said nothing. In January of 1976, he met with William Gulley, the chief of White House military affairs who was responsible for handling former presidents. Gulley had come to Annenberg's Sunnylands to deliver a regular briefing to the former president. But soon the former president decided to brief Gulley.

"I'm going to China," Nixon said quietly. And then added, "Don't breathe a word to a soul." Gulley overcame his momentary shock to ask what impact this trip would have for the president. Nixon brushed off Gulley's concerns and predicted that the upcoming New Hampshire primary would go Ford's way.

Gulley could not in good conscience honor Nixon's request to stay quiet. He immediately notified National Security Advisor Brent Scowcroft. But Scowcroft kept a close hold on the information—so close that when Secretary of State Henry Kissinger arrived at La Casa Pacifica on February 2, he didn't know of Nixon's plans. And Nixon did not divulge them to him.[18]

The public announcement of the trip came not from Nixon, but from China. On February 5, Han Hsu, the Chinese Liaison Office's deputy, gave the White House an advance copy of the press release announcing the news. Later that day, the Chinese government formally issued the release.

President Ford, a man not easily angered, was overcome with rage. He held his emotions in check as he called the former president from the Oval Office. Ford took the high road and wished Nixon well on the trip. If he had hoped the former president might ask for Ford's blessing, he was mistaken. Nixon talked at length about how important China was. Nothing was said about the timing of the trip or about how this might affect Ford's reelection prospects.

But once the Chinese government made the announcement, negative reactions began pouring in. If Nixon had hoped that the lingering emotions over Watergate had tapered off, he soon found that they had not.

In the Senate, Barry Goldwater suggested angrily that Nixon might extend his stay in China indefinitely: "If he wants to do this country a favor he might stay over there." And conservative patriarch William F. Buckley wrote that people would be so enraged that it would "aggravate sentiments of injustice that can only be exercised at the expense of Gerald Ford."[19]

Not all of the criticism was leveled in public. "You told me that President Nixon is acting without portfolio," Maine governor James Longley wrote to Ford. "If such is the case, the public deserves to know." But Ford remained quiet.

Not everyone criticized the move. Former Nixon speechwriter Bill Safire, now writing a column for the *New York Times,* interviewed his former boss for a column in which Nixon claimed he was going to China because the relationship begun in 1972 was now "more important" than when he traveled there as president.

Nixon arrived in Peking on February 20, 1976. He had flown on a Boeing 707 that the Chinese government had sent for him. Pat joined her husband on the trip, as did Jack Brennan and several support staff and Secret Service agents. It was a much more subdued affair than the official 1972 trip, but the media still couldn't get enough of it. Here was Nixon finally back in the public eye at the scene of his greatest triumph.

The next day, Nixon was hosted at a state dinner at the Great Hall of the People. The former president rose to make a toast. Wearing a dark suit and looking very much like he had four years earlier, Nixon spoke of how "the future of all the people in this world depends on the reliability and the capability and the determination of our two nations to work together...." It was a succinct summary of what Nixon believed and what he had tried to do as president: bring the U.S. closer to China and pull China away from the Soviets.[20]

Still, Nixon's return trip to China also included reminders that China was still a totalitarian state. After Nixon visited with Chairman Mao the next day, he toured Tiananmen Square and shook hands with ordinary Chinese citizens. When Nixon saw a man holding a young child, he asked him what he wanted the child to grow up to be.

"Whatever the party decides," the man answered grimly.

Nixon met with university students and with new premier Hua Kuo-fend and former minister Chiao Kuan-hua. At a dinner to wrap up the trip, Nixon and Hua both spoke. Hua spoke assertively about the "rapid" expansion of the Soviet Union. Nixon suggested that the relationship between the U.S. and China must continue to evolve:

"We shall not fail. We must not fail, because of the young people we saw at the university today." He added that it would be naïve to think that "the mere act of signing a statement of principle or diplomatic conference will bring lasting peace."[21]

After nine days, Nixon was exhausted but exhilarated. The trip had been everything he had wanted it to be. He had not been forgotten in China. Nor in America, for that matter. American newspapers covered the trip extensively. The *New York Times* keyed in on Nixon's closing remarks about how "signing a statement" would not "bring lasting peace," calling the ex-president's words "implicit criticism of President Ford and Secretary of State Kissinger" for their roles in the Helsinki talks the year before.

For a man who had grown accustomed to endless negative press coverage, to be taken seriously by the paper of record on a matter of policy represented an important step forward on the long road back.

Back home in San Clemente, Nixon basked in the glow of his first foray into the world after Watergate. He was delighted when Henry Kissinger called and asked if he would report back to the White House on his trip.

Yet reality soon set in. Most pressing of all, financial challenges still loomed over Nixon. After he had paid off his medical bills in 1975, he had had only five hundred dollars in his bank account. The advance money from the book publisher was spent on paying staff salaries. Clearly he needed to find more money, and he needed to do it quickly.

"He would sit there figuring away on his yellow pads," Khachigian would remember, "even when the sums just couldn't be made to add up, he would end up by saying, 'Oh, well, it will work out.'"[22]

As Nixon continued to construct his book detailing the events of his life and presidency, another book was making all the news in Washington.

*The Final Days* had been written by Bob Woodward and Carl Bernstein, the two reporters most closely associated with the coverage of Watergate. The book took a similar tack as their reporting of the scandal in the *Washington Post*. Nixon was portrayed as overly emotional, hysterical, and out of control in his last days as president. Though he never read the book, he did read excerpts. And they enraged him. The former president was particularly irked by the book's portrayal of Pat as a drunk.

"The nebulous, weak figure of *The Final Days* is not my mother," Julie Eisenhower—no doubt speaking for her father—told the *New York Times*. Though Nixon considered suing for libel, Bob Finch convinced him it would be a tough case to win.

Instead, Nixon returned to writing his own description of events to set the record straight. He worked day and night through the spring of 1976. One afternoon in July of that year, he and Pat relaxed in the patio area at La Casa Pacifica. Despite her husband's outrage over the book, on this particular day Pat had been reading reading *The Final Days*. And she had learned even worse news: her husband would be disbarred. Nixon himself had offered to resign from the New York State Bar. But rather than accept his resignation, the bar had chosen to publicly disbar him.

The impact of the book and the disbarment news hit Pat hard. The years of stress from being in the public light and the months of anguish over the loss of the presidency finally caught up with her. After sitting in the sun on the patio that afternoon, she felt suddenly sick, put down the book, and quickly returned to the house. David and Julie were in town on vacation and they were all supposed to meet at the pool later that afternoon. Pat emerged for the swim but did little more than sit on a step in the shallow end. Later, she managed to attend the dinner that Julie had prepared. "She said little and ate only a few bites," Julie remembered.[23]

She retired to bed. In the morning, she stumbled her way into the kitchen and struggled to open a new can of coffee. When Nixon arrived in the kitchen, he noticed his wife slurring her words.

After excusing himself to go to the office, Nixon went to the bedroom where Julie and David were staying. "I think your mommy's had a stroke," he told his daughter. He immediately called Dr. Lungren, who in the interest of time recommended that a doctor from nearby Camp Pendleton come visit. The military doctor took her blood pressure and found that it was 175 over 100.

Not long after, Pat Nixon arrived via ambulance at Long Beach Memorial Hospital. There the diagnosis was quick: she had suffered a stroke.

In the eighteen months since the resignation, Pat had been a constant source of strength to her husband.

"Dick," she often told him, "I don't know how you keep going."

"I get up in the morning just to confound my enemies," he once replied.

But now, back in Long Beach Memorial Hospital, the roles were reversed. Nixon found himself offering words of support.

He would come visit her every day in the hospital. He would kiss her and then grab her hand, saying, "Well, let me feel your grip." Often he would sit in the chair next to her bed and read telegrams that had come in from people around the country wishing her a speedy recovery. Often, Julie remembered, she seemed tired after just fifteen minutes of visiting.[24]

That's not surprising, given that the doctors had said publicly that "she may not walk normally" again. But Pat proved tougher than the stroke. After weeks of therapy at the hospital, she was well enough to return home. She had home health care available to her. But a long road still lay ahead of her.

One day while she was reclining again on the patio where she had first suffered the stroke weeks before, Pat spoke of the pain the last few years had caused her. With her husband, Julie, and David sitting near her, she spoke of the scandal that had brought down Nixon.

"Watergate is the only crisis that ever got me down," she said. "I guess it did because every day there were more ugly stories and there still are. It is just constant." Then she added sadly, "And I know I will never live to see the vindication."

Looking over at her husband, she added, "I don't think there's a man living who has more noble qualities, who is as kind and thoughtful and unselfish. He's always thinking about the country and not himself. Well, there just isn't anything small about him in any way."[25]

Watergate had taken a toll on Pat—emotionally, mentally, and now physically. But it never took a toll on her relationship with her husband. She remained his constant supporter.

———

As Pat continued recuperating at home, the presidential election season was in full bloom. The Nixons watched the campaign closely, and it was not lost on them that President Ford referred often to the last "two and a half years" and not to the last eight. Ford needed distance from Nixon. And while the Nixon family undoubtedly understood that, it still stung. It felt like Nixon's presidency was being erased from history.

Nixon had stayed quiet through the GOP primaries. President Ford faced a formidable opponent in former California governor Ronald Reagan. Reagan ran to Ford's right and sharply criticized the détente policies of "Dr. Kissinger and Mr. Ford." Of course, these were largely the same policies as Nixon's. Yet Nixon seemed to take little offense. Perhaps his political antenna picked up on the deep connection Reagan was making with conservative voters. Even if he didn't win the nomination, Reagan could win by losing. If the Democrats won in November, Reagan, assuming his health would hold up at his age, could take over the party in 1980.

In the end, Ford barely secured the nomination. But at the convention in Kansas City, Reagan stirred the crowd with his bold oratory, demanding that the GOP stand for "bold colors," not "pale pastels." But Reagan's time would have to wait. The immediate question was who Ford's vice presidential nominee would be. And here Nixon had definite opinions. His first choice was John Connally, who had served both as governor of Texas and as Nixon's treasury secretary. Nixon personally called delegates at the Republican convention in Kansas City to lobby for Connally. When that failed, Nixon tried calling Ford, but he was unable to speak with him.

In the end, Ford chose Kansas senator Robert Dole, a war hero who had been wounded in Europe at the end of World War II. Nixon knew and respected Dole. In fact, as chairman of the RNC in 1974, Dole had been loyal to Nixon. Interestingly, at that time Dole represented the conservative wing of the party; indeed, Reagan had given his approval to Dole's placement on the ticket. Nixon, perhaps anticipating a more conservative era looming for the party, did not object. In fact, ever the political strategist, he only worried about Dole's public persona. Nixon had struggled with his own challenges with his own personality in the television era; he knew how hard it was for an introverted person to come across as warm and engaging on television.

"He's able," he said of Dole, "but his personality is abrasive as hell." Then, correctly anticipating what would become years of Dole's gaffes on multiple presidential campaigns, Nixon warned, "he's going to cause a helluva lot of problems with the press. They better get somebody good to handle him, someone who can control him, limit his appearances to select audiences, or this guy's going to alienate a helluva lot of people."[26]

After the convention, when Gulley came from the White House for his usual briefing, Nixon said directly, "We know who our guy is. Now let's get to work."

Nixon believed the race was still winnable for Ford. But there was work to be done. Public opinion polls showed the president trailing the Democratic nominee, Georgia governor Jimmy Carter, by double digits. But Nixon told Gulley not to worry about the polls; the race would tighten as it got closer to November.

Nixon also told Gulley that he would send advice through Gulley and that he wanted it delivered directly to Richard "Dick" Cheney, who served as Ford's chief of staff. The former president's advice was predictably pragmatic, shrewd, and brutally honest.

"Don't worry about what you say about Nixon," he wrote in one piece of advice. "Murder me. I understand."

The gist of Nixon's strategy was to make the election a referendum on Carter, not on Ford. This was long before political strategists professionalized the art of the incumbent attacking his opponent rather than defending his own record. In 1976, the conventional wisdom was that an election should be focused on the incumbent.

Nixon, ahead of his time, urged Ford to go on the offensive and make the election about Carter.

"Carter scares the hell out of me," he told Gulley. "Scare the hell out of the American people about Carter's foreign policies. Bear down on it. He'll come close to making us a number two power."[27]

The Ford team, for its part, seemed eager to take the advice, if not to give credit to the source. Ford and his surrogates—most notable vice presidential candidate Bob Dole—went after Carter. And with each new poll that emerged that fall, the gap between the candidates narrowed, until it was too close to call heading into Election Day.

In the end, Carter won a narrow victory. Pundits were quick to point to Ford's pardon of Nixon as factor that had made the difference. Even Nixon agreed, to a certain extent. He expressed his sadness over Ford's fate to his daughter Julie, telling her that he bore "a great sense of responsibility for Ford's loss."

The Nixon political era had officially ended. A new Democratic administration would take over in January. And what would become of the remnants of the Republican Party? No one knew for sure. But Nixon had demonstrated in the advice and counsel he offered privately during the 1976 election that he still had one of the sharpest political minds around. Now, without a direct line to the White House anymore, Nixon would have to be resourceful about when and where he should offer his advice, and to whom. But if nothing else, he had proven to himself that he still had something to offer to the party and the country.

Chapter Six

# Interviews and Apologies

*"I'm a pretty fair poker player myself."*

As 1977 began, Nixon was thinking about television, of all things. It was time to get ready for his first television appearance since August 9, 1974.

Journalist David Frost had contacted Nixon back in the summer of 1975 about the possibility of doing television interviews. Frost was well-known for his wide-ranging interviews. In Nixon, he saw the chance of a lifetime—the first television interview with the only president to resign from office.

The president had already been toying with the idea of going on television and telling his side of the story. Plus, Nixon knew Frost. Frost had interviewed him earlier in his career. And Frost was shrewdly working through an intermediary—former Nixon aide Herb Klein, who eventually convinced his former boss to at least consider the interview request.

One of the most compelling reasons for Nixon to do the interview was to help solve his primary problem—money. Previously, many media outlets had balked at the thought of paying huge sums of money to Nixon. But Frost proved more than willing. Frost's production company, David Paradine Productions, offered to pay Nixon significant money for the interviews. It was an opportunity the former president couldn't pass up.

The deal came together after Swifty Lazar entered the negotiations. NBC, the other significant bidder, had offered as much as three hundred thousand dollars, but Lazar was now seeking more. When he and Frost spoke, he offered four one-hour shows in exchange for $750,000. Frost countered at five hundred thousand dollars. Lazar let NBC know about Frost's offer, and the network quickly raised its price from three hundred thousand dollars to four hundred thousand dollars. When informed of this, Frost offered to pay even more than his last offer of five hundred thousand dollars, but he wanted editorial control of the interview, and he wanted assurances that no other networks would interview Nixon before he did.[1]

In the end, they reached a deal: Frost would pay six hundred thousand dollars and get a piece of the profits. For his part, Nixon agreed to give no other interviews and gave control of the interview exclusively to Frost.

An ominous note was struck when Frost pointed out that the contract gave him control of the interview. Nixon brushed aside the warning.

"I'm a pretty fair poker player, myself," he said to Frost. "During the war, I won a helluva pot with less of a hand than you're holding."[2]

It was a remarkable exchange that foreshadowed what was to come in the interviews. Nixon seemed absolutely convinced he could handle any question thrown his way; Frost was equally convinced that he could destroy Nixon.

According to Frost, as he got out the check to make a down payment on the interview, Swifty Lazar interjected, "Can I have the check please?"

Nixon seemed shocked. Perhaps the constant worry over his financial challenges had caused him to want the money at that very moment. But Lazar, as his representative, would handle the money. Frost remembered that Nixon looked like a kid who had not been permitted to eat a "cookie" he had "just swiped from the jar."

The men shook hands and the deal was finalized. Later in the fall of 1976, Nixon had conducted his second negotiation with Frost over the interviews. This time the issue centered around timing. The former president wanted to do the interviews in August of 1977. Frost wanted to move much more quickly than that.

"As I recall," Nixon said when Frost objected to the late summer date, "we got a helluva rating [on] August 9, 1974."

Frost was unimpressed. He agreed that the ratings from the resignation had been huge, but he asked the former president, "What do you do for an encore?"[3]

Eventually they reached a compromise and Nixon agreed to conduct the interviews in March of 1977. Frost arrived again for another meeting in Nixon's San Clemente office in February. With the date of the showdown swiftly approaching, the two men abandoned the mostly cordial tone of past meetings for much more guarded postures.

When Nixon shook hands with Frost that day, he called him the "Grand Inquisitor." Frost answered that he was merely a "friendly neighborhood confidant." The new tone of subtle hostility would continue through the meeting and into subsequent conversations Frost had with the Nixon team in the runup to the March interviews.

"How do we know that you aren't going to screw us in the editing?" Colonel Brennan sharply asked Frost just days before the first interview.

"How do we know that you aren't going to screw us with stonewalling?" Frost shot back.[4]

Brennan had always opposed the interview. Like any staffer who fears his boss may be asked questions that don't have good answers, Brennan worried that Nixon was walking into a losing battle. And his frustration showed that day with Frost.

"Sixty percent of what this guy did in office was right," he said, raising his voice. "And 30 percent may have been wrong, but he thought it was right at the time. If you screw us on the 60 percent, I'm going to ruin you if it takes the rest of my life."

"If you screw me on the ten percent I'm going to ruin you if it take the rest of my life," Frost answered.

On March 23, 1977, at seven thirty in the morning, Frost met his team of researchers at the Beverly Hilton and then loaded them into his Mercedes Benz. Then he drove them an hour and a half to meet Nixon at the mansion of industrialist Nixon supporter H. L. Smith in Monarch Bay. In the living room of the house, Frost's team set up a makeshift television studio. The Nixon team helped by bringing some of Nixon's own souvenirs from San Clemente and placing them on the bookshelves to add to the set in the background of the interview.

Nixon dressed as he often did in a dark blue suit and a blue tie. He had studied for weeks with his research team back at La Casa Pacifica. "The only issue where there was a disagreement was on what to say about Watergate," Khachigian remembered. "Gannon, Sawyer, and Brennan wanted him to put it behind him and acknowledge some sort of wrongdoing. I told him not to give an inch." In fact, as Nixon prepared to meet with Frost for the tapings, he and Sawyer were only beginning the Watergate section of his memoirs. As the interviews started, no one on the Nixon team knew what he would say when pressed about Watergate.[5]

Inside the Smith mansion, Nixon used the master bedroom as his green room to prepare. The Nixon staffers used the den area as their gathering spot. As the two men entered the makeshift set in the mansion's living room, one of Frost's researchers, James Reston Jr., was surprised at how tall Nixon was. "He looked fit and healthy, well-tanned with an orangey hue," he recalled.

As Nixon and Frost sat down and the camera crew prepared to film, small talk ensued. Nixon spoke of the groundswell of support for Pat after her stroke. Frost, dressed in a crisp dark jacket and a striped grey shirt accented with a white collar, looked down at his notes before joking that the camera crew spoke only Turkish.

Frost was prepared. His team, led by Reston, had left no stone unturned in the research; they had even looked through the files of the Watergate prosecutors. And Frost had even gone through practice sessions with Bob Zelnick portraying a defensive Richard Nixon.

Frost's plan was to put Nixon on defense as soon as possible without being overtly hostile. The Frost team eventually wanted to set up a showdown over what had happened to the missing minutes on the tape and to trap Nixon into admitting he had played a role in the coverup. And they had what they believed was an ace in the hole. Frost team researcher Reston had interviewed former Nixon counselor Charles Colson. In the midst of the conversation, Colson had casually mentioned that there were tapes of conversations he had conducted with Nixon about Watergate. Reston had never heard any tapes that included Colson. Indeed, no one had. So Reston went to the federal courthouse and searched through the record of the Haldeman trial. And in the exhibits, he found five different conversations between Colson and Nixon. In one of them, the word "stonewalling" had been used. Nixon had no memory of these conversations, and he certainly had no knowledge that the tapes existed. Only Reston and Frost did. And they intended to use it. A memo prepared by Reston for Frost before the first taping said, "This is a trap for Nixon and should be sprung deftly."[6] Indeed, years later, Reston would refer to the videotaping sessions not as interviews, but as an "ambush."[7]

Once the cameras were rolling, Frost lost little time getting into the heart of the matter.

"Why didn't you burn the tapes?" he asked the former president. Nixon responded in longform with a treatise that ultimately suggested Haldeman was to blame.

Later in the first interview, Frost showed Nixon a tape of the resignation speech, which the former president claimed he hadn't seen before. Nixon offered some commentary on the performance—and a bit of humor. His advisors had told him that he "shouldn't gesture so much because your hands get in front of your face. Well, maybe that's good. Maybe the hands are better looking than the face."

But Frost was not laughing. He pushed Nixon to say how he thought history would remember his administration.

After several hours of taping, the first day's session ended. Nixon returned to La Casa Pacifica; Frost returned to his hotel in Beverly Hills. Some on the Frost team worried that the interviewer hadn't laid a glove on Nixon yet. They urged Frost to get tougher in the coming interviews and to try and stop Nixon when he filibustered.

A few days later, Frost celebrated a birthday. Celebrities came to the party, including Neil Diamond. But it was Sammy Cahn

Nixon with David Frost. (Courtesy of the Richard Nixon Foundation)

who brought down the house. Cahn changed the words of the song "Love and Marriage" to:

Frost and Nixon, Frost and Nixon,
Now, there's an act that's gonna take some fixin'.[8]

The interviewing continued, but Nixon more than held his own. The Frost team pushed the interviewer to get even tougher. As the two combatants settled into their places for another round on April 13, Nixon joked that an overhead plane that could be heard outside was CBS checking up on Frost. Frost didn't seem amused.

Frost's strategy was to open with a "litmus" question that was overly broad and then to work back toward specific elements of the question. On this day, he asked, "With the perspective of three years now, do you feel that you ever obstructed justice or were part of a conspiracy to obstruct justice?"

Nixon responded with an attempt to make the topic even broader than Frost had: "Watergate means all of the charges that were thrown at me during the period before I left the presidency."

Frost objected and tried to narrow the scope of the question again, suggesting that he wanted to know about "Watergate, the cover-up, and the events that sprang from that."

Then, laying his trap, Frost asked a series of questions about the Haldeman meeting on June 20, 1972, when Watergate had been discussed and then eighteen-and-a-half minutes of the audio-tape of the conversation had been destroyed. Nixon answered that he had had nothing to do with the tape's erasure and didn't know how it had happened. He described the conversations with Haldeman as nothing out of the ordinary: there had been no talk of a cover-up.

Frost pounced. He began reading excerpts from the transcripts of the Colson tapes. The excerpts included the word "stonewalling" and also this phrase: "The president's losses gotta get cut on the cover-up deal."

Nixon, in an apparent attempt to deflect attention from the evidence suggesting that he had played a role in the coverup, expressed confusion about what exactly Frost was quoting from.

"It hasn't been published yet, you say?" he asked.

But Frost wasn't giving an inch. "I think it's available to anyone who consults the record."

Nixon then offered some context for the content of the transcripts, saying, "I didn't know if anybody at that point—nobody on the White House staff, not John Mitchell, anybody else that I believed was involved" was involved "criminally."

This was the basic Nixon response to the Frost charges: yes, he may have talked about damage control on the tapes, but he didn't know that the damage he was seeking to control was a criminal enterprise.

Frost, seeking to exploit the moment, continued quoting from the transcripts.

Nixon listened nervously. Then he interjected, "You're doing something here which I am not doing and I will not do throughout these broadcasts. You have...you were reading there...out of context, out of order...."

The interview ended. Frost had finally prevailed in one of the exchanges thanks to a massive advantage he possessed—his team had searched far and wide for every scrap of information they could find on Watergate, while Nixon had yet to get to the Watergate section of his memoirs. He simply didn't know as much about Watergate as Frost did. Indeed, the researcher handling the Watergate section of the book for Nixon, Diane Sawyer, did not possess the Colson transcripts either. Armed with exclusive information, Frost had set the trap and executed it perfectly.[9]

If Nixon didn't realize the calamity that had fallen on him, his team did.

"The president of the United States made himself look like a criminal defendant with David as the prosecutor," Ken Khachigian bemoaned.

Sawyer, perhaps feeling bad about the level of Watergate detail that Frost possessed, added, "He hasn't written the Watergate part of his book yet. So none of us knew what he was going to say."

Nixon had said quite a bit in the interview. His explanation was not a bad one—that he hadn't seen the material and that any comments he made at the time of the tapes were made unaware that the coverup was a coverup of criminal activity. But in television, as in politics, a person explaining is a person losing. And on that day and in that taping, it was hard to escape the conclusion that Nixon had lost and Frost had won.

The sparring partners met up again at the Smith mansion a few days later. Frost continued to try to home in on Nixon. The former president, for his part, seemed a bit more introspective in this interview.

To him, the coverup had come about because he was fighting for his team.

"I knew their families," he said in explaining why it was hard to simply fire people on his staff accused of wrongdoing. Then, quoting British prime minister William Gladstone, Nixon said that a leader has to be "a good butcher. Well, I think that the great story, as far as the summary of Watergate is concerned...I was not a good butcher."

This was as close as Nixon had come in the interviews to expressing remorse. Still arguing that he had not known of any criminal wrongdoing at the time, he conceded that he hadn't done enough to hold his staff accountable.

But that wasn't enough for Frost. He wanted more. Frost's staff had been telling him for weeks that this wasn't an interview—it was a prosecution. Reston, in particular, wanted to see Nixon "confess" to the crimes.

Frost, no doubt with all his staff's promptings in his mind, pressed the issue.

"There are three things," he told Nixon, "that I would like to hear you say, and I think the American people would like to hear you say." Looking down at the table that sat between the two men as he read from his notes, Frost said that the first item he would like Nixon to address was that "there was probably more than mistakes, there was wrongdoing.... Whether it was a crime or not." Nixon sat uncomfortably as Frost continued with the words he thought people wanted to hear from Nixon: "I did abuse the power I had as president...." He ended with a third request for a Nixon admission: "I put the American people through two years of needless agony, and I apologize for that." Nixon sat watching impassively as Frost made his requests. The former president's head was tilted at an angle, and his eyes watched Frost closely. He occasionally looked off to the side as he processed the demands coming at him from the interviewer.

After Frost made his charges, Nixon began to speak, but Frost interjected again. "And I know how difficult it is for anyone and most of all you," he said about making an apology. "But I think people need to hear it. And I think unless you say it you're going to be haunted for the rest of your life."

As Nixon began to respond, he continued to look off in the distance, seemingly unsure of himself. When Frost interjected yet again, Colonel Brennan jumped into action. He furiously wrote out the words "Let him talk" on a piece of paper and held it up off camera where only Frost could see it. Frost misread the sign and thought it said "Let's talk." As a result, the interview came to a halt.

Frost and Brennan stepped away from the makeshift set for a brief but tense conversation.

"You've gotta let him do it his own way," Brennan said.

When one of Frost's producers demanded that Nixon make a full confession, Brennan pushed back again—then asked for time.

"Let me talk to him," he said and left for Nixon's holding room.

But while Brennan had been talking to Frost, Khachigian had been talking to Nixon. The old speechwriter had been through so many battles with his boss over the years and Nixon had always admired his ability to give tough, honest advice. Now the time had come for Khachigian to give the toughest advice of all.

"He wants me to say I'm guilty and I'm not going to do it," fumed the former president.

Khachigian, realizing how enraged Nixon was, decided to respond with questions rather than answers: "What do you want to say?"

As Nixon paced around the bedroom, he thought for a moment before responding. "Look, I'm not trying to blame anyone," he finally said. "I regret it. But if they want me to get down on the floor and grovel, never."

Khachigian, the consummate wordsmith, thought that Nixon had just created a more elegant solution than any he could have offered. "Mr. President," Khachighian said, "that's exactly what you tell Frost."[10]

As the two gladiators returned to the arena and prepared to go at it again before the cameras, Nixon seemed more composed. Perhaps his brief conversation with Khachigian had helped clear his mind. He knew what Frost wanted. But he also knew how to handle the interviewer's demands. Frost wanted him to say he was legally wrong; instead, Nixon would offer something less exciting, but more profound, to Frost. No, he wouldn't say he was legally wrong. But he would say he had been morally wrong.

With the cameras on, Frost continued to push for an apology. But Nixon, who had previously been on the defensive, now pushed back hard.

"It snowballed and it was my fault," Nixon responded. "I'm not blaming anybody else. I'm simply saying to you that, as far as I'm concerned, I not only regret it—I indicated my own beliefs in this matter when I resigned. People don't think it was enough to admit mistakes, fine. If they want me to get down and grovel on the floor, no. Never, because I don't believe I should."[11]

Nixon also told Frost that whether he was impeached or not was not important because "I have impeached myself." When Frost pushed him on this, Nixon explained that he had impeached himself "by resigning."

At last the interviews came to an end. Frost had them edited within weeks, and the first episode ran May 4. It was a ratings sensation, generating enough viewers to make it the most-watched news broadcast ever up to that time. Some fifty-five million viewers saw the performance. And although a Gallup Poll showed that most Americans felt Nixon was guilty of obstruction of justice, another 44 percent felt more sympathetic to him than they had been before the interviews.

For Nixon, there were no celebrations. He had done the interviews because he had to financially. But going over all the details of his downfall had proved to be an emotional ordeal. As he settled back into life at La Casa Pacifica, he was ready to return to some sense of normalcy. And that meant finishing the memoirs and starting to think about really stepping out into public. He had gone to China and he had appeared on American television in the Frost interviews. But he knew the time was coming when he would have to do more. With a book coming out, he would have the perfect opportunity.

As is typical with any writing, the editing of the book was turning out to be a challenge. The publisher sent editor Robert Markel to San

Clemente to review the material that had been written thus far and make recommendations. Markel thought the manuscript was becoming too long, but the Nixon staff resisted his suggestions.

"If you are going to know any of it," Frank Gannon said of Nixon's life story, "you have to know all of it."

Markel was unpersuaded. He told Gannon that it was important to tell the whole story but also to be "able to live it."

The issue was taken to Nixon. After hearing the arguments from both sides, he acknowledged that cutting material could leave only "the bones" of the story. But then he suggested that was fine, if it was the only way to do it.

Markel made a second appearance in San Clemente in April. That meeting was largely social, but Nixon did manage to talk about his goals for the book.

"I want people to read it," he said in describing why it was so important for him that the book be well written. "I want them to understand."[12]

To make the book more readable, Markel enlisted the help of a New York editor ironically named David Frost (Nixon took to calling him the "good" David Frost) and another editor, Nancy Brooks, who was from Texas. The two flew to San Clemente that summer and began their work in earnest.

The work went on through the rest of the summer and into the fall. The last remaining piece of the Nixon story to be resolved was what exactly he would say about Watergate.

When Diane Sawyer brought Nixon an outline detailing all the events of Watergate, he read through it all. Then, looking up from the document, he said simply, "This is the first time I've really understood everything that happened."

The former president then began a torrent of dictation that would eventually lead to 250 pages of content. Continuing what he had begun in the Frost interviews—the admission of moral, if not legal, mistakes—Nixon confessed in his dictation: "Instead of exerting presidential leadership aimed at uncovering the cover-up, I embarked on an increasingly desperate search for ways to limit the damage to my friends." While not enough of a concession for his critics, the statement was largely true: Nixon hadn't been involved in any way in the break-ins, and when he learned about them his goal was to protect his staff.

For his part, Markel generally liked the Watergate dictations. But he did feel like Nixon hadn't said enough about the missing eighteen-and-a-half minutes of tape. In October, he met with the ex-president and urged him to say more about the tape. Working with Nancy Brooks, Nixon wrote that while "the only explanations that would be readily accepted" were that either he or his secretary, Rose Wood, had erased the tape, he was emphatic in denying both. "I know that I did not do it. And I completely believe Rose when she says she did not do it."

With that, the manuscript of the memoirs was completed. Markel had told Frost and Brooks that he wanted the writing done by September. "It must not, it cannot, it will not go longer than that," he had implored in July. But even though the writing has stretched into October, Markel seemed pleased with the product.[13]

So did Nixon. At a celebration of the book's completion with his researchers, Nixon raised a glass for a toast: "To the book! And to the future!" he said after thanking them for their work.[14]

As 1977 came to a close, Nixon had begun finally to come to terms with Watergate. In the Frost interview he had offered an emotional apology for his "moral mistakes" while staunchly denying any legal mistakes. Even the formulation of the phrase "impeached myself" was a way of taking the matter out of the legal realm and placing it into the realm of personal responsibility. And in the memoirs, while not accepting any role in the actual criminal cover-up, Nixon took responsibility for "covering up" for his friends. This was now the Nixon line on Watergate: he had failed personally, but he had not committed a crime. He had impeached and punished himself by resigning from office. And he had been too loyal in trying to protect his friends. This is the same line he would return to any time Watergate came up for the rest of his life.

In a way, the Frost interviews and the memoirs had settled Watergate for Nixon. Now he was ready to move on. But a lingering question remained. Was the country ready to move on?

As 1978 began, Nixon was about to find out.

# Chapter Seven

# The First Steps Back

*"You've come back and I've come back."*

O n January 9, 1978, Richard Nixon celebrated his sixty-fifth birthday. He was joined at Casa de Pacifica by his family. As typically happened on his birthdays, calls from well-wishers came in from around the country. But one in particular meant the most to him. From a hospital in Minnesota, Hubert Humphrey called to wish Nixon well on his birthday. The two men had long been friendly rivals. After Nixon narrowly won the 1968 election, he felt genuine empathy for the Democratic candidate. "Pat and I know the heartache you and Muriel must be going through," he wrote to Humphrey in the days following the 1968 election, "to have come so close, then lost the biggest prize." Four years later, when Humphrey came up short in his bid to win the Democratic nomination again, Nixon wrote to console him again: "As friendly opponents in the political arena, I hope that we can both serve our parties in a way that will serve the nation." Nixon had always liked Humphrey; Humphrey had always respected Nixon.[1]

Nixon's birthday was not the first time the two men had spoken in recent months. On Christmas Eve, Humphrey had called La Casa Pacifica only to hear the voice of a discouraged Nixon on the line. Afterward, Humphrey, who was dying of cancer, told his family how disturbing the conversation had been. He seemed genuinely worried about his old rival's state of mind. He worried that Nixon was isolated and alone in California.

"No former president should live in exile from the nation's capital," he told his wife when he hung up the phone.

Humphrey was so worried that he had called Nixon again on Christmas Day. This time Humphrey called bearing gifts. He told Nixon that he only had a few days to live and said that when his body lay in state in the Capitol, he wanted Nixon to be there.

"Dick, I'm not going to be around much longer," he told Nixon. "There is going to be a memorial service for me in the Capitol Rotunda. I want you to attend that service."[2]

It was an extraordinary act of grace. Here, a man whom Nixon had vanquished during the presidential election in 1968—someone who could have found pleasure in the suffering that Nixon had endured—saw fit to include Nixon in his public funeral. At the end of 1977, the American people still gave Nixon overwhelmingly negative ratings in opinion polls. But Humphrey wanted to help bring him back, in a sense. He told Nixon that if anyone objected to his presence at the funeral, Nixon should say he was there "at the personal request" of Hubert Humphrey.

Nixon had been moved by the offer. Not that his former political rival gave him any choice as to whether he would accept it. "You must attend," Humphrey had told him. Now, on his birthday, Nixon could tell from the strained voice on the other end of the line that Humphrey was losing his fight with cancer. He sensed his old friend didn't have long to live. "He's only got a few days," he told Jack Brennan after the call ended. Then he gave unequivocal orders to his chief of staff: "I don't care what it takes, but I'm going to his funeral. Start working on it."[3]

When Humphrey died on January 13, Nixon issued a statement calling him a "dedicated patriot" who "commanded the genuine respect and affection of his political opponents and allies alike." Humphrey's death provided another reminder to Nixon of his own mortality. He had already suffered a political death and had very nearly suffered a physical one, as well. Yet Nixon found himself moved by the death of his friend and the grace that Humphrey had shown him.

On January 15, Nixon and Colonel Brennan boarded a United Airlines commercial flight to Washington. When he landed at Dulles around 9:20 that night, it marked the first time he had been back to Washington since the resignation. Indeed, echoes of Watergate still chased him as about a hundred protestors waited for him at the airport terminal.

The next day, Nixon joined President Carter and former president Ford at the service. Nixon, dressed in a black suit and black tie, sat stoically through the ceremony as Vice President Walter Mondale called

President Carter and former presidents Ford and Nixon together for the funeral of Hubert Humphrey. (National Archives and Records Administration)

Humphrey his "country's conscience." After the ceremony concluded, Humphrey's widow, Muriel, turned to shake hands with the Fords. When she got to Nixon, the former president kissed her on the cheek.

It was an extraordinary moment, unthinkable only a few days before. Here was Nixon at the U.S. Capitol honoring a former rival—and except for the protestors at the airport, no one seemed to object. Of all the ironies of Nixon's return to acceptance, none is more striking than the fact that Hubert Humphrey helped make it happen.

Back home in California after the funeral, Nixon was beginning to see some rays of light in early 1978. "He never talked about a 'comeback,'" son-in-law Ed Cox remembers of the days following the Frost interviews and the completion of the memoirs. "But he wanted to be active again." The Humphrey funeral had allowed him to re-enter Washington and be accepted as an elder statesman. He was eager to capitalize on this moment.[4]

The Frost interviews had marked a turning point in Nixon's post-presidential life. At last he had spoken publicly about Watergate. The public had watched him for hours. And the reviews had been mostly positive. Now he had been invited by a former Democratic rival to a place of honor at a state funeral. Nixon had seemingly come quite a long way since August 1974.

And Nixon's financial situation had improved, thanks to the payments from the Frost interview. With his financial status stronger and with the memoirs completed, Nixon began to think about what would come next. That year on his sixty-fifth birthday, Nixon confronted his future.

"I had to decide what to do with the rest of my life," he would write. "In a sense, this was a life-or-death decision. If a person quits after a defeat, he dies spiritually and will soon die physically."[5]

As Nixon looked back on the sixty-five years of his life, he couldn't help but reflect on the recent valleys he had been through.

He had wallowed in the sorrows of Watergate for nearly four years. He had faced a health crisis that nearly killed him. He had watched his wife suffer through a stroke. He had lived with constant financial pressure. And he had wondered how he would make a living.

But Nixon had endured. Despite the constant struggles of the nearly four years since his resignation, he had survived. But any survivor wants more than just to exist; he wants to live fully again.

Now for the first time since he resigned the presidency, Nixon truly was ready to live again. He wanted to be able to use his voice and his mind to be involved in public affairs again. And he fixed his eyes on a new and specific goal: using his status as a foreign policy expert to become a player once again in politics. Above all, Nixon was an intellectual, and such a person doesn't need public office to have a public impact.

"As I analyzed the world scene, I was profoundly troubled by the geopolitical momentum behind Moscow's expansionism and by the paralysis of political will in the Western world," he would remember. "I therefore chose to devote myself to advocating a more energetic and assertive American role in leading the free world, a stronger and more skillful strategy for the continuing East-West conflict, and a more far-sighted geopolitical approach to managing global affairs in a world with new emerging power centers in Europe and East Asia."[6]

Nixon's future would be based on his past: he would focus on foreign policy, the issue that had always motivated him most. It made perfect sense. The former president had long been seen as a savant on foreign policy. And he hoped his abbreviated presidency would be remembered for foreign policy triumphs, namely ending the war in Vietnam and opening the door to China.

Now in 1978, Nixon surveyed the foreign policy landscape and decided the time was right to enter the fray again. As he watched the policies of the Carter administration, he became agitated. Even at this early stage in Jimmy Carter's presidency, there were signs that the job—especially the role of the president on the world stage—was too big for him.

When Nixon learned at one of his briefings with Gulley that Carter had ordered a reduction in line officers in the military, he exploded.

"Who gives a damn how many generals and admirals there are anyway?" Nixon asked rhetorically. "When a war breaks out, right here in San Diego the marines have got a training facility that you damn well know about. They can turn out killers every ninety days. But it's no use turning out killers if you haven't educated the generals and the admirals to see the big picture and understand what has to be done."

This was Nixon's main criticism against Carter: he couldn't see the forest for the leaves. Carter was so bogged down in minute details that he had no sense of strategy.

Nixon also sensed that Carter was unknowingly undermining the power of the presidency. The man who famously approved the schedule of the White House tennis courts was not a man who had time to think strategically about how to use the power of his office. When Nixon heard that Carter had denied talking to the Justice Department about Robert Vesco, a fugitive financier who was suspected of involving the president's brother Billy in a bribery scheme, Nixon scoffed at the idea that no one at the Justice Department had paid attention to Carter's overture in the case of his brother's associate. "When the attorney general gets a memo from the president," he told Gulley, "he shits in his pants."[7] Nixon believed Carter almost certainly had spoken to his attorney general about the matter and felt there was no way that either person didn't remember the conversation.

For Nixon, Carter's presidency presented the perfect opportunity to speak up again and to make an impact on foreign policy decisions in Washington. For that purpose, he would choose a familiar vehicle and write a series of books. Nixon had always enjoyed the writing process, whether it was writing his recent memoirs or his *Six Crises* book in 1962 detailing six major moments in his career up to that point. Now he would write policy books outlining his vision for America's place in the world and what America's strategy should be.

But if Nixon wanted to be back in the public's eye, then writing books would only take him so far. He would also have to start appearing in public again. His memoirs, published that spring of 1978, enjoyed largely positive reviews and strong sales. Was now the time to start making public appearances? Nixon began discussing the possibility with staff and family.

Meanwhile, to celebrate the launch of the book, he hosted a reception at La Casa Pacifica where he handed the first three copies of the book to his wife and daughters. A few days later in late May, he hosted three hundred prisoners of war who had returned from Vietnam. Nixon went all out in throwing a party for them: alcohol was served at six different stations around the pool and flowers had been placed all around the house. It was hard to know who enjoyed themselves more—the Vietnamese heroes or Nixon. The former commander-in-chief autographed a copy of his book for each man.

A few weeks later, Nixon ventured up the Pacific Coast Highway to Angel Stadium in Anaheim. The California Angels were playing against the Kansas City Royals. Nixon enjoyed being at the stadium. Before the game, he even spent a few minutes talking baseball with announcer Dick Enberg.

"I remember the last time I was here was the 1973 Opening Day and I hope it's a good omen," he said with a smile. Then he flashed his encyclopedic memory for facts. "That day I remember Nolan Ryan pitched, the Angels won 3 to 2. And Frank Robinson, playing his first game for the Angels, hit one over the left field wall." He even recalled that Steve Busby had been pitching for the opposing Royals that day.[8]

Later during the game, he spoke with a local sportswriter and bragged about the strength of the Angels lineup. "Now you can take all this advice and go to Las Vegas, put some money down and win yourself a trip to Hawaii, or Peking, if you want."

By the end of June, the first public steps of Nixon's comeback had taken place. He had appeared on television, attended a state funeral, released a successful book, and hosted hundreds of former prisoners of war at a publicized reception. Now it was time to go even further. And the choice for his next public outing was a strategic one.

As a presidential candidate in 1968, Nixon had campaigned on the idea of revenue sharing. The idea was that the federal government should send some money directly to local governments with no strings attached. The local entities could use the money as they saw fit. Eventually, a bipartisan bill that had originated with Democratic congressman Ed Koch of New York emerged from Congress. Nixon signed the legislation in 1972. Like many of the domestic achievements of his administration, Nixon felt that it had been overlooked in the shadow of Watergate.

But it had not been forgotten in the town of Hyden, Kentucky, which was home to five hundred people. This coal-mining town had used revenue-sharing money from the federal government to construct a recreation center. And since revenue sharing had been a Nixon program, the reliably Republican town decided to name the new center after Richard Nixon. The dedication for the building was set for July 2, 1978.

Nixon received an invitation to the dedication not long after his foray into Anaheim. He wanted to go. It made sense on so many levels. This had been his program; these were his voters. But was it too soon? Would he risk a new batch of "cover-up" stories from the media? The Humphrey funeral had been different; he had the cover of the Humphrey family, who wanted him there. But now he would not have such a luxury. Critics in the press would likely pounce and accuse him of reengaging in politics.

Nixon weighed all the pros and cons and decided to attend. He was ready to be seen in public. He was ready to take another step on the journey back. He would take the risk.

Nixon left San Clemente for the airport early on the morning of July 1. When he arrived at the London-Corbin Airport in Kentucky, he looked out from the plane's window and saw more than a thousand people waiting to greet him. Many in the crowd were wearing Nixon campaign gear from 1972. As Nixon exited the executive jet, a local high school band began playing "Hail to the Chief." Instinctively, Nixon decided to work the crowd. Just like he had during the 1972 campaign, he went to the fence line and shook hands with supporters. Some were holding signs with the old Nixon slogan from the 1972 presidential campaign: "NOW MORE THAN EVER." Nixon shook hands before making his way to a makeshift stage where a microphone had been set up.

"I really appreciate your coming out," he said in his first public speech since leaving the White House. For a man not known for outward displays of emotion, Nixon seemed genuinely moved by the crowd. For the people to "come out to the airport and stand in the hot sun...that's just the nicest thing you can do."[9]

Nixon then made his way to the car waiting to drive him to Hyden. After spending the night at the Appalachian Motel, he rose the next morning and went over his remarks for the day's event. Around eleven thirty in the morning, the Nixon motorcade left the hotel and began the drive to the community center. As the cars pulled up, Nixon could see the brown brick building with the roof sloping from right to left. Just below the roofline, the words "Richard M. Nixon Recreation Center" could be seen on the building.

As Nixon got out of the car and headed inside, he could see the crowd, which numbered about four thousand. "I hope it's not too soon," he said, wondering if he had made the right decision in making such a public move.

He needn't have worried. The people in the crowd had been chosen for their Republican credentials. So the former president was in little danger of any hecklers greeting him on this day. Besides, it had been almost four years since his resignation. The American people had been through a lot in those four years. They had seen the failures of Ford and Carter. And they had watched the Frost interviews and seen Nixon in anguish over his fall from power. After four years, people were beginning to be ready to show grace to the former president.

The program that day began with the introduction of local officials. Then, the time had come—Nixon would at last address a public event in the U.S. It was the first such event since Watergate.

Warm applause greeted him as he was introduced and made his way to the microphone. As he placed his hands on the sides of the podium, he looked very much like he had as president. Wearing a dark blue suit and looking fit, Nixon smiled at the crowd. A sign attached to the front of the podium read, "Thanks for Courage Under Fire." Though he couldn't see the sign, he could see the support from the crowd. He quickly launched into a classic Nixon speech. Politics in America is always a game of choices, and no one understood this better than Nixon. As a candidate and as a president, he had always tried to demonstrate the choices people faced and the consequences of those choices: the Silent Majority versus the elites and the free world versus the Communists. Perhaps no one ever framed issues as choices better than Nixon. Now, as a former president, he did so again.

He spoke to the Hyden audience that day about two Americas. In one America, people were being told that the country needed to adjust to changing times and not try to lead the world. This thinly veiled shot at the Carter administration was quickly followed up by his description of a second option.

"Let me tell you about another America," he said—a country made up of people "who have not lost faith in America, who believe American should be strong...." The crowd erupted in cheers as a smile creased Nixon's face. After all those years and after all those setbacks, he still had it. He could still work a crowd.[10]

The speech went on for forty minutes. But it only took one minute to prove his point—Nixon was back. He had taken a risk in going public; all it would have taken to ruin the narrative of a comeback that day would have been one angry heckler demanding he go to jail. Instead, he got cheers. The public, it seemed, was ready to forgive.

Some members of the media were not so ready. *New York* magazine, for example, had recruited Dick Tuck to cover the event. The selection of Tuck spoke volumes about the magazine editors' intentions. Tuck was an infamous political trickster who had spent years trying to undermine Nixon. During Nixon's gubernatorial campaign way back in 1962, Nixon had arrived at an event in a Chinese restaurant where Tuck had decided to make an issue of a previously reported loan from Howard Hughes to Nixon's brother. "What about the Hughes loan?" read signs in Chinese held by members of the crowd.

This was the man chosen to cover Nixon's comeback. He was not a serious journalist.

Still, he managed to secure an interview with his nemesis. After some small talk about politics, Tuck got to the point. "My editors at *New York* magazine were hoping that I'd come back with a signed confession," he told the former president. Tuck then admitted without such a confession he wouldn't have anything to write in his story.

"Don't worry, you'll think of something," Nixon deadpanned. The interview ended. Ironically, for all his animus toward Nixon, Tuck still respected the man's mind and his ability. Years later, shortly before his death in 2018, Tuck shocked guests at the celebration of his ninety-third birthday by saying of the current Republican president: "Donald Trump couldn't carry Dick Nixon's shoes."[11]

As Nixon left Kentucky that day in 1978, he was experiencing a glimpse of the happiness that had eluded him since Watergate. He still commanded an audience; he still had something to say; he still could be a voice on issues that mattered to him.

It was a small victory that day in Hyden, Kentucky. But long wars are won with small battles. And for Nixon, it was now time to start thinking about his next strategic moves. Like any commander, Nixon wanted to pick favorable terrain for his next battle. So for his next public foray he chose Joe Graham Post #119 of the American Legion in Biloxi, Mississippi. This would be another safe place for Nixon to speak—a Southern town in front of military veterans. Colonel Brennan called this the "friendly faces" strategy, and the Nixon team would have been hard-pressed to find any friendlier faces than these.

There seemed to be good news all around Nixon that summer of 1978. In August, his daughter Julie gave birth to his first grandchild— Jennie Elizabeth Eisenhower. An overjoyed Nixon took pen to paper to welcome his granddaughter.

"In the years ahead you will have many happy moments," the letter read. "But in life you must expect some disappointments and sadness. At such times you will always be sustained by the fact that so many people love you very much."[12]

Nixon went on to note that Jennie's "Great Grandfather, President Eisenhower, had the great gift of being able to light up a room with his smile. My fondest wish, which I know will come true, is that you will have that same gift."

The letter was signed, "RN."

The good times continued into the fall. In November, Nixon flew in a private jet to the event in Mississippi. On his way, he stopped and greeted fans in Dallas and then later in Shreveport. At the airport in Shreveport, Nixon reveled in the crowd's chant of "Keep coming out!"

"Don't worry, I will," he responded. "Officially, you can say, 'I'm out!'" The crowd roared its approval. But the media in attendance were appalled. A *New York Times* editorial excoriated his comments. "The implication is that, beyond the formal pardon issued by President Ford," the editorial read, "a merciful Judge Nixon has now ruled that a manly Defendant Nixon deserves to be 'out.'"

If Nixon ever bothered to read the editorial, he didn't act like it. Like anyone emerging from the throes of a personal calamity, he was starting to feel alive again. In Mississippi, Nixon took a giant stride forward in his journey out of the darkness of his despair. Just like the old days when he was campaigning for office, Nixon spoke to a cheering crowd inside the Mississippi Coast Coliseum. For his remarks on this occasion, Nixon spoke more personally about his past challenges. As a reference point, he talked about the hurricane the region had experienced in 1969. While some had thought it would take decades to rebuild, he told the crowd that he knew it wouldn't.

"I knew there was a spirit no hurricane could possibly break," he said. Then he referred to conversations he had conducted with Mississippians in the aftermath of the storm in 1969: "You can come back, and when you do, I'll come back to see what you've done."

Then, Nixon delivered his most deliberate statement of his intent since the resignation. "You've come back," he said to roars from the crowd, "and I've come back."[13]

---

If the Nixon comeback had now achieved successes in the United States, it made sense to take the elder statesman and foreign policy guru to an event overseas. Sure, he had been to China in 1976. But those had largely been private meetings. In November, he flew to Paris, appeared on the French television program *Les Dossiers de l'écran*, and even answered questions from callers.

Then it was on to the main event in Great Britain. For years, Nixon had maintained a relationship with a young Tory backbencher in the British Parliament named Jonathan Aitken. They had talked earlier that year about Aitken setting up meetings in England for Nixon should he want to come. Then on November 3, Nixon had called his friend unsolicited.

"I'm thinking of coming to your country towards the end of the month," Nixon announced. "I've had an interesting invitation to address the Oxford Union." He then asked Aitken if he should consider accepting it. Aitken urged him to decline. He told the former president that he would be greeted with a hostile crowd eager to debate him.

Nixon was unconcerned. "As the conversation continued," Aitken remembers, "it became apparent that he was not seeking advice: he had already made up his mind to go to Oxford."[14]

Aitken went to work making arrangements for the trip. And he encountered no shortage of opposition to the visit, including the strong disapproval of the British Foreign Office. But Aitken found an ally in the leader of his own Conservative Party.

"I would be absolutely delighted to meet President Nixon," Margaret Thatcher told him. With Thatcher's support, the speaker of Parliament, George Thomas, reversed his previous decision not to host Nixon. "What a woman! What courage!" Thomas told Aitken after learning that Thatcher wanted to meet with the former president.[15]

When Nixon landed in London on November 29, he was buoyed by his recent success in Paris. The very next day, he arrived at the crucial event on his itinerary—the Oxford Union. As he drove to the event with Aitken in a black Daimler limousine, Nixon took note of the protestors outside the event.

"Rhodes Scholars from Ivy League schools, I bet," he quipped as he heard chants of "Jail to the Chief." Nixon seemed to enjoy the protest. He was back in the arena again, and he relished the fact that the opposition thought enough of him to come out and protest publicly. Once he entered the hall and began his remarks, Nixon felt right at home. Few people could talk off the cuff with such recall and precision. Nixon delivered a classic overview of world affairs and called himself a "realist" in international policy.

Afterwards, when the question and answer period began, Nixon was on top of his game.

Asked about the Cold War, he said he "liked the Russians" but didn't like the "Communists."

On Cambodia, he didn't give an inch: "Accusing the United States of invading the North Vietnamese occupation zones in Cambodia is the equivalent of accusing the Allies of invading German-occupied France in 1944."

Inevitably the conversation turned to Watergate. And here, as he had with Frost, Nixon struck a balance by accepting moral responsibility while trying to provide some context for his overall presidency. "Some people say I didn't handle it properly, and they're right," he admitted. "I screwed it up. And I paid the price. Mea culpa. But let's get on to my achievements. You'll be here in the year 2000 and we'll see how I'm regarded then."

As the event concluded, the crowd rose to its feet to applaud him. Later that night, he made his way to the House of Commons, where he was thoroughly impressed with the leader of the Conservative Party.[16]

"Wow, you can see how she became leader," he told Aitken after he met Thatcher. "She's really got it."

He then gave another tour de force of a speech on international affairs to a group of Parliament members, including some Labour Party members. The tone of the meeting and the reaction of the crowd was largely the same as it had been at Oxford—Nixon was favorably received.

According to his friend Aitken, this was more than just the British exercising decorum and being polite. He sensed something more profound. "What Nixon was encountering was the first manifestation of the swing in international opinion away from the obloquy that had been heaped on him at the time of Watergate," he would write.[17]

Before ending the trip, Nixon met with several other prominent figures, including Benjamin Disraeli's biographer, Robert Blake. Nixon had always admired the British prime minister who defied the Russians in Europe. Nixon paraphrased a line from Blake's book about Disraeli being a man who "was never long defeated and would always make a comeback." Blake was struck by the comment and later conceded that Disraeli and Nixon shared many similarities, including the ability to "bounce back."

As Nixon said goodbye to Aitken, he thanked him and commented on the favorable reviews his appearances in England had garnered. Then, suddenly, his eyes moistened. "You have to stay in the arena," he told his friend. "Even when you're down and bleeding and being kicked in the nuts, you have to get up and fight back. You can always do it. And when you feel you can't go on, you must do it."

As he shook hands with his friend he added, "If the cause is great enough, it's always worth fighting back...."[18]

———————

On his way back home to California, Nixon landed first in New York City. The city had long been important to him. It was here that he had gone into exile after his humiliation in the 1962 gubernatorial race. And though he resented the pretentiousness of the city, he respected its importance in finance, law, and media. "It's the fastest track in the world," he would say.

While staying at the Waldorf Astoria, he met up with Pat. Ed and Tricia, who lived in the city, joined them as well. Because Christmas was approaching rapidly, the Nixon family even made time for some shopping.

But the trip to New York was intended for business as well as pleasure. While there, Nixon decided to grant an interview to a friendly member of the press. Nick Thimmesch had at one point been a young Nixon staffer. Now he was a syndicated columnist. Thimmesch was eager to be the first to interview the former president about his trip to Europe.

The *Saturday Evening Post* had commissioned the article. With international events often in the news, Thimmesch asked Nixon about his thoughts on world affairs. The former president was brutal in his critique of what he saw as the failed policies of the Carter administration. He mocked the idea that Carter could somehow change the behavior of individual countries by championing human rights.

"'Look boys,'" he imagined Carter saying to the Saudis, "'until you unveil the women we won't buy your oil.'" Ever the realist when it came to foreign policy, Nixon said the goal on the world stage was to build relationships and maintain allies. And if that meant remaining quiet about human rights issues in those countries, then so be it. He told Thimmesch, "The bottom line is to keep friends of the United States. I don't approve of kicking our friends in public."

Echoing the famous "dictatorships and double standards" argument of a Georgetown professor named Jeane Kirkpatrick, he drew a sharp distinction between Communist countries and

non-Communist ones. "Those are authoritarian states," Nixon said
of Iran and the Philippines, "but they don't threaten their neighbors
and they are our friends."[19]

Later, Nixon met with some other conservative journalists, including William Buckley, the founder of *National Review*. Buckley had
long been ambivalent about Nixon and was known to be much closer
to Reagan politically. Yet now he found Nixon to be moving toward
the right in his international policy views. In the interview with Buckley, Nixon went out of his way to criticize Carter's approach to the
Cold War; he said there was no one at the State Department who
could handle Leonid Brezhnev.

"Nixon today gives the impression of being much more hard-line
on relations with the Soviets than he was as president," Buckley
observed in his magazine. Buckley even added that Nixon's comments seemed closer to "the kind of criticism being offered by the
'New Right.'"[20]

It was a shrewd observation. But Nixon didn't see himself as moving to the right; he saw Carter moving the country to the left on
foreign policy. And he feared that Carter's perceived weakness did
not bode well for the U.S. in the ongoing Cold War standoff. Always
the strategist, Nixon sensed that the late 1970s called for a tougher
posture from the U.S. He was already beginning to think about what
a Republican president in the 1980s might be able to do in confronting the Soviet Union.

As the Nixons celebrated Christmas back home at La Casa Pacifica, for the first time in years there was much to celebrate. Nixon
had enjoyed a successful 1978, relatively speaking. The Frost interviews had enjoyed massive ratings across the country, and Nixon had
fared reasonably well in the exchange. His memoirs had been completed and released. And most importantly, Nixon had begun making public appearances again. The Humphrey funeral, as well as the

trips to Kentucky and Mississippi, had all been very successful in the minds of the Nixon team. And Nixon had made a triumphant foray into Europe. He was even back to conducting interviews with reporters again.

But every journey out of a place of despair includes reminders of what came before. That December, H. R. Haldeman was released from Lompoc Federal Prison after eighteen months in jail. Nixon had stayed in touch with his former top White House advisor and written to him and called him while he served his time. But the warm relationship had cooled. It wasn't easy for Haldeman to go to prison. And he particularly resented the Frost interviews. While in prison, he had decided to get his revenge with a pen. He wrote a book called *The Ends of Power*. In it, he pretty much laid the responsibility for Watergate at Nixon's feet. Later, he would express regret for the book and essentially blame his co-author for the Nixon allegations.

When Haldeman left the prison, he drove to his home in Los Angeles. There, he received a surprising phone call.

"Merry Christmas," Nixon said, as Haldeman picked up the phone. "And welcome back."[21]

Chapter Eight

# The Move to
# New York

*"The fastest track in the world."*

A s the year 1979 dawned, Nixon devoted himself to writing his way back into public life. He not only excelled at writing, but he enjoyed the process, too. He loved to recline in his chair with his feet propped up on the ottoman, legal pads filled with his scribbling on the table beside him, a pipe in his hand, and his Irish Setter—King Timahoe—sitting at his feet. He would hold forth there with his team of writers surrounding him. He found that talking his way through the book helped him not only remember the past more clearly, but to see the future more clearly, as well.

As Nixon saw it, his presidency had centered on one issue: foreign affairs. "Nixon didn't care about domestic politics," remembered Hugh Hewitt, a young staffer who joined his staff in 1978. "Foreign policy mattered most." In Nixon's mind, while history would judge him harshly on Watergate, it would inevitably have to deal with his achievements on the world stage. Here he felt that he had a strong case to make. He also believed that his administration's

foreign policy successes—whether opening the door to China, creating détente with the Soviets, or ending the Vietnam War—should not
merely be stories for the history books, but also be lessons for the
challenges America still faced as it approached the 1980s.[1]

And Nixon's mind was still a well-oiled machine on any subject
related to foreign affairs. One day, Hugh Hewitt brought his parents
to meet the boss. "What's going to happen in China?" Hewitt's
mother asked, trying to make conversation. Two hours later, Nixon
finished his answer.[2]

On foreign policy, Nixon not only knew a lot, but also had a lot
to say. The first book he began working on in early 1979 was *The
Real War*, which would essentially serve as Nixon's rebuttal to the
Carter administration. Ironically, President Carter had tried to gain
Nixon's cooperation on foreign policy. In negotiating formal diplomatic relations with China—a leftover matter from Nixon's 1972
trip—Carter found the Chinese difficult to work with. When Deputy
Prime Minister Deng Xiaoping recommended that Nixon take part
in the talks, Carter sent for the exiled president.

Carter didn't want Nixon to be there. He was busy trying to
secure Democratic votes in the Senate for the SALT II Treaty, and
publicly inviting Nixon back to the White House was no way to curry
favor with the Left. Still, Deng drove a hard bargain, even suggesting
at one point that he might visit Nixon in San Clemente unless Carter
invited him to the White House.

That Carter begrudgingly did so indicates that Nixon's comeback was, if anything, ahead of schedule. Less than five years after
leaving office, here he was being invited to a state dinner at the
White House by a Democratic president. It was one thing for
Hubert Humphrey to invite him to the state funeral; it was quite
another for the sitting Democratic president to invite him back to
the White House.

On January 29, 1979, Nixon's car arrived at the White House gate and was quickly waved through. Once inside, the former president was taken to the second floor to the family residence. There he found President Carter waiting with Deng. He shook hands with the American president and then turned to greet Deng. He had never met the Chinese leader before.

They departed later for the state dinner in the East Room. There were a few audible groans from the crowd when Nixon's name was announced upon his entry into the room. But if it bothered him, he never let on. Nixon made his way to his table, where he was joined by National Security Advisor Zbigniew Brzezinski, Ambassador to China Leonard Woodcock, and Chinese Minister for Science and Technology Fang Yi, among others.

Nixon was in his element. Surrounded by members of the foreign policy intelligentsia and back in the White House, he felt perfectly at home. Still, a bit of melancholy filled the air.

Nixon became nostalgic at the sounds of the Marine band playing as it had during his presidency. "You know they are playing the same songs, the songs they played when I was here," he said.[3]

His attempts at small talk during the dinner were sometimes awkward.

"How did you meet your husband?" he asked Ambassador Woodcock's wife.

"In a hospital," she responded.

"Is there something wrong with Ambassador Woodcock?" Nixon replied.

"No, Mr. President," the ambassador answered for his wife. "I'm perfectly fine."

Still, as the dinner went on, the fellow guests at Nixon's table warmed to him. Brzezinski asked the former president to list the world leaders he most admired.

"You won't catch me naming them because each one is different," he replied. He did, however, say that he was especially fond of de Gaulle, Mao, and the Shah. He then looked across the table at Fang Yi. Knowing that Fang would report everything Nixon said back to Deng, the former president added one more name to the list of foreign leaders he admired: "Chiang Kai-shek"—the nationalist Chinese leader who had fought the Communists for control of China.[4]

Before the night ended, Nixon had all the guests at his table sign a menu that he could take back to Pat. He seemed genuinely pleased with how everything had gone. He had been back at the White House, talked foreign policy with Carter's top experts, and even had managed to get under the skin of the Chinese by praising their bête noire—Chiang Kai-shek.

The next day, Nixon got the chance to speak directly with Deng. He met with Deng privately for two hours. At the end of the discussion, it was decided that Nixon would come and visit Peking.

This was a somewhat more successful private negotiation than the one conducted by the Carter administration. In his first foray back into the world of Washington politics, Nixon had achieved more than he could have ever hoped for—he had entered the White House again, met with a foreign leader, and been accepted for the most part. He even had the chance while in Washington to reconnect with old D.C. friends—including the recently freed John Mitchell, who had served several years in prison for his role in Watergate.

For his part, President Carter probably hoped that by extending an olive branch to Nixon he could win the former's president's favor as negotiations with China went forward. But if Carter thought he had won Nixon over, he thought wrong. Nixon returned home and began working furiously on *The Real War*, his answer to Carter's foreign policy. Nixon saw the book as his chance to shape the election of 1980 by highlighting the dangers the country faced on the world stage. And if anything, his visit to the Carter White House had left him even more convinced that a new president should be elected in 1980.

"If the U.S. chooses a president who will not stop the president's drift toward Soviet strategic superiority, [then] the Chinese—survival-minded above all—will move toward rapprochement with the Soviet Union," he said to his old staffer, William Safire, now a columnist for the *New York Times*. Nixon viewed his opening to China as a masterstroke not because it allowed U.S. zoos to import pandas or because it made for good political photo-ops. He saw it as important because it had exploited a divide in the relationship between the Chinese and the Soviets. While many on the political Left applauded the opening to China as an idealistic gesture, Nixon himself always viewed it in realistic terms. It was about dividing enemies and protecting American national interests. He worried that this distinction had been lost on the Carter State Department.[5]

As the writing of the book continued in California, Nixon started to think again about another tactic to get himself back into the public eye—a move back East. He was now four years short of his seventieth birthday, and he wanted to maximize what time he had left. The trip to D.C. had confirmed for him that the public was ready. And a recent Gallup survey had found that he was now one of the country's most admired people.

And there was no time to waste if Nixon was going to be a player in the 1980 election. Already candidates were lining up to run for the Republican nomination. Not surprisingly, Nixon thought his former treasury secretary, John Connally, was the best option. But he had met with several of the other candidates considering running. And he had been around politics long enough to recognize real talent when he saw it. One of those potential candidates, in particular, caught his attention.

"Reagan is a good listener," Nixon told Safire, "and not just for show."[6]

---

On May 24, Nixon took a break from writing the book to announce that he was selling La Casa Pacifica and finally making the move to the "fastest track" he often spoke of—New York. Nixon had personal as well as political reasons for the move. Two months earlier on March 14, Tricia had given birth to his first grandson—Christopher Nixon Cox. Nixon had flown out to New York just days after the birth. He loved holding the little boy and talking to him. But after a few days, it was time to return to California. The pull of another grandchild added to his desire to move East.

And so La Casa Pacifica was sold to a group of Nixon friends. Inevitably, the sale raised eyebrows in Washington. Democrats in the Senate soon pushed for and passed a "Sense of the Senate" resolution suggesting that the former president should pay the government back for items the government had installed at the house.

If the Senate Democrats hoped to get Nixon's attention, they succeeded. Outraged, he wrote a letter to the General Services Administration demanding that "all items in question be removed." Nixon's letter, which was released publicly by Colonel Brennan, argued that the installation of almost all the items had been insisted on by the Secret Service.

If Democrats were going to play games, then Nixon would match them. He noted in his letter that it was true that he himself had installed a flag pole. But, he added, "I am forwarding my check in the amount of $2,300 to the United States Treasury by express mail today" to pay for it.

Satisfied that he had gotten the best of the exchange with his enemies in Washington, Nixon turned his attention to where he would live in New York. After much deliberation, the Nixons chose East 65th Street, close to where their new grandchild lived. The three-story townhouse offered the Nixons a library where the former president could read and write, four bedrooms, and even a garden in the back.

With his future in New York settled and his past in California winding down, Nixon could again focus on world affairs. And there was much on which to focus. He was worried about events in Iran and about the Carter administration's handling of them. The Shah had been exiled, and Nixon decided to fly down and visit his old friend in Mexico.

"You've got to keep fighting," he told the deposed Iranian leader. "You could fade away, but that's the easy way out." Afterward, he spoke with the press and blasted the Carter administration's handling of the situation.[7]

"If the United States does not stand by its own friends," he warned in a not very veiled shot at the White House, "we are going to end up with no friends." At this point, Nixon still viewed the Islamic Revolution through the lens of the Cold War. He didn't seem to foresee that the uprising could lead to trouble for Americans in Iran in just a few short months.[8]

Back home from Mexico, he and Pat finished packing a lifetime of memories in boxes for the move. But before moving out, Nixon made sure to take advantage of the California home. That September, he held a reception in honor of his old friend John Mitchell, who had been recently released from prison. Nixon felt the time had come to honor the man who had done so much for the Nixon presidency and who had paid such a price for that service.[9]

On September 3, 1979, a mariachi band performed while food from a favorite Mexican restaurant of Nixon's, El Adobe, was served to a reunion of Nixon staffers who came to honor John Mitchell—the mastermind of Watergate.

It was a night filled with memories and flooded with emotions. Perhaps no one enjoyed the event more than Mitchell himself. After a while, the tapping of a spoon could be heard on a wine glass signaling to the crowd that it was time to listen. The two hundred and fifty guests—including Ray Price, Bill Safire and Ron Ziegler—grew quiet.

Mitchell himself spoke to the crowd: "We who have served in the Nixon administration can be proud of some monumental accomplishments." He then added a great understatement: "Although that's not to say we didn't run into a few skids along the way."

When Nixon spoke, he praised his attorney general and said, "John Mitchell has friends and he stands beside them." Nixon respected Mitchell immensely. The two went back years, to when they were law partners in New York. Then Nixon had hired Mitchell to run his presidential campaign. Following that, he made him attorney general. While Mitchell served his time in prison, Nixon called every week to check on him. If Mitchell ever watched the Frost interviews and saw Nixon suggest that Watergate might not have happened had the attorney general done a better job minding the store, he didn't let on. In fact, on this night, it seemed very much like the two men were again best friends.

In his brief remarks, Nixon also told the crowd about the new book he was working on, promising that it would be devoted to discussing the foreign policy challenges America would face in the coming years.[10]

The next day, the New York Times—one of Nixon's least favorite publications—ran a story on the event headlined "The Ex-President's Men Reunite at San Clemente."[11]

Nixon was riding high following the Mitchell event as he made plans for yet another trip to China. China was essential to Nixon because it was essential to his presidential legacy.

He made a short trip with Ed Cox and Colonel Brennan. While there, Nixon met with Deng to continue the conversation they had begun in Washington. Nixon did visit an oil refinery while in China, but he had already refused the offers of American oil companies who wanted him to help get them into the Chinese oil business. At a banquet in Peking, Deng and others toasted the former president for all he had done for China. "When drinking the water, don't forget those who dug the well," said one official in his toast. Nixon got the message—he would never be forgotten in China.[12]

By the end of 1979, Nixon was preparing to launch his new book and begin his new life on the East Coast. In San Clemente in late 1979, he reviewed the galleys of *The Real War*. He made a few edits and sent them off to his editor, Michael Korda, at Simon & Schuster in New York. The book was set for release the following May.

As he finished editing the galleys, he saw the news of the American embassy workers being taken hostage in Iran. Shocked at the images from Iran, Nixon saw the embassy takeover as proof that the Iranians were "an irrational people" governed by "an irrational leader." Still, he knew that the man who had ended the Shah's reign should not be underestimated. The Ayatollah, he feared, was "crazy like a fox."

Chapter Nine

# The 1980 Election

*"I have a gut feeling that your victory
will be far greater ... than predicted."*

T he story of the hostages in Iran dominated news coverage
in early 1980. And the Carter administration's seeming
inability to do anything about it only added to the growing
interest in the upcoming presidential election.

The 1980 Republican presidential primary had essentially
begun in 1976 when Governor Ronald Reagan stole the show at
the convention with an impromptu speech after he narrowly lost
the nomination to President Ford. "There is no substitute for victory," Reagan told the delegates in his stirring remarks, which made
little mention of President Ford. The next morning, Reagan—who
was signing the convention credentials for one of his aides, Martin
Anderson—wrote, "We dreamed, and the dream lives on."

During the 1976 fall campaign, Reagan made token efforts to
help the Republican ticket. But when Ford narrowly lost to Georgia
governor Jimmy Carter, the stage was set for Reagan to make one
more run in 1980. Not that he would be the only Republican running. The struggles of the Carter administration virtually invited

Republican candidates to join the fray. Senator Bob Dole, who had served as Ford's running mate in 1976, announced his plans to run. So did Nixon's favorite contender, former Texas governor and former treasury secretary John Connally. Former UN ambassador and RNC chairman George Bush of Texas also announced his candidacy.

But all eyes were on Reagan. The charismatic former governor of California had always been something of an enigma to Nixon. Though friendly, the two weren't really friends. At this point in their relationship, Nixon's remarks about Reagan's gifts could sound almost like backhanded compliments.

"Reagan can give a good speech" was a frequent comment he made to friends who sometimes weren't sure if it was genuine admiration of the former governor's oratorial skills or a way of saying he didn't have any substance. And the Watergate Tapes revealed a 1972 conversation Nixon had had with Haldeman in which the president suggested that Reagan "was not pleasant" to be around and, without a trace of irony, called Reagan "strange." Reagan, for his part, found Nixon odd. The naturally smiling man found it difficult to connect with the introverted Nixon.[1]

But by early 1980, Nixon began to warm up to the idea of Reagan. He had spoken to the candidate several times and told friends he was impressed. This was high praise, indicating that Nixon was impressed with Reagan's questions during their foreign policy talks (which were mainly monologues by Nixon). And if Nixon had worried that Reagan didn't have the gravitas for the job, the events in Iran were beginning to convince him that Reagan's decisiveness might be just what was needed in American foreign policy.

Though Carter's public approval numbers eventually rose in the immediate aftermath of the hostage crisis, the public soon became concerned that the president had no strategy for ending the crisis. On ABC News, Ted Koppel began a new nightly program to cover the events in Iran called *Nightline*. And every night the show reminded the American people that the crisis was nowhere near being resolved.

In early 1980, Carter ordered a commando raid that ended in disaster. When Nixon was briefed about the mission by Defense Department staffers, he asked why more helicopters hadn't been used. "It's not like we don't have 'em," he said in a critical comment that was likely reported back to the White House.

Nixon was more concerned not with the tactical failures of one operation, but with the strategic failures of the entire administration. He was particularly worried that Carter had allowed the entire stand-off to be focused on the hostages—thus empowering the Iranians. "I think that one of the major errors that President Carter made at the outset," the former president told Barbara Walters in an interview on ABC, "was to indicate that his primary, and, in fact, it seemed to me, his only concern at the beginning, was the lives and safety of the hostages. They are important. But the moment you do that, you are inviting blackmail. They know you'll pay any price in order to save those lives and we could never do that."[2]

While the hostage crisis dragged on, the Republican presidential primary was heating up.

Though he maintained a public posture of neutrality during the 1980 Republican primary, behind the scenes Nixon kept a close eye on two candidates in particular: John Connally and Ronald Reagan. His obsession with Connally stretched back nearly a decade to when he had recruited Lyndon B. Johnson's close friend from Texas politics to join his administration. "Nixon loved strong men," Ken Khachigian later remembered. "That's why he stuck with John Mitchell for so long. And it's why he liked Connally so much." Connally was the exact opposite of Nixon: he liked shaking hands with voters, he exuded a natural charm, and he possessed major self-confidence. But the former Texas governor possessed something else—baggage.

Scandals had plagued Connally for much of his career. Surprisingly, the one president brought down by a scandal seemed unconcerned about Connally's shady past. "He had a total blind spot when it came to Connally," Khachigian said. "I told him Connally couldn't get elected. But he thought he could."[3]

Still, Nixon kept his options open. And if Connally couldn't get the nomination, then perhaps Reagan could. "They weren't close personally at the time," Khachigian said, "but Nixon certainly appreciated his political ability." Reagan, like Connally, had many of the political attributes Nixon admired but never possessed: his handsome face looked good on camera, and he maintained a steady air of confidence. Even if Nixon didn't think Reagan had the sharpest mind, he respected him as a formidable political talent. "He always said, 'I have a great mind, but Reagan has a great gut,'" Ed Cox remembered.[4]

Nixon's ambivalence about the upcoming 1980 election had been visible to his friends and associates well before the election season began. A former aide named Rob Odle had visited Nixon that spring and found him fixated on presidential politics and world affairs. Odle had worked on the Nixon campaign in 1968 and then in the Nixon White House. He still proudly carried a worn-out brief case that he had collected from a trash can at campaign headquarters in 1968. He had noticed the initials "RMN" on it and asked secretary Rose Woods if it had been Nixon's. "Yes," she answered, "the boss got a new brief case." Odle couldn't believe his luck. He also remained close personal friends with Ed and Tricia Cox. But it had been a while since he saw his old boss.

"He's working on a book so don't stay too long," Rose Woods advised Odle as he arrived for his meeting. Nixon greeted his guest wearing his typical blue business suit. The president seemed to be in especially good spirits.

"You are really in a great mood, sir," Odle said as he sat down across from Nixon's chair and ottoman. Nixon mentioned the new pope in Rome and said, "I'm really happy about what's happening there."

The two men exchanged favorable comments about Pope John Paul II. But while Odle, a Catholic, expressed his hope for what the pope would do in the church, Nixon seemed much more interested in geopolitics. "John Paul will be tough, cunning, and efficient," Nixon said, using adjectives that he would normally apply to a head of state he admired. Then he made a prediction: "He will go to Communist countries. I told Pope Paul to do that but he never did."

Odle remained unconvinced. But Nixon persisted: "What's going to happen is he's going to set off a spark. He said, "This is going to give the Poles back their pride and that's going to set off a spark."

The conversation then shifted to Iran. "He foresaw that Iran would be a major foreign policy issue for years to come," Odle remembered. "He was very concerned about its strategic location and geopolitical importance." And he feared that President Carter relied too heavily on the diplomats at Foggy Bottom. "The State Department people," he said, "they're all McGovern people." Nixon told Odle that eventually Iran would be a more important foreign policy challenge than anything else in the Middle East.

After that, the two men talked about the upcoming presidential campaign. After Odle said he had attended fundraisers for both Connally and Reagan, Nixon asked for a comparison of the two candidates. "I told him Reagan looked old and tired and Connally had it together. At the Reagan event, the candidate didn't even speak until after ten o'clock in the evening." Nixon nearly came out of his seat, saying, "I've told Reagan to never go on after eight!" Then he added, "No advance man!" The comment surprised Odle; he hadn't realized the extent of the conversations going on between Nixon and Reagan.

Nixon then asked what Odle thought of the only other living former president. "Weak and disappointing," Odle said of Ford. Then he mentioned that Susan Ford had taped commercials selling Subarus.

"What's a Subaru?" Nixon asked.

"A car."

"What?" Nixon incredulously asked. "Can you imagine Tricia selling cars? They would have indicted us for that."[5]

---

After a surprising win in the Iowa Caususes, George Bush rode what he called "the big mo" into New Hampshire, where he hoped his East Coast pedigree would give him an advantage.

But at a debate at a local high school in Nashau, New Hampshire, during the first week of February, the race took a turn away from Bush. A dispute erupted between the Bush and Reagan camps over the debate rules shortly before the debate was scheduled to begin. Reagan's team had effectively put up the money for the event, operating on the theory that he needed debates and public appearances to reach as many people as possible. When Reagan began speaking into the microphone to explain to the assembled crowd what the delay was about, the moderator, John Breen, spoke over the public address system.

"Turn off Mr. Reagan's microphone," he instructed the crew working in the sound booth.

The crowd gasped as Reagan stood, picked up his microphone and raised his voice, saying, "Mr. Green, I am *paying* for this microphone!"

It was vintage Reagan—he got the details wrong (the man's name was "Breen" not "Green") but he got the big picture right (he was paying for the event and no moderator should boss around a presidential candidate). The clip of the exchange—which included the crowd erupting in approval as Reagan told off the moderator— was played on news broadcasts around the state and across the nation. As America watched a helpless and indecisive president dealing with a hostage crisis in Washington, it saw a strong and decisive candidate in New Hampshire. Reagan was on the rise. A few days later, he went on to the win the New Hampshire Republican Primary. After that, he was well on his way to winning the Republican nomination.

If strength and decisiveness were what the country was looking for, they were also the traits that Richard Nixon increasingly thought were needed in Washington. That summer the Iran Hostage Crisis became personal for him when the deposed Shah of Iran died. The Carter administration's only comment came through the State Department. "His death marks the end of an era in Iran, which all hope will be followed by peace and stability," the statement read in part.

This outraged Nixon. He found the history of Carter's treatment of the Shah nauseating. In 1977, President Carter had traveled to Tehran where he toasted the Shah for "the admiration and love which your people give you." This announcement came as news to the Iranian people, many of whom loathed the dictator. At around the same time, Ayatollah Ruhollah Khomeini was creating a grassroots movement of Islamic revolutionaries. By 1979, the Shah was facing an uprising from the people Carter had thought loved him. When the Shah was forced to flee the country and seek asylum, President Carter offered to accept him in the U.S. The Shah had declined as he wanted to stay in the neighborhood in the remote hopes he could return to power in Iran. But it was not to be. Khomeini had filled the power vacuum in Iran and created the Islamic Republic of Iran.

It was at this point that Carter had begun to reconsider his support for the Shah. His ambassador in Iran, William H. Sullivan, warned the White House that granting asylum to the Shah "would almost certainly result in an immediate and violent reaction" in Iran.

But when news broke in October of 1979 that the Shah had been diagnosed with cancer, domestic pressure mounted on Carter from both outside and inside the White House. Inside, National Security Advisor Brzezinski urged the president to allow the Shah to enter the U.S. for medical treatment. Outside, prominent Republicans were pushing for the same thing. Henry Kissinger blasted the president for making the Shah look like "a Flying Dutchman looking for a port of call." Carter, largely for humanitarian reasons but also looking to garner Republican and Democratic support for the SALT II Treaty, decided on October 21 to grant the Shah access to the U.S. for medical treatment. It proved to be a fateful decision, which led directly to the militants seizing the U.S. Embassy.

All of this backstory was very much in Nixon's mind in the Summer of 1980 as the Shah's death was announced. And it still angered him. So much so that he decided to do something about it. He made plans to fly to Cairo and attend the Shah's funeral. It was the ultimate slap in Carter's face.

When Nixon arrived in Cairo with his son-in-law Ed Cox and several Secret Service agents, he was greeted by reporters. Nixon did not hold back. Carter's treatment of the Shah? "One of the black pages of American foreign policy history." What about the official State Department statement on the Shah's passing? "The administration didn't even have the grace to point out that he had been an ally and friend of the United States for 30 years."[6]

But his most savage words were directed at Carter himself. Without naming him, Nixon pointed to the contrast with how Anwar Sadat had handled the Shah. "I think President Sadat's guts in providing a home for the Shah in his last days at a time when the U.S. turned its back on one of its friends is an inspiration to us all," he said.

The comment showed the depth of Nixon's anger. The former president sensed how real the challenge was in the Middle East and how ill-quipped Carter was to handle it. The presidency, it seemed, was too big for Jimmy Carter. Nixon had talked throughout his career about the need for a leader to take charge. "Get on top of the job or the job will get on top of you," he would frequently counsel. Now it seemed painfully obvious that the job of president was on top of Carter. And he showed little sign of knowing how to get out from under it.

After attending the funeral and a dinner that Sadat held for him in Cairo, Nixon traveled with his entourage back to the U.S. It was time to do something, once and for all, about the ineffective Carter White House. And with the 1980 presidential election quickly approaching, Nixon knew just what to do.

―――――――――

By the summer of 1980, Nixon had settled into a familiar routine in his new hometown. Each morning he would rise early and walk the two miles from his townhouse to his office in the Federal Building in New York City. Along the way he would buy coffee and the morning newspapers. Once in his office, which was located on the thirteenth floor, he would begin working. The office itself was ordinary. "The bigger the office the smaller the man," Nixon often observed. And here at the New York Federal Building, he lived by his own rule. In his office there was a desk, a phone, a coffee table, and some photos of Nixon and foreign leaders. Next door his top aide, Nick Ruwe, worked in his own office. Ruwe had worked as the assistant protocol chief at the White House and had been hired by Nixon when Colonel Brennan left to work in Washington with John Mitchell.

Each day the two men would follow the same ritual. Ruwe would go through all the mail and Nixon would make calls. At lunch, Nixon would often eat salmon from a tin container while seated at his desk. In the afternoon, Nixon would make his way back to his house. There he would rest and read and think.

And there was a lot to think about. By this time, Governor Reagan's momentum, which had begun in New Hampshire, had spread throughout the other primary states. He would win the nomination that summer at the Republican National Convention in Detroit. And Nixon, though originally a fan of Connally's, was now on board with Reagan.

Nixon had an advantage in dealing with Reagan—he knew so many of his top staffers. William Casey had served in the Nixon administration, as had Lyn Nofziger. In addition, a former Kissinger protégé named Richard Allen was serving as the Reagan campaign's top policy aide on foreign policy. And Nixon had been friendly for years with Mike Deaver, Reagan's indispensable advisor on all things image. These men kept Nixon up to speed on what was going on inside the campaign. And Nixon wasn't shy about offering advice.

But not all of Nixon's work to help Reagan was behind the scenes. When it came to foreign affairs he knew his reputation was strong enough that he could occasionally comment publicly. One such moment came after the *New York Times* argued that John Anderson, the independent candidate also running for president, possessed more experience in world affairs than the former California governor.

"I find that in fact Governor Reagan made four official trips abroad at the request of the White House between 1969 and 1973," Nixon wrote in response to the *Times*. According to the former president, Reagan had been "well-received" in the sixteen countries that he had visited on behalf of the Nixon White House.[7]

Nixon also granted a few television interviews in which he tried to appear fair and balanced but was actually shilling for Reagan. When the candidate makes a mistake, he said on the *Today Show*— referring to several Reagan gaffes on the campaign trail—it's the staff's job to "go out and take the heat." Nixon then added sharply, "And that's what the Reagan staff had better learn." The comment gave the appearance of Nixon being critical of Reagan; actually, he was defending Reagan and shifting blame to his staff.

Then Nixon turned to the incumbent in the White House. If Reagan's weakness was "his words," then Carter's weakness was "his record."

In another interview, Nixon went a step farther. After praising Carter's intellect and work ethic, he called his administration a "tragedy for the country" and castigated him as "ineffective president."

This would prove to be Nixon's public strategy through the fall of 1980—appear to be neutral, but use every opportunity to sideswipe Carter and remind voters of his failures as president. But sometimes his public comments went a step too far. In one interview with *Parade*, Nixon suggested that he might have a role helping a President Reagan: "something like a counselor or negotiator." He added that he "would be available for assistance and advice."[8]

The interview sent Reagan aides into a fury. The last thing the campaign needed was the suggestion that Reagan would be bringing Nixon into his administration should he win. The Nixon comeback had made progress, but the public was likely not ready for Nixon to have a formal role in a presidential administration. One Reagan aide, speaking to the press anonymously, said the former president was "hallucinating" about a role helping Reagan.

This was too much for Reagan himself. He had always admired Nixon and thought he deserved to be respected as a great foreign policy mind. He called and apologized to Nixon for the words of the anonymous aide; Nixon assured him that there was no need to apologize.[9]

Meanwhile behind the scenes, Nixon continued to work the phones and talk to senior Reagan aides. In 1980, presidential debates were still a new feature of elections. Indeed, there had been only once since the Nixon-Kennedy debates of 1960—the 1976 Ford-Carter debate. So there was some discussion within the Reagan camp about whether to agree to a debate with Carter. There were plenty of Reagan aides worried about the possibility of another Reagan gaffe.

Nixon had no such concerns. He reached out to Reagan's deputy campaign manager, Robert Gray, and sent a memo in which he personally lobbied for a debate. He joked that he wished he could give advice on winning a presidential debate, "but I don't have that experience." The memo argued that Reagan couldn't ignore the fact that the debate could have "220 million Americans watching him" and that was an opportunity he should not pass up.[10]

In October, just a few days before the election, Reagan and Carter met for their only presidential debate. What Nixon had likely sensed—that Reagan's camera-friendly presence would contrast well with Carter's stiff persona—proved true. Nixon had sent pages of debate suggestions on various foreign and domestic policy topics to Mike Deaver, Ed Meese, and even Mrs. Reagan. He needn't have worried. Reagan was ready. Reagan pounced during the debate when Carter accused him of opposing Medicare earlier in his career. "There you go again," he said before methodically describing how he had supported a different version of Medicare in the early 1960s. The firm response combined with Carter's sheepish expression created a powerful moment for Reagan.

But it was in the closing statements that the contrast was the most dramatic. Carter awkwardly talked about having a conversation with his daughter Amy about nuclear war. It was a missed opportunity to leave a lasting and favorable impression with the viewing public. Reagan did not make the same mistake. In perhaps the most famous closing ever delivered in a presidential debate, Reagan urged voters to enter the polling place and ask themselves a question before pulling the lever: "Are you better off than you were four years ago?"

Elections are always about choices, and Reagan had perfectly framed the American people's choice in the 1980 election. With hostages in Iran, double-digit inflation at home, and uncertainty around the country, many Americans did not feel that they were better off.

Nixon felt increasingly good about Reagan's odds in the closing days of the campaign. When a poll appeared showing that Reagan could lose New York state, Nixon reassured the Reagan team about his new home state. He called and told a campaign aide that Reagan would in fact win New York state. The Reagan team dismissed the idea; they were still preparing for a close election.

Nixon felt so confident of Reagan's chances that on November 4 he sent a handwritten note to the candidate. "I have a gut feeling that your victory will be far greater than most of the pollsters and political columnists have predicted," he said.

The former president also praised the candidate for proving the critics wrong at every turn. "They said you were a hard-hearted bomb thrower and you convinced millions of Americans who saw you on TV that this caricature was false," Nixon wrote. He added that "the nation and the free world would be counting on" Reagan's leadership.

"I know you will not let them down," he ended the letter, signing it, "Dick."[11]

But even as Nixon reveled in the chance to play a part in Reagan's rise behind the scenes, he could never leave Watergate entirely behind. Just days before the election, Nixon testified in a courtroom inside the Federal District Court in Washington, D.C., where Edward S. Miller, a former chief of the FBI's intelligence bureau, and W. Mark Felt, a former acting associate director of the FBI, were on trial for violating the civil rights of the Weather Underground.

The two men argued that they had authorized break-ins and wiretaps of Weather Underground members, but said that they had done so for national security reasons. As a witness for the defense, Nixon said he had indeed wanted the FBI to get tough with the Weather Underground. He further suggested that with America engaged in the Vietnam War at the time, he had viewed these actions as part of the war effort; after all, there was evidence of connections between the Weather Underground and foreign governments.

But most important, Nixon argued on the stand, was stopping the Weather Underground bombings that had cost twenty-three Americans their lives. The former presidnet firmly stated that he had authorized the aggressive tactics so that he could prevent "innocent people" from being killed. In the end, the jury found the two men guilty anyway. Nixon was saddened by the verdict. It would not be until Felt's death in 2008 that journalist Bob Woodward revealed Felt had been his famous "Deep Throat" source; without Felt's insider information, it seems unlikely that Watergate would have ever brought Nixon down. Nixon never suspected Felt was "Deep Throat." In fact, when President Reagan pardoned Felt, Nixon wrote to Reagan, "Pat and my reactions were the same: 'Thank God for Ronald Reagan.'"[12]

With the trial over, Nixon returned to his regular routine in New York and prepared for Election Night. It was everything he could have hoped it would be. Reagan won in a landslide. And as Nixon had predicted to the skeptical Reagan campaign staffers, Reagan carried New York state.

With a new administration preparing to take over, Nixon was hopeful that new foreign policies would be put in place.

On November 17, he sent an eleven-page memo to the president-elect. He urged him to focus on the economy in the early months of the presidency. "Unless you are able to shape up our home base it will be almost impossible to conduct an effective foreign policy," Nixon wrote. He went onto to suggest that "the time to take the heat for possibly unpopular budget cuts is in 1981, not 1982 or 1984," referring to congressional elections and the presidential election.

This proved to be one area where the former president and the incoming president were not aligned. Reagan had little interest in cutting spending; he believed that inflation was a product of monetary policy and that Fed chairman Paul Volcker's policy of high interest rates would eventually bring inflation down. He also believed that the stagnant economy could best be primed with fiscal policy, especially through tax cuts. Reagan's subsequent economic plan of increased spending and reduced taxes was not an orthodox Republican approach to economics at the time.

Nixon's memo also included suggestions on personnel—all the way from cabinet posts to staff positions. For secretary of state, he recommended Al Haig. For attorney general, he suggested William French Smith. For CIA head, he recommended William Casey. "I hope I have not been presumptuous in making some of these suggestions," the ex-president ended the memo. It is a testament to Nixon's revival that the incoming president accepted all of these recommendations—although Reagan likely already had the same people in mind. As Reagan prepared to take office, Nixon not only had direct access to the president, but direct personal relationships with all of the senior staffers making foreign policy, as well. He had come a long way since 1974 and the dark days of Watergate.[13]

And Nixon also possessed another means of influencing the new administration's worldview through his latest book. *The Real War* had been released earlier in the year largely to critical reviews. Yet the book sold well. Few in America doubted Nixon's ability to scan the world and provide analysis of foreign policy. And with the seemingly endless run of Carter's failures on the foreign stage, people were eager for a new approach on international affairs.

What undoubtedly inspired the critical reviews the book received was the perceived sharp turn to the right that Nixon seemed to take. Nixon's target in the book was the Carter administration; more specifically, the target was Jimmy Carter. In almost apocalyptic terms he declared that America was "at war." Then using a poker analogy, he suggested, "All but one of our cards are face up on the table. Our only covered card is the will, nerve, and unpredictability of the president."

In some ways, Nixon used the book not to describe Carter, whom he viewed as lacking all these traits, but Reagan. The former president suggested that the foreign policy of the future would require "placing limits on idealism, compromising with reality, at times matching duplicity with duplicity."

Nixon went on to draw a distinction between the United States and the Soviet Union, labeling it a difference between "Good and Evil, Light and Darkness, God and the Devil." Nixon used the history he knew firsthand to frame the coming challenges. Citing his years as Eisenhower's vice president, he wrote that Ike later regretted his decision to halt the British attempt to retake the Suez Canal. Nixon used this to story to argue for a more aggressive posture in the Cold War.

He specifically called for a dramatic increase in defense spending. "We can afford a vastly increased defense effort," he wrote, "if we decide to. We can carry the twilight war to the enemy—if we decide to."[14]

One person who seemed to be fully in sync with these views was the new president-elect. Reagan had sharply criticized the weakness of the Carter administration's foreign policy and promised a more robust response to events like the Soviet invasion of Afghanistan. In fact, Reagan was so convinced this was the right course that he was willing to risk the election on it. When an advisor urged him to tone down his foreign policy views during the campaign, Reagan remarked that the American people were perfectly entitled to know how strongly he held his foreign policy views and how fervently he intended to carry them out. If that bothered them, then they should vote for Carter. Reagan, perhaps influenced by Nixon's evolution toward a harder line in *The Real War*, correctly believed that most Americans were ready for a more decisive commander-in-chief.

A few days after the election, Nixon sat in his study in his town house and worked on a new introduction for the paperback version of *The Real War* that was being readied for release. "I am confident that President Reagan and the members of his administration will have the vision to see what needs to be done and the courage to do it," he wrote, pointing to the message of the following pages as the roadmap for foreign policy in the 1980s. He sent a personalized copy of the book to the president-elect.

Nixon wasn't going to leave anything to chance. Just six years earlier he had been forced out of office and into a political exile unlike anything ever seen before in American history. He had faced physical challenges and almost died just a few months later. He had had to fight his way out of debt and begin the long process of public rehabilitation. Now at last he could see the fruits of his labor. His books sold briskly, he could go out in public, and he could even deliver public speeches on politics. But best of all, he had been an important, if small, part of the successful election campaign of a Republican presidential candidate. Not only that, but he also knew and liked the president-elect. Nixon was back—not as a political and public force himself, but as an elder statesman behind the scenes. He had access and he had some influence, and he intended to use it. Indeed, he already was.

Not long after the election, Nixon appeared at the Russian Embassy for a celebration of the Bolshevik Revolution. In front of his old friend Henry Kissinger, Nixon spoke to Soviet Ambassador Anatoly Dobrynin about the incoming president.

"There will be a new style," he said to the ambassador about Reagan, and "it will be different."[15]

# Chapter Ten

# Advisor to the President

*"Don't change a game plan that is working."*

**"T**his letter is a first," Nixon began a note to Nancy Reagan on January 12, 1981. "Former presidents on many occasions have given advice to their successors and have written about the presidency. None as far as I know have written to or about the role of first ladies."

Nixon had always admired Mrs. Reagan's strength. And as the new president prepared to take office in a few days, Nixon had little doubt of how important Mrs. Reagan's voice would be. He started his back-channel diplomacy with the incoming White House by reaching out directly to the first lady.

"You are blessed with intelligence, charm, and beauty," he continued as he lavished his praise on the former Hollywood starlet. "You have subordinated your own career to that of your husband's." Nixon then praised the iron hand in the velvet glove, which so many on the Reagan team had experienced. "The way you have conducted yourself has helped Ron achieve one of the greatest election victories in American history. Don't change a gameplan that is working."

The former president went on to give specific advice for dealing with the press: "The general rule should be to reward your friends and ignore your enemies." He gave advice on helping to smooth the relationship between the administration and Congress: "I would suggest that on occasion it would be useful if you were to have luncheons in the State Dining Room for congressional wives...."

He also urged the future First Lady to make sure to include conservatives on the guest lists at White House parties. To illustrate his point, he said he had often told Kissinger that instead of having a "séance with the *Los Angeles Times*" on trips to California he should see the Reagans. He never did. "He tells me now that he thinks this was a great mistake," Nixon wrote.

He also wrote that Connally talked to him about campaigning with Reagan in Texas after he dropped out of the race. "He called me on the phone and told me he was amazed," Nixon wrote, "he hardly saw anyone he knew at Reagan's rallies." Nixon's point was that Reagan was reaching a new and different crowd. And he wanted Mrs. Reagan to continue doing just that in her role of controlling invitations to the White House. Given the chance to invite someone from Wall Street or someone from Main Street, Nixon wrote, "take Main Street."

He went on to discuss renovations at Blair House, hiring a new White House chef, and the importance of using Camp David "in the middle of the week as well as on weekends." Nixon ended the letter by again praising Mrs. Reagan: "You look like a first lady, act like first lady and talk like first lady. You will bring beauty, class, and dignity to the White House."[1]

Meanwhile, Nixon—and the nation—prepared for Inauguration Day on January 29. The Reagan presidency began differently than other presidencies. Under the advice and counsel of Mike Deaver, Reagan decided to hold the inauguration on the west side of the U.S.

Capitol. Rather than staring at the Supreme Court building like so many of his predecessors, Reagan would look out on the vast expanse of the National Mall. The symbolism was not lost on the Reagan team—early Americans had often pointed their rocking chairs toward the West to sit back and look toward the future. Now, the oldest president ever elected up to that time would look West as he spoke of American renewal.

That renewal would have a strong conservative bent to it. "In this present crisis, government is not the solution to our problems," Reagan said, clearly referencing the staggering inflation and recession facing Americans at home. He said that "government is the problem." The new president suggested that limited government was the future of American government: "From time to time, we have been tempted to believe that society has become too complex to be managed by self-rule, that government by an elite group is superior to government for, by, and of the people. But if no one among us is capable of governing himself, then who among us has the capacity to govern someone else?"

Near the climax of the speech, Reagan waxed poetic, saying that those who believed there were no heroes left in America "just don't know where to look." The speech—and the subsequent announcement that the Iranians were releasing the hostages—provided just the beginning the new administration wanted.

Nixon was quiet about the speech in public. Privately, he had offered some suggestions to Reagan staffers. And one of the main speechwriters who worked with Reagan was Ken Khachigian.

Nixon undoubtedly approved of the speech and clearly appreciated Reagan's gifts as a communicator. And he also saw that one of those most responsible for Reagan's carefully crafted image was Mike Deaver. Deaver had served Reagan in California and many considered him to be a master of political stagecraft. Deaver was famous for his image wizardry. But the unassuming, longtime political aide always downplayed his genius. "I didn't make Reagan," he would tell people, "Reagan made me." Deaver also liked to joke that his only role in staging Reagan was to "light" him well and fill up "the space around the head." Reagan did all the rest. Nixon quickly began cultivating a relationship with the publicity wizard. Memos and letters came forth from his New York office that provided Deaver with many suggestions, including a unique idea that Nixon developed to capitalize on Reagan's communication skills.

Nixon had suffered from his own shortcomings as a public speaker, most famously in the debates with Kennedy in 1960. So he reveled in the fact that the GOP standard-bearer possessed a unique ability to communicate big ideas in simple ways.

To take advantage of this, Nixon suggested a new idea to Deaver. Years before, Deaver and Nixon had discussed the importance of taking advantage of modern forms of communication. "You will recall the conversation we had in San Clemente several years ago," Nixon now wrote, "about the use of radio. Why not exploit the president's unique ability in using this medium?"

The former president went on to urge that a "weekly ten-minute radio talk on Sunday evenings" would allow the new president to "dominate the Monday papers." It would also allow Reagan to bypass the Washington press corps and speak "directly to the American people." Deaver loved the idea, although he changed it to Saturday rather than Sunday in order to influence the Sunday morning news talk shows. On April 3, 1982, Reagan delivered the first of what would be 331 Saturday radio addresses during his presidency.[2]

Nixon praised another Deaver initiative—the first lady's anti-drug campaign. He called the plan a "ten strike." He reassured Deaver, saying, "Don't be concerned that the Washington 'witches' in the press try to knock it down as an attempt to change a poor image. Just as the heathens worshipped the idols they built, so the media must always worship the myths they have created."[3]

As the weeks rolled by, Nixon stayed in touch with Deaver. He continued suggesting ideas to him. When Reagan met with the returning hostages from Iran, Nixon suggested that Reagan use a similar meeting to tie up some loose ends from the Vietnam War. "It occurred to me that without any publicity whatever that he could invite the same POWs who had dinner with him in Sacramento to have a private dinner with Nancy and with him at the White House," he suggested. Deaver appreciated much of Nixon's counsel, but he was only interested in Reagan's best interests. He wasn't particularly interested in reopening the Vietnam issue. That idea of Nixon's was ignored.[4]

Meanwhile from his townhouse in New York City, Nixon carefully observed as the Reagan cabinet nominees went before the Senate for confirmation. One of the most controversial was the one Nixon cared about most—Al Haig—to be secretary of state. Nixon never knew that Haig had worked behind the scenes to help push him out in 1974, and he remained close to him. He regarded Haig as a tough soldier who was just the right man for the job at the State Department.

When Haig's role in Watergate became an issue in the Senate hearings, Nixon found himself in the crosshairs. The Senate committee wanted the Watergate tapes. These were technically controlled by the National Archives, but Nixon had the authority to release them. He told the Senate it would take a subpoena to get the documents. He was outraged that the very presidential materials that had been denied to him could potentially become public. Eventually the standoff ended. Haig was confirmed, and Nixon was ecstatic. Haig, Nixon said, was "the meanest, toughest, most ambitious son of a bitch I ever knew. He'll make a great secretary of state."[5]

Back home in New York, Nixon began holding stag dinners at his townhouse. Thinkers, writers, and influencers were invited to join him for drinks and dinner. Among those who would dine with him from time to time were Hugh Sidey of *Time* magazine, the economist Alan Greenspan, and his old friend and columnist Bill Safire. After dinner, Nixon would serve drinks and talk politics. He would hold court on topics ranging from the Reagan White House to the NFL. And he never failed to fascinate his audience. He also began reaching out to younger and more conservative writers and became friends with R. Emmett Tyrrell, who was the editor of the conservative publication the *American Spectator*.

On March 30, 1981, as Nixon was going about his daily routine in New York, news broke from Washington—the president had been shot. As Reagan was leaving the Hilton Hotel in Washington after giving a speech, John Hinckley Jr. had fired a series of shots at him, including one that bounced off the presidential limousine and into Reagan's side. Nixon was horrified. Having been president himself and having watched as John Kennedy was assassinated in 1963, he couldn't help but have an emotional reaction to the event. He watched the endless news coverage as doctors worked to save Reagan at George Washington University Hospital in Washington.

Nixon felt compelled to comment publicly. Through his daughter Tricia, he issued a statement to the press that he was "thankful" the president had survived and that he and Pat were "praying for the recovery of all the wounded and for the president's recovery." His measured tone was in stark contrast to that of his friend Al Haig who embarrassed himself—and damaged his position in the Reagan administration—by declaring from the White House Press Briefing Room that he was "in charge" while the president was in the hospital.[6]

By early April, the reports from George Washington Hospital were encouraging—Reagan was on the mend. The bullet had stopped just short of his heart, and the doctors had been able to remove it. By the end of the month, Reagan not only returned home to the White House, but was also preparing to address Congress. Surviving the assassin's bullet gave the Gipper new momentum to push for his agenda.

Much to Nixon's chagrin, Reagan chose to focus his attention on his plan to cut taxes. In a stirring address to Congress, Reagan went all in on his economic agenda. As he stood at the podium in the House of Representatives, wave after wave of applause came over him.

"You wouldn't want to talk me into an encore, would you?" Reagan said. From there he had the Congress—and the country—in his hands. He pushed for sweeping reductions in the marginal tax rates as a way to get America's economic engine humming again. After the speech, the White House would claim that it was inundated with calls, letters, and telegrams supportive of the president's tax cuts.

One observer who remained skeptical was Nixon. He believed that Reagan should have focused his newfound political capital on what he saw as the most important issue—facing the Soviets. And he feared the impact the tax cuts might have on Reagan's foreign policy.

In a conversation with Peter Peterson, who had served as his commerce secretary, Nixon sharply critiqued Reagan's economic strategy. "He would have been smarter to go slower," he said. "If he had asked for, say, five percent, he could have sold it on the Hill. Now, he can't, and the Soviets know it."[7]

Nixon's concern was that Reagan would get bogged down in a quagmire of negotiations with Congress over tax cuts while the Soviets watched. This would do little to deter recent Soviet aggression in places like Afghanistan. "We'd be better off politically unified behind a smaller figure," he told Peterson, adding that a smaller tax cut would "scare the hell" out of the Soviets because it would indicate that Reagan was ready to compromise and move on to foreign policy.

But Reagan often surprised the experts. And his economic recovery package proved to be such a case. The president worked aggressively to court "Boll Weevil" Democrats like Phil Gramm of Texas. And by the summer, enough conservative Democrats had pledged their support and the tax cut package was passed. Reagan signed it into law in August at his ranch near Santa Barbara.

Nixon took the high road publicly and supported the president. While in Washington state to attend his niece's wedding, he headlined a fundraiser for the King County Republican Party. In his remarks, he said that because of the "Reagan Revolution, the whole direction of the country is going to change. It's already changing." He added, though, that it would take "at least eight years" to undo the Democratic policies of the last generation.[8]

After securing his signature domestic policy victory early in his first term, Reagan was now ready to do exactly what Nixon wanted him to do—focus on foreign policy. And Nixon was ready to help Reagan do just that.

------

While Reagan had been busy looking for votes for his tax cut bill that summer, Nixon had been busy looking for a new home. In June, the Nixons purchased a fifteen-room contemporary home in Saddle River, New Jersey, for one million dollars. It was situated on more than four acres with a swimming pool, a tennis court, and a wine cellar. Nixon would maintain his office in New York and commute into the city each day. The new location would give the family more space to host and entertain. Nixon had become especially concerned when he saw girls at the Catholic school across the street from his New York townhouse smoking marijuana. He didn't want his grandkids to see anything like that. Now in the New Jersey countryside, they wouldn't.

The Nixons then sold their townhouse on East Sixty-Fifth Street. The Syrian government was looking for a residence for its delegate to the United Nations and agreed to purchase the Nixon townhouse for $2.6 million. By September, the Nixons had moved out and were fully relocated to their new place in Saddle River.

―――――――

On October 6, a few days after moving into the new house, Nixon sat in his new study editing another book manuscript when Al Haig called from the State Department and revealed that Anwar Sadat had been assassinated at a military parade in Egypt. The parade had been organized to celebrate the Egyptian military's seizure of the Suez Canal in October 1973. At the end of the procession this year, assassins had emerged from their military truck and began firing at the dignitaries. Sadat refused to cower and faced the gunmen directly. He was immediately shot and killed.

After Haig outlined the events to Nixon, the former president asked if a delegation had been formed to represent President Reagan at the funeral. Haig indicated that no final decisions had been made. "Well," Nixon responded, "whatever the president does, I am going to go."[9]

Nixon was not alone. Carter was also planning to attend. And since President Reagan had decided to defer to the Secret Service and not attend for security reasons, he decided to include President Ford and send the three living ex-presidents to represent him.

Before leaving for Cairo, the three presidents met at the White House for a brief reception with President Reagan. Following hors d'oeuvres and drinks, the current president and his three predecessors stepped onto the South Lawn for a brief ceremony. Nixon, in a dark suit and blue striped tie, stood immediately to Reagan's right as the president took the podium. Though he had attended a state dinner with President Carter in 1979, that had been a closed press event. This time, here he was at last—back at the White House in full view of the public. It was his first time on the South Lawn since he had departed in Marine One in August 1974.

Reagan delivered brief remarks praising Sadat as someone who had "stood in defiance" of those who threatened peace. As he concluded the speech, he looked to the three men surrounding him and offered a "a heartfelt thank you to these men here, these three who are making this mission on behalf of our country. I thank you, and if I may, in the language of my own ancestry, say: Until we meet again, may God hold you in the hollow of His hand."

The former presidents then boarded the marine helicopter and lifted off on their way to Andrews Air Force Base. The irony could not have been lost on Nixon—just seven years before he had made this same journey in the moments before his presidency officially ended.

President Reagan welcomes former presidents Ford, Carter, and Nixon to the White House on their way to represent him at the funeral of Anwar Sadat. (National Archives and Records Administration)

"I kind of like that house down there," he joked to the other former presidents as the helicopter flew off of the South Lawn.[10]

The flight to Cairo was a long one. A number of congressional leaders were on board. Nixon made sure to stop and visit with each one. He showed signs that his personal Watergate battle had ended. When he spotted the *Washington Post*'s Haynes Johnson, who had covered the Watergate scandal, Nixon politely asked him how he was doing. And when he came across Senator Charles Percy, he seemed unconcerned with the Senator's support for his impeachment. "Chuck Percy has stood by presidents in foreign policy," he said as he shook the man's hand.

Once they had arrived in Cairo, the former presidents were under tight security at the hotel. The next day at the funeral, the air was thick with tension as the Secret Service worried about a possible terrorist attack on three former presidents. The U.S. delegation wore bullet-proof jackets underneath their suits. And when the funeral procession went past the very reviewing stand where Sadat had been murdered just a few days earlier, the bullet holes could still be seen.

Still, no incidents materialized and the funeral ended without any issues. But when Carter and Ford arrived at the airport for the return trip home, Nixon was missing. They learned from Haig's staff that Nixon would be traveling separately to Saudi Arabia. Much confusion ensued about the origin of this side foray into the Middle East and whether the Reagan administration had approved it. In fact, Nixon had worked with Haig on visiting Saudi Arabia, Jordan, Tunisia, and Morocco. But questions remain as to whether Haig kept the White House informed. Since the trip was unofficial and since the White House probably would have been concerned, it seems likely that Haig provided vague details at best to President Reagan. The final and official version of events was that Haig had told Reagan, but that the president had forgotten about it—an unlikely story, but one that the White House stuck with as Nixon's trip unfolded.

After making his way through four Middle Eastern countries and meeting with officials in each one, Nixon landed in Paris, where he set up at the Crillon Hotel. He then worked with the American Embassy in Paris to issue a public statement about his trip. The Reagan administration was keen to use Nixon's trip—and his public statement—to endorse its own plan to sell $8.5 billion worth of Airborne Warning and Control System (AWACS) planes to Saudi Arabia. Israel was not happy about it. And the plan had stirred up much debate in the U.S.

Nixon's friend Richard Allen, now serving as Reagan's national security advisor, asked the former president to issue a statement about the trip and specifically comment on the AWACS sale. In his statement, Nixon praised the sale and suggested that "if it were not for the intense opposition" of Israeli prime minister Menachem Begin that it would not be controversial. He also blamed "parts of the American Jewish community," a comment that accurately represented the domestic politics of the issue but invited criticism that he was essentially blaming American Jews. Allen sent the piece around to his colleagues at the White House and called it "splendid" and "exactly what we had hoped he would do."[11]

The trip—and Nixon's report—represented another step forward in his journey back. Here was the only president who had been forced to resign the presidency, and yet he was not only representing the current American president at a state funeral in Egypt, but he also was meeting with leaders of key countries in the Middle East and publicly commenting on the wisdom of the controversial Reagan arms policy in the Middle East.

The media devoted ample attention to Nixon's comments. The *Washington Post* stated plainly that this recent foray into the politics of the Middle East had continued his "rehabilitation." And *Time* approvingly called him a "ubiquitous elder statesman without portfolio."

---

As the first year of the Reagan administration came to a close, Nixon was pleased with how his friend was doing. "I like and admire [Lech] Walesa," he wrote to Reagan after *Time* magazine selected the leader of the Polish Solidarity Movement for its "Man of the Year" award, "but in my book, *Time* missed the boat: President Reagan should have been Man of the Year." Sure, Nixon was trying to flatter the president, but he also believed the country was in far better hands than it had been with Jimmy Carter.[12]

Back home in New Jersey, Nixon recovered from the long trip and read the reviews. He could see that his work was paying off. But he knew a real legacy would require more than a trip around the world and some positive news clippings. He wanted a presidential center where he could define his own legacy once and for all.

Chapter Eleven

# A Home for the Nixon Library

*"To hell with 'em. We'll go to Yorba Linda."*

The concept of the presidential library is a fairly new one. It was Franklin Roosevelt who signed the legislation and Herbert Hoover who became the first former president to build a place where the public could visit a museum and a scholar could research his papers. Before that, presidential papers were housed in Washington, D.C. The goal of the presidential library was to take presidents out of Washington and put them back into the places from which they came. If people wanted to get a real understanding of a president, the thinking went, they needed to see where he was from and how his beginnings had shaped him.

The fight for a Nixon library had begun almost the minute he left the White House. And as in so much else of Nixon's career, he had to fight a unique battle. That's because Congress had passed and President Ford had signed legislation requiring that all of Nixon's papers stay in Washington because of their importance in the ongoing Watergate litigation. Nixon's lawyers had immediately challenged the new law, arguing that Nixon was being singled out

Inside the Richard Nixon Presidential Library and Museum. (Jeremy Thompson)

with special rules. He was, but in 1974 most people didn't care. He was still viewed negatively by so much of the public.

Nixon knew that litigation could take years, but he was eager to get moving on the library. So on April 26, 1975, at the Annenburg Estate, plans were announced to build a Richard M. Nixon Presidential Library on the campus of Pat's alma mater, the University of Southern California. The USC Board of Regents and USC president John Hubbard joined Nixon in making the announcement.

At that time, Nixon told reporters that he was "very pleased" with the arrangement and that he looked forward to the day when scholars could undertake "historical research and public study" on his papers. Even the faculty and staff at USC seemed genuinely excited. "I'm exhilarated," school librarian Roy Kidman told the press. "It's like the biggest thing that ever happened to USC," added student Karen Kennedy, "except the national championship."[1]

The deal hinged on Nixon's ability to secure his papers from the government. The Presidential Records and Materials Preservation

Act—the legislation Ford had signed—did not give the federal government ownership of the documents, but it did give the government possession. Nixon's litigation challenged this, and the case went all the way to the Supreme Court. Two years after he had made the announcement about the arrangement with USC, the Supreme Court ruled 7–2 that the law dealing with the Nixon papers was legal because Nixon represented a "legitimate case of one." Later that year, employees of the General Services Administration began storing the Nixon/filed deep inside the National Archives in Washington.

This impasse was enough to keep matters from moving forward at USC Indeed, from 1977 until 1981, little progress had been made toward creating a Nixon library on the college's campus. Then in 1981, a chance encounter between two unlikely allies changed the plans for the Nixon library. While attending an event in New York on July 28, 1981, Nixon spoke with Duke President Terry Sanford. Sanford was a liberal who had served as governor of North Carolina and had seconded the nomination of John F. Kennedy for president in 1960. Yet he saw the value of having the archives of Duke's most famous alumnus on campus. On the spot, he asked the former president about placing his library at Duke. Nixon demurred and changed the subject to football, joking that Duke should hire his friend George Allen as its coach.

But the library itself was no joking matter. And Nixon was far more interested than he had let on to Sanford. Nixon still fondly remembered his law school alma mater as the place that gave him a chance. He had survived on a $250-per-year scholarship provided by the school, supplemented by working in the law library. He would never have gone on to a successful political career had it not been for Duke. Plus, Duke had a prestigious academic reputation. With the USC negotiations lagging, why not consider Duke?

In early August, Stan Mortenson, Nixon's lawyer, visited the campus on two separate occasions to see if Duke would indeed make sense for the Nixon library. He liked what he saw and reported back favorably to his boss. Meanwhile, President Sanford pitched the idea internally at Duke. There, the reaction was not so positive.

"We know more about presidential papers than Terry Sanford," jeered Duke professor Lawrence C. Goodwin when the proposal became public. "We know what presidential libraries are. They're not archives; they're shrines."[2]

Goodwin was not entirely wrong. Modern presidential libraries are not only places to host the archives, but they are also museums with exhibits extolling presidents' virtues, with gift shops where photos and t-shirts of the presidents can be purchased. Did Duke—a traditionally left-leaning institution—want a Nixon museum on its campus? The answer coming back to Sanford from the faculty was a resounding no.

"It would be an albatross around Duke University for years to come," Duke professor H. Sheldon Smith told the *Washington Post,* "an object of censure, scorn, and derision."[3]

Sanford persisted. He understood the risks, but he also saw the benefits. "I would have been ashamed of myself if I would have been afraid to propose this," he said publicly of the proposal. "I think it indicates integrity, courage, and institutional self-confidence on Duke's part. I think it would hurt our image if we turned it down."

Sanford was about to learn the truth in Kissinger's famous joke that academic politics is so vicious because the stakes are so low. In the summer of 1981, college professors at Duke left their comfortable offices and the editing of their syllabi for the opportunity to take shots at the former president. And to someone like Sanford, who had spent his life and career toiling in the vineyard of the Left, it proved to be too much.

When the Duke Academic Council took a formal vote on the project, Sanford's efforts came up short. The proposal was voted down 35–34.

The house where Nixon was born in Yorba Linda, California. (Jeremy Thompson)

At this point, there were few options left for the homeless Nixon library. One possibility was San Clemente, the California town where the Nixons had lived for so long. A beautiful plot of land overlooking the ocean was chosen. "We were looking for a focus for tourism," San Clemente mayor Scott Diehl said, "and we thought the Nixon Library could do that for us."[4]

Nixon followed events closely through his longtime aide Ken Khachigian, who faithfully attended hearings at San Clemente City Hall. But as with USC before, the initial excitement over the plan devolved into a long grind of years of negotiations.

The reflecting pool on the grounds of the Nixon Presidential Library. (Jeremy Thompson)

Things began encouragingly when the San Clemente City Council voted in 1984 to approve preliminary plans for the library. But controversy soon ensued as the 16.7-acre site was to be connected to a 253-acre commercial and residential development that was being called the Marblehead Coastal Plan. The strategy was that the developer of the site, the Lusk Company in Irvine, would receive approval from the city for the entire project and then donate the land for the library on top of a bluff overlooking the ocean.

The city of San Clemente had hoped to agree to terms with Lusk in July 1987. But a council member urged delay, saying, "Nixon needs us more than we need him." Khachigian reported the comment back to Nixon. And it was too much for him.

"To hell with 'em," Nixon raged. "We'll go to Yorba Linda." So the site of Nixon's birthplace was purchased and some buildings were cleared so that a presidential museum could be built. On November 7, 1987, the *Los Angeles Times* reported that Nixon would build a "twenty-five million dollar library next to the house where he was born" in Orange County. The Richard Nixon Elementary School, located next to the site of Nixon's boyhood home, had experienced declining enrollment for years. The city and the school district agreed to demolish the building to make room for the Nixon presidential library. This would give the library six acres of land on which to build.[5]

Nixon, for his part, seemed genuinely excited to be going home to Yorba Linda. But John Whitaker, executive director of the Nixon Foundation, made sure the press knew how disappointed the Nixon team was in the four-year process they had just been through in San Clemente. "We expected it to take some time but never that long," he told the *Los Angeles Times*. But at long last the search for a home had ended. Now planning and fundraising could begin. But one challenge remained—Nixon's papers. The former president had still not been able to reach an agreement with the federal government over the status of his presidential papers. They were still in Washington. This meant that the Nixon Library and Museum would be mostly a museum. The pre-presidential papers and post-presidential papers would be located in the new facility in Yorba Linda. But the post-presidential papers were controlled by the family and not open to researchers. So tourists and history buffs would be the main target of the new facility, not researchers or scholars.[6]

Meanwhile, it was becoming clear that Richard Nixon's career could not yet be consigned to a museum. He still had plenty to say.

# Chapter Twelve

# Navigating the Turbulence

*"The leader must organize his life…*
*to make the big plays."*

B y the fall of 1981, Nixon had already published three books and was editing his fourth. *Leaders* represented a bit of a departure for Nixon. Rather than take an issue such as foreign policy and hope that key people like Reagan would read it, he had decided to take key people in history and write profiles defining the characteristics that made them great. Nixon had worked closely with his old friend and aide Ray Price in New York. Price and Nixon loosely structured their book on the model of Churchill's *Great Contemporaries*, and the idea was for Nixon to write about and reflect on people he had been with in the arena.

"I had to have known them.…" Nixon said of his criteria in choosing the figures in the book, and they had to have "made a difference—by building their nation, by saving it, or by moving the world in some other singular way." Nixon also noted that each of the people in the book had been in "the wilderness" and had returned to "lead his nation out of a moment of supreme crisis."[1]

Nixon's choices were revealing. He included chapters on his hero Charles de Gaulle and on Winston Churchill, Douglas MacArthur (whom Nixon wrote about in a chapter including his thoughts on Japan's Shigeru Yoshida), Konrad Adenauer, Nikita Khrushchev, David Ben-Gurion, and Golda Meir, among others. Nixon told anecdotes about each leader and included some of his or her axioms. But permeating each chapter was Nixon's own personal take on what made the leader in question successful and what defines leadership in general. And Nixon shrewdly offered his own personal reminiscences about each figure, which helped bring the book to life.

Telford Taylor, reviewing the book for the *New York Times*, couldn't help but like Nixon's eye-witness viewpoint of the leaders in the book: "By far the most interesting passages are those in which Mr. Nixon describes his personal encounters with his subjects. While some of these accounts are routine, those dealing with de Gaulle, Adenauer, and especially Khrushchev, Zhou Enlai and Leonid Brezhnev (to whom Nixon devotes a portion of the chapter on Khrushchev) are fascinating." Taylor quoted from the Khrushchev chapter:

> In their personal diplomacy Khrushchev and Brezhnev were similar to Lyndon Johnson. They felt compelled to reinforce their words with some sort of physical contact. Khrushchev's tactile diplomacy was almost always menacing.... When Brezhnev reached out to touch or grab my arm, he sought to implore, not to bully. But should these gentler means fail to persuade me, Brezhnev could also apply sheer muscle. What struck me most about Brezhnev was his emotional versatility. At one moment he would speak with what seemed to be perfect sincerity about his deep desire to leave a legacy of peace for his grandchildren.

In the next he would assert with unequivocal determination his right to control the destinies of other nations all around the world.

Taylor wrote that parts of the book represented something close to Nixon coming into his own as a writer and historian. "Furthermore," he wrote, "the style of these parts is fluent and poised—not unduly self-laudatory and with few wasted words. Indeed, this reviewer came away from the book with a sense that Mr. Nixon was far more relaxed—and successful—when dealing with foreign potentates than when confronting domestic problems in Washington or California and that his own most pleasant memories are for the days in Paris, Bonn, Moscow, and Peking. It is noteworthy that the only American leader on whom Mr. Nixon focuses is General MacArthur."[2]

It was indeed noteworthy. Nixon had not included his former boss Dwight Eisenhower, yet he had included MacArthur, who had famously ridiculed the idea of Ike becoming president by calling him "the best clerk" he had ever had. The omission was not lost on the public—or the Eisenhower family. "I hate the association of the name Eisenhower with the name Nixon," Milton Eisenhower later said in expressing the family's reaction to—and even gratitude for—Ike's exclusion from Nixon's book.

Toward the end of the book, Nixon managed to take shots at some familiar suspects. Years before conservatives were complaining about "fake news," Nixon accused television of having "shortened the public's attention span." He also portrayed the media as an entity filled with a "pervasive left-wing bias." Academia came under fire, as well. Tenured professors too often lived in the "stratosphere of the absurd." And bureaucrats were not spared either. Nixon accused federal civil servants of being "institutionally lethargic," and even

worse, "politically active for liberal causes." He made this argument
decades before conservatives would attack "the deep state" for continuing to implement the Left's policies no matter which party won
the elections.

A leader, Nixon was saying, had to overcome the bias of the
media, the academy, and even the civil service to get things done. He
did not explicitly apply this analysis to his own presidency. He did,
however, write that a leader must not be judged until enough time has
transpired. Quoting de Gaulle, who was quoting Sophocles, Nixon
wrote of the leaders in his book—as well as of himself—that "one
must wait until the evening to see how splendid the day has been."

The book represented another milestone as Nixon added "historian" to his list of accomplishments. The reviews were ambivalent,
but the book sold briskly. And on its publication in 1982, Nixon sent
out copies to friends, and even rivals. Invariably, he would autograph
the book with a specific note to the recipient. Occasionally, Nixon
would receive a note back. One that may have surprised him came
from his rival in the 1972 presidential race—George McGovern. The
note simply read, "History will remember you as one of the great
peacemakers of the twentieth century."[3]

By early 1982, the Reagan administration was beginning to experience internal controversy.

In January of that year, National Security Advisor Richard Allen
found himself in hot water when news was leaked of an FBI investigation into possible bribery. Allen had essentially intercepted a payment
from a foreign reporter. The Japanese media outlet routinely paid for
major interviews and the check was supposed to be a thank you for
Mrs. Reagan. Allen grabbed the check as a way of keeping Mrs.

Reagan out of trouble. Eventually, the investigation showed that he had violated no laws. But the leaked story had done the damage, and Allen was forced out in January 1982.

Meanwhile, David Stockman, Reagan's Office of Management of Budget director, fell prey to the ancient Washington temptation of a fawning profile from the press. In his case, it came during a series of interviews with William Greider for a story that eventually ran in the *Atlantic Monthly*. Stockman appeared dismissive of the 1981 tax cuts package. "None of us really understands what's going on with all these numbers," he told Greider, referring to Reagan's economic agenda. The article appeared in December 1981 and created a frenzy of talk in Washington about how Reagan's own team didn't believe in Reaganomics.

In January 1982, Nixon wrote to Reagan to reassure him. And, as only a former president can, he told the current president that the fault lay with the staffers. Nixon wrote that "the problem all conservative administrations face is that those who are loyal are not bright and those who are bright are not loyal." In case Reagan should wonder whom he was referring to, Nixon was explicit. "Allen is loyal but unfortunately not bright enough," he wrote. "Stockman is bright, but as anyone who reads the entire *Atlantic Monthly* interview article as I have would conclude, he is simply not loyal to the Reagan economic policy."[4]

Nixon himself was not wild about Reaganomics, but few issues could get him riled up more than staff disloyalty. It outraged him to read Stockman—a former advisor to Reagan's 1980 presidential rival John Anderson—essentially questioning his boss in print.

Still, Nixon was largely pleased that Reagan's major domestic policy agenda had been accomplished with the passage of the tax cuts. Now the president could cast his eye overseas.

But even there, trouble loomed. Nixon's friend and personal choice to head Reagan's foreign affairs was losing support. Al Haig had always been an acquired taste. He possessed a competent management style but had an abrasive personality. And ever since the assassination attempt—when Haig was perceived to have essentially declared himself temporary president—many in Reagan's inner circle had grown suspicious of the secretary of state. Haig had never been accused of having a small ego. But now questions were growing about whether Haig could be a team player and subordinate his own interests to those of the president.

Late in the spring of 1982, events in the Middle East forced Reagan's hand. Israel had invaded Lebanon. Reagan, possessing a far shrewder mind on foreign affairs than his critics realized, understood the Israelis' thinking. For years, terrorists from the Palestinian Liberation Organization had used Southern Lebanon as a staging ground to launch terrorist attacks into Israel. From Israel's point of view, the counterattack against Lebanon was not an invasion of a sovereign country, but was a strike against rogue terrorists. In their minds, it was an act of defense—not an offensive measure. Indeed, the Israelis called it "Operation Peace for Galilee."

Haig shared this view for the most part. He went to the president and urged him to say nothing publicly. Reagan was sympathetic with Haig's position and with the goals of the Israeli operation. But he also understood how it would look in the eyes of the world—like the invasion of a sovereign nation. The president initially gave Haig what he wanted. No statement came from the White House in the initial hours of the attack. But a day later, Reagan's instincts had been proven correct. Israel was being widely condemned for the attack. The leader of the free world could no longer remain silent. On June 6, Ambassador Jeane Kirkpatrick joined the other members of the United Nations Security Council in passing a resolution demanding that Israel withdraw from Lebanon.

Enraged, Haig called Nixon to vent. In his mind he had been undermined by the president, and he believed he should resign as secretary of state. Nixon pushed back. He told his old friend to relax and let things play out. But Haig was never one to be an observer.

On June 13, he appeared on a Sunday morning talk show and was asked about the possibility of American troops being sent to Lebanon to help restore the ceasefire. "We're going to have to look very, very carefully at what will be necessary to provide a stable situation in Southern Lebanon," Haig responded.

It would be his last public comment as secretary of state. The president had finally had enough. Earlier that week, Haig—ignoring Nixon's advice to lay low—had complained bitterly to new National Security Advisor William Clark about how he had been undermined. It was that display of histrionics that sealed his fate. Clark reported the conversation back to Reagan.

One of the great myths about Ronald Reagan is that he was blindly staff-driven and never questioned or challenged subordinates. Yes, he hired people he trusted and he delegated authority. But if someone lost his trust, he didn't hesitate to make a move. Al Haig found that out the hard way on June 25. He was summoned to the Oval Office, where the president gave him a document. As he read it, Haig saw that it was Reagan's acceptance of his resignation. Haig had just been fired.

Within minutes of the meeting ending, Reagan called Nixon. He probably suspected that the former president would be upset to see his old friend unceremoniously dismissed from the State Department. But Nixon understood Haig's shortcomings as well as anyone. And he was pleased when Reagan told him that he would be offering the job to another Nixon friend, George Shultz. Nixon later spoke to Haig by phone. Still later, on June 28, Nixon told the press that "Secretary Shultz will carry on." And then he took one of the complaints Haig had made and turned it into a virtue for Shultz. "If there has been any sniping or guerrilla warfare against the secretary of state, as Secretary Haig has indicated, let me tell you, you're not going to see anything publicly about it from Secretary Shultz." The reason? Shultz "will not tolerate it."[5]

Nixon likely felt for Haig. But he understood politics well enough to know that Reagan deserved a secretary of state he could trust. And so the choice of Shultz seemed fine at the time. Nixon believed that Schultz was capable of doing the job and lacked Haig's obnoxiousness. Besides, Nixon had to keep his ties to the administration in order to have any influence. The former president could and would try to work with Shultz. His statement to the press was his way of giving Reagan some cover and signaling to Shultz that he wanted to be a resource for him.

Haig's departure could have been the end of Nixon's foreign policy counsel to the White House. But he managed to navigate it carefully and his relationship with the president seemed just fine. "I criticize him privately and praise him publicly," he told the press in describing his relationship with Reagan.

That fall, Reagan's party took a beating at the polls. Midterm elections are always a challenge for the party that controls the White House, and November 1982 proved to be no exception. Still, the Republicans maintained a majority in the Senate. And that meant the president would still be able to govern effectively, especially on foreign policy. He had campaigned in 1980 promising to confront the Soviets. As 1983 began, Reagan was ready to make good on this promise. And Nixon's advice and counsel would become even more important to him.

Chapter Thirteen

# The Evil Empire

*"The United States wants peace;
the Soviet Union wants the world."*

In late 1982, a group of former Nixon staffers gathered at the Marriott Hotel in Washington. A banner greeted them that read, "Welcome Class of '72." The occasion was the tenth anniversary of Nixon's forty-nine-state electoral landslide. The former president arrived wearing a dark suit and a bright smile. Nixon looked happy, and he was. He had a friend in the Oval Office, he was making public appearances again, and his books were selling. Nixon's spirits soared as his made his way around the ballroom shaking hands with Pat Buchanan, John Mitchell, Chuck Colson, and others.

In his brief remarks to the group, Nixon quoted from his favorite Theodore Roosevelt passage: it was "the man in the arena" who counted and not the "cold and timid souls who know neither victory nor defeat." Nixon added with emphasis that none of his former staffers present at the occasion were "timid souls."

Nor was the current occupant of the White House. On March 8, 1983, President Reagan arrived in Orlando, Florida, to deliver a keynote address to the National Association of Evangelicals. In a speech that touched on everything from domestic policy to NATO, Reagan spoke directly about the Soviet opposition. Using a phrase that would make news around the world, Reagan did not hold back: "Yes, let us pray for the salvation of all of those who live in that totalitarian darkness—pray they will discover the joy of knowing God. But until they do, let us be aware that while they preach the supremacy of the State, declare its omnipotence over individual man, and predict its eventual domination of all peoples on the earth, they are the focus of evil in the modern world."

And Reagan wasn't finished rebuking the Soviets. He urged his Evangelical audience to "beware the temptation of pride—the temptation of blithely declaring yourselves above it all and label both sides equally at fault, to ignore the facts of history and the aggressive impulses of an evil empire, to simply call the arms race a giant misunderstanding and thereby remove yourself from the struggle between right and wrong and good and evil."

The national media were aghast. "When a politician claims that God favors his programs," sneered Anthony Lewis in a column in the *New York Times*, "alarm bells should ring." Lewis was especially appalled that Reagan urged the audience to avoid "the temptation of pride." He castigated Reagan for aggressively blaming the Soviets. He faulted the president because he "applied a black-and-white standard to something that is much more complex."[1]

According to Lewis, Reagan didn't understand the history of the arms race: "One may regard the Soviet system as a vicious tyranny and still understand that it has not been solely responsible for the nuclear arms race. The terrible irony of that race is that the United States has led the way on virtually every major new development over the last 30 years, only to find itself met by the Soviet Union."

Lewis' comments were more critical than correct. As it turned out, Reagan did understand the terrible irony of the arms race. And he was appalled at where it had left the country. Reagan particularly took umbrage at the doctrine of Mutually Assured Destruction (MAD). This was the theory in place for much of the Cold War that said the Soviets couldn't launch a nuclear attack because the United States would reciprocate in kind. Thus, mutually assured destruction kept the world safe. Ironically, MAD essentially had become official U.S. policy with Richard Nixon's signing of the 1972 Anti-Ballistic Missile Treaty that restricted defensive systems. But the idea had predated Nixon; the Johnson administration had first proposed the idea out of concern that the rush for a defensive system would lead to yet another arms race.

Reagan thought that MAD was indeed mad. And he had wondered for years if a different method of protecting the U.S. from a nuclear attack would work better. His speech to the Evangelicals was the first step in a two-pronged plan. First, Reagan would call out the "evil" that he saw in the Soviet Union and in the Soviets' actions around the world. Second, he would propose a new approach.

As far back as his days as governor of California, Reagan had been intrigued by the possibility of creating a defensive system for the nuclear era. Even as Lyndon Johnson and Defense Secretary Robert McNamara were exploring ways of limiting nuclear defense, Reagan began thinking that expanding nuclear defense might be the answer. In 1967 he had met with a physicist at the Lawrence Livermore National Laboratory named Edward Teller who suggested that technology such as lasers could potentially be used to knock down a nuclear weapon in route to its target. Now as president, Reagan was toying with the idea again. Earlier in 1983, he had met with the Joint Chiefs of Staff and expressed his dismay about the current policy of MAD. They agreed and told the president that new technologies such as kinetic energy could possibly help block a nuclear missile once it was launched. Reagan seized the idea.

Speaking from the Oval Office on the night of March 23, 1983, Reagan asked the nation, "Wouldn't it be better to save lives than to avenge them? Are we not capable of demonstrating our peaceful intentions by applying all our abilities and our ingenuity to achieving a truly lasting stability?"

Then he made his major announcement: "Tonight, consistent with our obligations under the ABM Treaty and recognizing the need for closer consultation with our allies, I am taking an important first step. I am directing a comprehensive and intensive effort to define a long-term research and development program to begin to achieve our ultimate goal of eliminating the threat posed by strategic nuclear missiles."

The plan to create a defensive shield protecting the U.S. from a nuclear attack would be called the Strategic Defense Initiative (SDI). It came under withering criticism almost immediately from Democrats like Senator Ted Kennedy, who mocked it as "Star Wars," after the popular George Lucas science fiction films. But Reagan forged ahead despite the criticism. He believed that if technology could create offensive weapons it could also create defensive ones.

And he found an unlikely ally in Nixon. The former president was intrigued by the idea—not so much as a matter of defense policy, but as a matter of diplomacy.

Almost from the beginning of the SDI debate, Nixon doubted that technology would be able to produce the impenetrable shield Reagan hoped to create. "Too much of the debate has focused only on the possibility of developing a one hundred percent leak-proof population defense which even the strongest proponents agree could not be developed until the next century," he wrote to his friend, Admiral U.S. Grant Sharp. But Nixon worried that the U.S. "counter-force missile silos" could be vulnerable to a first strike from the Soviets, and thus believed that the U.S. had "no choice but to go forward with an SDI program" to at least protect these silos.[2]

In addition, Nixon, as always, was playing a long game. He viewed the new Reagan policy as a tool to be used in negotiations down the road with the Soviets. And Reagan, perhaps taken aback by the negative reviews of his plans, sought out Nixon's advice even more. Not long after first unveiling the SDI program to the nation, the president wrote to his friend and thanked him for his part in "alerting our nation to the steady, relentless nature of Soviet military expansion, and the need to devote more of our resources to defense."

Major White House policy announcements never happen in a vacuum. And Reagan taking the initiative with SDI was in part a response to growing pressure on the president to meet with the Soviets. Reagan was willing to meet with Soviet leaders, but, he later joked, "they kept dying on me." Nixon's old rival Leonid Brezhnev died in 1982, followed by the brief tenures of Yuri Andropov and then of Konstantin Chernenko.

Still, as Nixon knew, the pressure on Reagan to meet with the Soviet leader would not relent. But Nixon did not think Reagan needed to rush into a summit meeting.

Nixon met privately with new National Security Advisor Bud McFarlane to discourage a "get acquainted" meeting. And he wrote directly to Reagan, warning, "Some well-intentioned advisors will urge you to agree to such a meeting because it will pull the teeth of the peace at any price groups and be reassuring to some of our jittery allies aboard." That much was true, he conceded in his note to the president, "but only temporarily. Unless something substantive comes out, the effect of an atmospheric meeting wears off very quickly...."[3]

Nixon believed that meeting for the sake of meeting made no sense. He continued this line of reasoning in his conversations with the national security advisor. He urged McFarlane to establish a meeting only once an agenda could be agreed upon. But one sticking point prevented that: SDI. The Soviets had reacted with outrage to Reagan's proposal to expand the arms race into the skies. Reagan had expected this reaction. But he also wanted to meet with the Soviets. Paradoxically, Reagan wanted to build a defense shield, but he also strongly favored eliminating entire classes of nuclear weapons.

McFarlane was a perfect connection point for Nixon. The two men had been friends for years, and McFarlane welcomed advice from the elder statesman. Indeed, McFarlane often found himself frustrated by President Reagan, though he appreciated his many gifts. "Reagan," he would famously say later, "knows so little but accomplishes so much."

In Nixon, McFarlane found a sympathetic ear. The former president, too, had often been critical of Reagan but had always respected Reagan's political gifts. And he sensed that Reagan might/able to do something to help end the Cold War. In aid of that outcome, Nixon would continue to advise not only the president, but also his national security advisor.

"I often called him to talk about my frustrations," McFarlane later remembered, "which could center on my relationships in the White House or most usually by difficulties in overcoming President Reagan's inability to understand foreign policy." Though he didn't always share McFarlane's harsh assessment of Reagan as a statesman, Nixon offered his friend much more than words of encouragement. "He would say, 'Put it to him this way,' or 'Put it to him that way,'" McFarlane recalled. And when the national security advisor used Nixon's phrasing with the president, "it often worked."[4]

That fall brought events that changed the equation in favor of Reagan's position with the Soviets. On September 1, 1983, Korean Air Lines Flight 007 left Anchorage, Alaska, on its way to Seoul,

South Korea. The commercial flight had deviated slightly from its flight path and accidentally entered Soviet airspace. Soviet fighter planes soon tracked the plane and fired warning shots, which the Korean Air Lines pilots most likely never noticed. The Soviet pilots then destroyed the plane with air-to-air missiles. All 269 passengers and crew members were killed.

Initially, the Soviets denied any responsibility for the attack. But the evidence was overwhelming. Then the Kremlin claimed that the plane was on a spying missing. But the rest of the world was having none of it, and neither was the American president. Speaking from the Oval Office on the night of September 5, 1983, Reagan spoke bluntly of the tragedy: "Let me state as plainly as I can: There was absolutely no justification, either legal or moral, for what the Soviets did." He contrasted the Soviets' actions with those of other countries: "Is this a practice of other countries in the world? The answer is no. Commercial aircraft from the Soviet Union and Cuba on a number of occasions have flown over sensitive United States military facilities. They weren't shot down. We and other civilized countries believe in the tradition of offering help to mariners and pilots who are lost or in distress on the sea or in the air. We believe in following procedures to prevent a tragedy, not to provoke one."

In that speech, Reagan never used the phrase "evil empire." But he didn't need to. The Soviets had proven Reagan's point with their actions. No one could doubt that they could not be trusted. And that was the very reason Reagan was pushing for a defensive system.

Other consequences flowed from this incident. Eventually the Reagan administration pushed for the commercialization of Global Positioning Satellite (GPS) technology so that other planes would not drift off course. But perhaps the most prominent side effect of the KAL 007 tragedy was that it strengthened Reagan's hand going into an election year. The economy had already begun to respond to his tax cut package and was growing again. Now the American public could also see that a strong hand was needed in the White House to deal with foreign events.

But they also saw a soft hand from Reagan at times. In the fall of 1983, the president signed legislation establishing a national holiday for civil rights icon Martin Luther King Jr., thus defying many in his own party. Pat Buchanan, one of Nixon's former aides, used his syndicated column to attack the president's decision. He wrote that "by the day he died on that Memphis balcony, Dr. King had become as polarizing, as divisive, as negative a force as there was in national politics."

On September 24, Nixon wrote to Buchanan to disagree politely. While acknowledging that King's personal life had been scandalous, he pointed to his role as a public figure. "On balance, what we have to recognize is that Americans need heroes," Nixon wrote, "and that the only perfect man died on the cross. And black Americans, because of their special background, need them most of all."[5]

As 1983 neared its end, Democrats were lining up to run against Reagan. The fate of American foreign policy would depend on the outcome of the 1984 election. Reagan privately told aides he wasn't sure he should run. But his friend in Saddle River, New Jersey, was quite sure. America, Nixon believed, needed Reagan. And he was prepared, once again, to do his part to help Reagan win at the polls.

Chapter Fourteen

# The 1984 Election

*"I urge you to bite the bullet*
*and do what is necessary...."*

As 1983 neared its close, Richard Nixon kept his eye on his place in history. He continued to make public appearances and work on books. But he was also looking for ways to reach even more people. No medium had done more for his rehabilitation than television did with the Frost interviews. What if he could appear on television again to talk about his presidency, only without an antagonistic interviewer like David Frost? A deal was negotiated with CBS to show a ninety-minute interview conducted by his former aide, Frank Gannon.

Gannon interviewed Nixon for more than thirty-six hours over the course of nine different days. Nixon proved more relaxed taking questions from his former aide. Before the interview was shown on *60 Minutes*, the stately figure of Morley Safer appeared to introduce the segment and downplay any concerns critics had about CBS purchasing the interview.

"When we looked at the videotapes we saw a Richard Nixon talking with astonishing candor," Safer told his audience on the night of April 8, 1984. "We never heard a president speak that way on the record. So we purchased the broadcast rights to an hour and a half of those 38 hours. Mr. Nixon was paid a fee by the company which produced the tapes and, in addition, has a profit participation in the worldwide sale of the memoirs."[1]

In the interview, Nixon—dressed in his usual dark suit and blue tie—spoke about Watergate and even used the phrase "smoking gun" when talking about the tapes. It was the "final blow, the final nail in the coffin. Although you didn't need another nail if you were already in the coffin, which we were." This was another attempt by Nixon to accept moral responsibility without acknowledging any legal responsibility. But now, more than five years after he first tried it on television with Frost, Nixon knew the public was more accepting of his explanation. Time heals most wounds.

But if the public accepted it, the media did not. John Herbers, reviewing the televised interview for the *New York Times*, characterized it as "another step" in Nixon's ongoing effort to "erase the stigma of Watergate" and rehabilitate his public image. Herbers was sharply critical of the choice of Gannon as the questioner, yet he acknowledged that Gannon asked tough questions. Indeed, at one point Gannon asked if Nixon was sorry for Watergate. Herbers seemed mainly angry not at Gannon, but at Nixon. He saw the interview as more of a cover-up and lambasted CBS for airing it. "Tonight's segment made no important disclosures that could be called news," he sneered.

Herbers was not entirely wrong in suspecting that the interviews had been scripted. Nixon had indeed worked closely with Gannon in the run-up to the interviews. "I know that you will be tempted to insert questions about me," he wrote to Gannon on June 16, 1983, after some of the tapings had already been completed. "I think I am far more effective talking about others than about myself." As for questions Gannon might ask about other leaders,

Nixon had advice there too. "Again here I think that like the questions on the presidency, we should try to bring out what to average people will be unexpected characteristics and/or achievements." He further suggested that Gannon propose answers to the questions, and he thought Gannon might peruse his book *Leaders* to get a sense of how those answers might be worded. Nixon was careful not to overstep, however. He congratulated Gannon on his stage presence and said, "I think your questions have been right on target in both tone and substance and that you will come [across] very well on the tube."[2]

Nixon was right. The interview proved to be a success. It showed Nixon taking stock of his career and acknowledging his shortcomings. Besides, Watergate was old news at this point. Politics had moved on. In the spring of 1984, most people were focused on the upcoming presidential election. And so was Nixon.

His first task was to ensure that Reagan ran for reelection. "You *should* run and you will win in 1984," he wrote to his friend in the Oval Office. "Bush has been a fine companion and a good soldier—but only you can hold the party together and give the Reagan revolution a chance to be permanent rather than temporary."

He then struck a more ominous note—Nixon had been concerned for some time about the quality of Reagan's staffers after the Stockman and Allen episodes. Now, he took the opportunity to urge the president to make changes. "I know that because of your innate decency and loyalty to your friends that you are repelled at the thought of dropping people who are loyal to you but who are not effective on the stump or on TV," he wrote. "But I urge you to bite the bullet and do what is necessary to field a tough, intelligent, hard-hitting team for the 1984 campaign...."[3]

Nixon often spoke to colleagues about the importance of a leader being tough—or, to use the words of William Gladstone, to be a "good butcher." Now with the 1984 election on the horizon, Nixon urged Reagan to pick up the ax and start chopping.

But who got cut seemed less important than who was doing the cutting. Nixon wanted the public to see Reagan as a strong, decisive leader. After suggesting that the president make changes to his staff, Nixon added that it would have a side effect that could benefit Reagan greatly. If "done the right way, as I'm sure you would, it increases your stature at home and abroad as a strong leader who will not tolerate ineffectiveness."

By the spring of 1984, the presidential campaign was in full bloom. Reagan was indeed running again, as Nixon had hoped. And the Democrats seemed to be in a race to the left, which also pleased Nixon. In the end, former vice president Walter Mondale won the nomination over a spirited challenge from Colorado senator Gary Hart. And Nixon continued to expand his public presence. In May, the American Society of Newspaper Editors held its annual convention in Washington. Nixon agreed to deliver a speech. Ironically, this was the same group that Nixon had spoken to in 1973 during Watergate when he defiantly proclaimed his innocence. It was a measure of how successful his comeback had been thus far that he was invited back to speak to the same group and that he was so well received. Nixon even told the newspaper editors that his philosophy on the media was "when they give it to me, I give it back in kind, and that's just the way it's going to be." He then commented on the nature of the relationship between reporters and politicians. "I don't think the press has changed," he said. "And as far as I'm concerned, I probably have changed some. There has to be an adversarial relationship between press and candidate."[4]

Perhaps no industry is more transactional than the media. Reporters often fall prey to the charms of their subjects, especially when they are given exclusive or extensive access to them. Nixon's new relationship with the press was generating some of the best news coverage of his career. With the presidential campaign in high gear, what better source for the media to interview than Nixon? In June he told a reporter that the Soviets' decision to boycott the Los Angeles Olympics was a mistake. "They think they can hurt Reagan in the next presidential election, but I think they're wrong," he said. "That's their intention and they won't change their minds. Absolutely not." He went onto add that perhaps the Olympics could move to a neutral site to avoid politics in the future. Nixon had become something of a go-to source for reporters looking for insight.

In July, Nixon unexpectedly showed up at a Smithsonian reception commemorating the twenty-fifth anniversary of the famous "Kitchen Debate" he had held with Krushchev in Moscow. He appeared in the Great Hall at the Smithsonian looking fit and healthy. Just as in his old campaign days, he worked the crowd and shook hands before delivering brief remarks.

"It is difficult to believe it all happened 25 years ago," Nixon said to the audience. "Do we look 25 years older?" The crowd laughed as Nixon reveled in the moment. The former president then referred to a brief tape of some of the exchange with Kruschev that was shown to the crowd that night. "The last round was a five-hour off-the-record debate that I am sorry to say was not on tape," Nixon said. Then he joked, "We had a lot of other things on tape that I wish were not recorded." The crowd roared with laughter.

Nixon went on to say that he respected Khrushchev, who possessed a "fast mind, a marvelous sense of humor and he was highly combative. He was a man of great warmth and totally belligerent." As he left the venue, Nixon shook more hands, signed autographs, and even posed for some photos.[5]

A few days later, John Herbers wrote about Nixon again in the pages of the *New York Times*. This time it was to note the tenth anniversary of the resignation and marvel at the former president's return to prominence since leaving the White House. In an article called "After Decade, Nixon Is Gaining Favor," Herbers expressed shock at how far Nixon had come. "A decade later he has emerged at 71 years of age as an elder statesman, commentator on foreign and domestic affairs, adviser to world leaders, a multimillionaire, and a successful author and lecturer honored by audiences at home and abroad," he wrote. After recounting the Watergate debacle and "the long road back" that Nixon had traveled, Herbers noted that Nixon's net worth was now estimated at $3 million, in large part thanks to his books and public events.[6]

In fact, in the first ten years following Watergate, Nixon had done more than just survive as a former president—he had unknowingly established a template for future ex-presidents to follow. Before Nixon, former presidents in the modern era mostly stayed behind the scenes. Truman had returned to Missouri and Ike split his time between his farm in Gettysburg and summers in Palm Springs. Neither of them made many public appearances or waded into public issues.

But Nixon, largely because he wanted to rehabilitate his name —and in any case was never one for retirement—chose a different path. He made money from delivering speeches and writing books. He gave interviews with the media in which he tried to shape public opinion on important national issues. He became something of an elder statesman. The Nixon template is the template used by former presidents to this day.

———————

By May 1984, the Reagan and Mondale teams had their sights trained on each other. The Mondale team thought their candidate would look best in debate settings that fall with the president. When a Reagan aide was quoted in the press saying that the president would agree to multiple debates against the challenger, Nixon decided it was time to circulate another memo among Republican luminaries. In his New York office, Nixon penned a memo detailing his thoughts on the upcoming race. "The set speech rather than the debate is Reagan's best forum," he wrote. "No one can challenge him in that regard. An incumbent is always at a disadvantage in a debate. He has no choice but to defend, as was the case with me in 1960, Ford in 1976 and Carter in 1980. This time Reagan will have to defend and Mondale will be on the attack."

On the issues, Nixon believed Reagan held the high ground. He could run on his economic record and on national security. "Incidentally," he wrote, "if Mondale tries to pick up Hart's "new ideas" theme, my answer would be, 'The people voted for a new idea in 1980, and it works.'" On foreign affairs, Nixon was still concerned about the pressure for a "get acquainted" summit. "I think this would be a major mistake," he wrote. Nixon was also worried that at this point in the political calendar Reagan might feel pressure to invite Mondale with him to the summit. Better to leave summitry to the second term.[7]

Having outlined his thoughts on the upcoming election, Nixon returned to his own writing. Of all the elements of Nixon's post-presidency, he most excelled at writing books. In May 1984, news emerged that he was under contract for yet another book. With the Cold War raging and President Reagan defending his staunch foreign policy in the 1984 election, Nixon chose to revisit the lessons of Vietnam and the fight against Communism. The new book, it was announced, would be called *No More Vietnams*.

"It's Mr. Nixon's opinion about why we went into Vietnam, what in his view we did right and wrong and what we can learn from that now," his literary agent, Swifty Lazar, told reporters. "It touches on Central America, although it has a global viewpoint. He believes that we shouldn't repeat the mistakes of Vietnam in other parts of the world."[8]

More evidence of Nixon's return to prominence appeared when the book proposal was shopped around publishing houses. A bidding war ensued with Arbor House offering a 15 percent "topping privilege" promising to raise the highest offer from another publisher by 15 percent. "I wanted to make it worth his while," Arbor House publisher Eden Collinsworth said, "and perhaps discourage competitors from making a very determined bid." The strategy worked. Warner Brothers, which had published *The Real War* in 1980, bowed out of the bidding, saying that Arbor House's offer was beyond where "we wanted to go."

And Nixon was experiencing not just professional success, but happiness at home, as well. On June 20, Julie and David welcomed their third child, Melanie Catherine (Alexander Richard, their second son and Nixon's second grandson, had been born in 1980). Nixon was overjoyed. "It's not uncommon," Julie said at the time, "to receive a phone call from my father's secretary announcing, 'The president is on the phone.'"[9]

But not all was well for Nixon in the summer of 1984. On July 4, Pat was taken to the hospital for a pulmonary infection. The year before she had suffered another mild stroke. The combined impact of these health setbacks left Nixon worried about his wife. He even considered selling the New Jersey estate and moving to a smaller place back in the city. "It's a question of whether she wants the burden of a big house," he remarked.

But Pat didn't mind the burden at all. She especially enjoyed the scenery in Saddle River. "Julie," she said one night to their daughter, "even though it is fall and the flowers are almost gone, it is still so beautiful. The leaves make a garden in the sky."

That fall, the Reagan team ran a nearly flawless campaign complete with television ads proclaiming that it was "morning in America." The Gipper, as he had been known since he had starred in a Hollywood movie as the legendary Notre Dame football player years earlier, seemed well on his way to a smooth reelection until the first presidential debate with Walter Mondale on October 7 in Louisville, Kentucky. There, as Nixon had feared, Mondale gained the upper hand. For once, Reagan's gift for communication failed him. The president appeared tired, and even old. He struggled with his responses. The Reagan team later would blame staffers for "overpreparing" him with books of information on various policy matters. The phrase "Let Reagan be Reagan" was borne out of concern over how poorly the first debate had gone and the insight that Reagan would need to be his old self in the second and final debate.

One observer who did not share Republican dismay over Reagan's debate performance and its impact on the election was Nixon. He had known Reagan would struggle in the debate since, as he had written in May, the president would be on the defensive. And watching the debate with Pat in their Saddle River, New Jersey, home, Nixon sensed Reagan wasn't on top of his game. But he also knew that Reagan had a handful of aces: the economy was booming and Mondale was a personification of the failed Carter years. To Nixon, the test for Reagan would be whether he could resist overreacting to one poor debate performance and stay the course for the duration of the campaign.

After the debate, Nixon called Reagan and congratulated him on his performance. Reagan disagreed with Nixon's assessment; he thought he hadn't done very well. After the phone call, Nixon decided to reassure Reagan in writing. In his memo, after acknowledging Reagan's concern that he had not been in "top form for the first debate" Nixon pointed to the positives. As someone who had been judged the loser by those watching his debate with Kennedy on television and the winner by those listening on radio, Nixon believed that there was a difference between the visual appearance of Reagan and the substantive arguments he had made. On the latter, Nixon thought Reagan had done better than he realized. He told the president that "your performance on substance could not be faulted. In fact, right after it ended Pat turned to me and said 'Mondale lost.'"

Reagan's real problem was managing expectations. "Only because he did better than expected and you did not knock him out of the ring did the media seize on the opportunity to make it appear as if he had won." Still, the expectation game worked both ways. Now that the media was ridiculing Reagan's performance, it would become "an advantage to you. You go into the debate Sunday as an underdog...."

Nixon's broader point in his message to Reagan was that the president was on track. Even the seeming shift in the polls toward Mondale was to be expected. "What we are seeing is the predictable pattern of registered Democrats returning to their party as the election draws closer."

Nixon remained convinced that Reagan would not only win in November, but that he would win big. He wrote, "you will win an overwhelming victory in the popular vote on Election Day and a decisive victory in the electoral vote approaching the one you achieved in 1980."[10]

A few days later at the second presidential debate, Reagan directly addressed the concerns about his first debate performance. When asked a question about his age, Reagan quipped, "I do not believe age should be an issue in this election. I will not exploit for political purposes my opponent's youth and inexperience." The crowd roared with laughter; so did Mondale. That moment effectively ended any concerns about Reagan's ability, and it essentially ended the election.

As Nixon had predicted, Reagan won in a landslide and became the first president since Nixon himself to carry forty-nine states.

Nixon wasted little time in congratulating the president and his team; he quickly began offering more advice. Nixon saw clearly that the second Reagan term would be dominated by foreign affairs and that the Republican president had a unique chance to shape history. Nixon met with Chief of Staff James A. Baker shortly after the election and urged a second-term domestic policy that would strengthen Reagan's hand overseas. Specifically, he wanted the White House to reduce deficits. "A defense budget which makes it impossible to reduce the federal deficit weakens our foreign policy," he told Baker in a follow-up communique to their meeting. "One which makes it possible to reduce the budget deficit strengthens our foreign policy."[11] Though Nixon had been moving to the right on foreign policy, he still represented orthodox Republican philosophy on economics. He didn't like deficits and didn't much care for the large Reagan tax cuts that he thought helped create them.

As the 1984 holidays approached, Nixon celebrated with his family at his home in Saddle River. It was a happy time. Ten years after Watergate, he had reemerged from the abyss as an influencer and confidante to Reagan and his senior staff. Now as his second term began, the president fixed his eyes on the Soviet Union. He and his friend in Saddle River could not have imagined the dramatic events that lay ahead in the coming four years.

Chapter Fifteen

# The Sage of Saddle River

*"Beneath the velvet gloves he always wears*
*there is a steel fist."*

He had them in the palm of his hands. On April 22, 1986, Richard Nixon went into the lions' den and emerged almost as unscathed as Daniel. The event was a speech to the American Newspaper Publishers. Looking better than ever and dressed immaculately in a dark blue suit, the former president gave a tour de force speech on foreign policy issues at a luncheon speech the *Associated Press* had helped set up. Sitting in front of him were publishers from newspapers all across the country, including Katharine Graham of the *Washington Post*.

Nixon gave a ringing endorsement of Reagan's foreign policies, particularly the administration's efforts to confront Soviet aggression. He even suggested that the Soviets were afraid that the Reagan-backed Contras in Nicaragua might prevail and inspire other uprisings in other outposts of the Communist empire. On politics, he went further than he had before in predicting a Republican victory in the 1988 election.

177

But the highlight of the event came during the question-and-answer period after Nixon's remarks. Watergate inevitably came up. But when he was asked what the greatest lesson he had learned from Watergate was, Nixon smiled and looked confidently at his audience.

"Just destroy all the tapes," he said to roars of laughter from the crowd. And one of those laughing the most was Katharine Graham. It was her paper that had done the most to end his presidency, and yet she couldn't help but be impressed by this performance. After the speech, she made her way over to Nixon to shake his hand. Not long after the event, another of her publications, *Newsweek,* took her advice to publish a profile of the former president. When reporters from the magazine approached Nixon about interviewing him for the profile, Nixon played his cards shrewdly. He knew that a positive feature from a Graham-controlled organization marked yet another turning point for him. So he wanted to make the most of the opportunity.

Initially, he told *Newsweek* he would not agree to an interview. Then, as the negotiations continued, he made a counteroffer: he would agree to the interview if the article was made into a cover story. The magazine, no doubt with Graham's blessing, agreed to the terms.

The cover of the magazine that spring featured a smiling Nixon and the headline "He's Back: The Rehabilitation of Richard Nixon." Inside, readers saw a lengthy article about Nixon's post-presidency rehabilitation, as well as a series of photographs. But perhaps the most striking part of the feature was the interview that was posted under the title, "The Sage of Saddle River." In the interview, Nixon did little to deny his rising influence in Washington.

"As far as President Reagan is concerned," he said when asked about his relationship with the current president, "I talk to him quite regularly. Usually he calls me from Camp David, usually after he has had one of those, you know, tough decisions. For example, he called me after the Libyan business [the U.S. bombing of Gaddafi's compound], and we chatted a bit about it. It's a very natural relationship."[1]

When asked how he thought history would remember him, Nixon gave an answer that was familiar to anyone who had ever discussed the matter with him: "Without the Watergate episode I would be rated, I should think, rather high." But with Watergate, "it depends on who's doing the rating." This was a constant theme of Nixon's—that history was too often written by historians who leaned left.

The former president went out of his way to encourage any historian he didn't think was a liberal. One of his favorites, a former Dole Senate staffer named Richard Norton Smith, burst onto the scene in the 1980s with a biography of Thomas E. Dewey that became a finalist for the Pulitzer. Nixon would write to Smith and compliment him as an "honest historian." It's a telling remark that demonstrates how Nixon viewed the rest of Smith's colleagues.

Nixon continued to plow away at his work either in his New York office or at his home in Saddle River. One day that April while he was working in Saddle River, he decided to go out for lunch. He and an aide drove down the New Jersey coast before stopping at a Burger King on Route 72 in Ocean County. If Nixon wondered how the general public viewed him, he got a positive answer that day. He made the rounds inside the restaurant, shaking hands and signing autographs for patrons. An employee named Doreen Johnson took him his food and even got a photo with him. After eating a Whopper, he left a signed note for the restaurant owner that read, "Best wishes to Burger King, home of the Whopper. Love, Richard Nixon."[2]

Back at home, Nixon again set his sights on events in Washington. New rumors of a potential second summit between Reagan and Gorbachev were beginning to surface. Nixon believed it was inevitable that the two men would meet again because so much had been left unresolved in Geneva. And as he had before, he wanted to do his part. This time he would not only try to influence Reagan, but he would try to influence Gorbachev, as well.

———

In July 1986, Richard Nixon traveled to Moscow. A Kremlin spokesman described Nixon as coming to Moscow as "a private person, a tourist." But the former president wasn't interested in sightseeing. He had a mission.

This trip represented Nixon's first meeting with Gorbachev. British prime minister Margaret Thatcher had famously called the Soviet leader a "man we can do business with" after she met him, and Reagan himself had seemed to connect with Gorbachev at Geneva. Now Nixon would size him up and report back to the White House. One of the people helping to arrange the trip was Anatoly Dobrynin, the Kremlin's foreign policy adviser and Soviet central committee secretary. He had previously served as envoy to the United States, and Nixon had known him since his own presidency.

Gorbachev, for his part, likely saw a meeting with Nixon as another way of demonstrating that he was a different kind of leader—one who was open to conversations with leaders (and former leaders) from around the world. Just before Nixon arrived, Gorbachev met with American broadcast executive Ted Turner, who had helped found the Goodwill Games—an Olympic-style competition between nations that was held that summer for seventeen days in Moscow. Gorbachev, leaving behind the drama of the last two Olympiads, played the gracious host and told Turner the games were a "real positive force in U.S.-Soviet relations."[3]

On July 19, Nixon got his turn. After several days of meetings with government officials, Gorbachev staffers ushered Nixon in to see the Soviet leader. He met with Gorbachev for nearly two hours.

Gorbachev made quite an impression on the American. "I have met with three of the principal postwar leaders of the Soviet Union—Nikita S. Khrushchev in 1959 and 1960, Leonid I. Brezhnev in 1972, 1973, and 1974, and Gorbachev in 1986," he would remember. "Gorbachev is by far the ablest of the three." He even went so far as to say that Gorbachev was in the same "league" with some of his favorite leaders in history, like Churchill and de Gaulle.[4]

"He received me in a more richly decorated room than those in which I had met Khrushchev in 1959 or Brezhnev in 1972 and 1974," Nixon said.

> Earlier in the week I had had a highly detailed, two-hour meeting with Soviet President Andrei A. Gromyko and the foreign-affairs adviser Anatoly F. Dobrynin about arms control and a wide range of other issues. Even though Gorbachev had spent the entire previous day with the Politburo, it was clear from his questions and comments that he had acquainted himself with everything that had been said in my earlier meetings. This permitted him to use his own time to refine nuances or to cover new ground. All in all, it was the most impressive performance I have witnessed in nearly 40 years of meetings with world leaders.[5]

During the meeting, Nixon urged Gorbachev to take advantage of the remaining years of the Reagan administration and get a deal on arms control. He told the Soviet leader that the American president was "enormously popular" and that Reagan needed to "have a stake in a new, improved U.S.-Soviet relationship." If Gorbachev didn't reach a deal with Reagan before the American left office, that could create additional problems for the Soviets. In fact, it could "create a situation where President Reagan might become a powerful critic" during his post-presidency. Nixon watched as the Soviet leader listened carefully to the translator. "I don't believe anything I said during the conversation had a greater impact on him," he later told Reagan.[6]

Inevitably the conversation turned to the one major sticking point in the U.S.-Soviet negotiations—the White House's insistence on SDI. Gorbachev tried to downplay the issue by telling Nixon that contrary to an American talking point, it was a "myth" that the Soviets were against SDI because of the potential financial strain it would put on them to keep up. "His major objection," Nixon later reported to Reagan, was that "if it went forward there would be a massive spiral in the arms race."[7]

After returning to Saddle River, Nixon prepared a twenty-six-page summary of the conversation for the president. In it, he suggested that Reagan press ahead with another summit. He also returned to his suggestion that Reagan use SDI as a bargaining chip. To counter Gorbachev's obstinance on SDI, Nixon suggested that Reagan propose trading "restrictions on deployment [of SDI] for reductions in Soviet missiles."

Nixon hoped his meeting with Gorbachev would prove helpful to Reagan; but it had already been helpful to himself. Nixon aide John Taylor made sure stories about the trip appeared in the *New York Times* and the *Washington Post*. And the memo to Reagan mysteriously found its way to *Time* magazine, where it was reprinted in its entirety.[8]

That fall, plans were announced for a second Reagan-Gorbachev summit. This one would be held in October in Iceland.

———

The Reykjavík Summit would become famous in history for what didn't happen there. Reagan and Gorbachev talked extensively about eliminating an entire class of weapons. Reagan pushed his idea of a nuclear-free world and Gorbachev responded in kind. But as the negotiations neared the end, the Soviet leader insisted that any deal must include Americans abandoning the Strategic Defense Initiative. Reagan refused. The summit collapsed and the Cold War seemed further away from ending than it had in years.

Reagan felt betrayed. He told the American people that he wouldn't abandon SDI because he would never compromise "our freedom or our future." Yet the event, seen at the time as a diplomatic disaster, set the stage for a later agreement. By essentially walking out on Gorbachev when the Soviet leader came after SDI, Reagan had shown the world that he would never agree to a deal that didn't preserve the possibility of defense against nuclear weapons.

Nixon, for his part, now found himself worried about Reagan's idealism. Ironically, the man most associated with détente now found himself to the right of Ronald Reagan. Nixon's major concern was that Reagan had offered too much in Iceland. Eliminating nuclear missiles would leave the Soviets with a strategic advantage because the Soviet Union's conventional military was so much larger than the American one.

Meanwhile, the negative reviews of the summit were soon eclipsed by a scandal that shook Washington, D.C. Allegations emerged that the Reagan administration had illegally sold arms to Iran in the hopes of gaining the release of American hostages. In addition, some of the money had been sent to support the Contras fighting the Communists in Nicaragua. At the time, Iran was subject to an arms embargo and Congress had prevented further funding of the Contras through passage of the Boland Amendment. Washington immediately became obsessed with the scandal and whether it might bring down the Reagan presidency. Almost from the moment that the news of "the Iran-Contra Scandal" broke comparisons to Watergate began to circulate.

One observer who did not share the view that Iran-Contra represented another Watergate was Richard Nixon. On December 10, Nixon spoke to a group of Republican governors in Washington. After sharing his thoughts on world affairs, Nixon addressed the new controversy. For starters, he said, "Watergate was a domestic matter. This is a foreign policy matter." And in very candid remarks, he pointed to an even more important difference, saying, "Watergate was handled…abysmally. This is being handled expeditiously."

Then Nixon proceeded to give his audience some insight into how the mess had gotten started in the first place. Reagan's goal, Nixon told the governors, had been to create ties with moderates in Iran who "would be less anti-American than the current government." Furthermore, Reagan wanted to "get our hostages back"—referring to the Americans that were being held in Lebanon by Iran-linked Islamic militants. This, combined with the administration's desire to "get aid to the Contras at a time when Congress was denying aid" had created the decision-making environment that led to Iran-Contra. Nixon made sure to distinguish between Reagan's policy goals, which he called the president's "right and responsibility," and the "execution," which was "something else."

Nixon laid the blame for the fiasco squarely on the president's staff. Reagan's team had "screwed it up" in combining what should have been separate efforts to free the hostages and court moderate Iranian leaders. Left out of Nixon's remarks was the fact that his friend Bud McFarlane had been directly implicated in the scandal. Instead, Nixon sharply criticized marine lieutenant colonel Oliver North for "skimming" the profits and then using the money to help the Contras.

Nixon told the governors that this last piece—the funding of the Contras—was the real problem. "That was illegal, apparently," he said. But he was careful to defend the president to the governors. "But President Reagan didn't know that," he said. "I know that because he just was not involved in details. He has told me so. I believe him."

Not surprisingly, Nixon's main focus in the opening stages of the scandal was to fight for the president. "He [Reagan] is going to continue to serve as president," he told the audience. Then he directly addressed those who were blaming the president for the scandal. "To his critics, I say, 'Get off his back.'"

Nixon used Reagan's reputation as a leader who delegated authority to explain how the scandal could have happened. Reagan, Nixon said, was a "big-picture man" who thought his role was "deciding big issues and then delegating to subordinates the carrying out of these things." This allowed overly zealous staffers to "screw up" the policy and create the scandal. Nixon's overall message was clear—the Republican governors should stand by Reagan.[9]

The speech represented Nixon at his best or worst, depending on one's point of view. He would stand by his friends and put spin on the issue to help defend them. It wasn't just political friends that Nixon stood behind. For years he had maintained a friendship with Woody Hayes, the pugnacious head football coach at Ohio State University. When Hayes was fired in 1978 after punching an opposing player in the final moments of the Gator Bowl, he received a sympathetic letter from Nixon. "When you win you hear from everyone," the former president wrote with words he had used often to describe how he felt after Watergate, "when you lose you hear from your friends." The feeling of goodwill between the two men was genuine and mutual. After a game in Los Angeles in 1974, Hayes took the time to drive down to La Casa Pacifica to visit the recently deposed president. And two years later after Pat suffered her stroke, Nixon received a kind letter from Coach Hayes. "You and I are about the two luckiest men in the world from the standpoint of marriage," the coach wrote to the president. "I know you will agree that neither of us could have done better and neither of us deserves to do so well."[10]

When Hayes died on March 12, 1987, the family asked Richard Nixon to deliver the eulogy. He was delighted and honored to do so.

Nixon arrived early for the service at First Community Church in Columbus on the morning of March 18, 1987. There he was greeted in the church library by the church's pastor, the Reverend Jeb Stuart Magruder. Magruder had worked for Nixon and served time for Watergate. After getting out of jail he had attended Princeton Theological Seminary and became a pastor. The two men had not seen or spoken to each other since Watergate. Nixon was genuinely moved to see his old aide and asked questions about his life since politics. "Fate has its strange way of working things out," Reverend Magruder said.

After their brief reunion, Nixon, dressed smartly in a black suit, was ushered into the sanctuary. The packed auditorium waited for Nixon's turn to take the pulpit and honor their hero. He did not disappoint. "I wanted to talk about football," Nixon said in describing the first time had met Hayes decades before, "and Woody wanted to talk about foreign policy. You know Woody," he said, pausing for effect, "we talked about foreign policy."

Then Nixon delivered a tour de force defense of the controversial football coach. "Over the next 30 years, I got to know the real Woody Hayes, the man behind the media," he told the audience. "I found that he was not the Neanderthal know-nothing that some people thought, but that he was a Renaissance man. A man with a great sense of history, and a profound understanding of the great forces that rule the world. I found that instead of just being that tyrant that you sometimes see on the ballfield, he was actually a softie, a warm-hearted man."

Nixon lavished praise on the coach's toughness and his will to win. The heart of the oration described the risks that Hayes had taken throughout his career. The former president noted that the coach had won his third national title in 1969. "He could have retired then at the top," he observed. "But he didn't. He wanted to go on and do more. If you think of why he didn't retire, you must remember that Woody knew there were risks. After all, there's a rule of life: If you take no risks, you will suffer no defeats. But if you take no risks, you will win no victories."

As Nixon neared his conclusion, he surprised many in the audience and in the media by confronting the greatest controversy and most infamous moment of Hayes' career—the night at the Gator Bowl when he punched a player and was fired the next day. "Woody was not one to play it safe," he said. "He played it to win. The incident at the Gator Bowl in 1978 would have broken and crushed an ordinary man. But Woody was not an ordinary man. Winston Churchill said, 'Success is never final and failure is never fatal.' That was Woody Hayes' maxim. He was never satisfied with success and he was never going to be discouraged by failure."

It was an extraordinary moment; not just for what it said about Hayes but for what it said about Nixon. Here he was challenging Hayes's critics to remember not just one night at the Gator Bowl but all the other great moments that had come before it. And he was saying that even after Hayes had lost everything, he had still made something out of nothing in the remaining years of his life. Nixon's eulogy served as a powerful tribute to Woody Hayes, but it was also one of the most introspective statements he ever made about how he felt about failure and why he persisted in staying in the arena.[11]

# Chapter Sixteen

# The Public Critic

*"The judgment of tomorrow's history
would severely condemn a false peace."*

In 1987, Nixon continued to worry about the aftereffects of Reykjavík. There were rumors in Washington that a new summit was being discussed. The Reagan administration remained interested in the idea of reducing an entire class of nuclear missiles. That spring, Secretary of State George Shultz traveled to Moscow to continue working with the Soviets on a potential deal to eliminate mid-range missiles.

This was Nixon's primary concern. In some ways, Reagan had pursued diplomacy with the Soviets the way Nixon wanted; he had used SDI as a means of getting the Soviets to the table. But in other ways, Reagan was way off the Nixon script. Talk of entirely eliminating nuclear weapons disturbed the former president. In fact, it disturbed him so much that he decided to do something he had never done before—sharply criticize Reagan in public.

Nixon decided he wanted a partner to join him in criticizing the president. And there was only one man who had the gravitas to join him in speaking out—Henry Kissinger. The relationship between the former president and his national security advisor had always been a complicated one. But their thinking on world affairs had always been similar. Now the two men decided to issue a joint public statement criticizing the "zero option" that Reagan was proposing, which would essentially eliminate all medium-range missiles. Kissinger was traveling in Europe in April, but he and Nixon spoke by phone and worked on an op-ed outlining their concerns.

On April 26, 1987, Nixon shocked Washington and dominated the news when the seventeen-hundred-word essay he co-authored with Henry Kissinger questioning Reagan's negotiations with the Soviets appeared in the *Los Angeles Times.*

"Every president has an understandable desire to assure his place in history as a peacemaker," the two men wrote. "But he must always remember that, however he may be hailed in today's headlines, the judgment of tomorrow's history would severely condemn a false peace. Because we are deeply concerned about this danger, we who have attended several summits and engaged in many negotiations with Soviet leaders are speaking out jointly for the first time since both of us left office."

Nixon and Kissinger urged the Reagan administration to alter its course in the ongoing talks with the Soviets. They wanted any potential removal of intermediate-range nuclear weapons from Europe to be directly connected to reductions in the Soviets' overwhelming advantage in conventional forces.

"If we strike the wrong kind of deal," Nixon and Kissinger wrote, "we could create the most profound crisis of the NATO alliance in its 40-year history—an alliance sustained by seven administrations of both parties."[1]

If Nixon and Kissinger were hoping the column would become the topic of conversation in Washington, they must have been happy. Everyone was talking about it.

The White House was blindsided by the op-ed. "We welcome comments from all sides," White House spokesman Dan Howard said tersely to reporters. "Our position is that we are still in consultation with our allies. Beyond that, we are not going to say anything further about the…treaty, except that we expect hard bargaining."

The Reagan administration was particularly incensed by the op-ed's charge that the ongoing negotiations put pressure on NATO. "I don't think it's going to prove divisive at all," Assistant Secretary of Defense Richard Perle said. "For a long time now, the alliance has agreed that the elimination of intermediate nuclear missiles was the Western negotiating position, and in the Western interest. The only remaining issue that needs to be resolved is how to handle some of those shorter-range systems."

And it wasn't just the people inside the Reagan administration pushing back on the Nixon-Kissinger op-ed. James Reston mocked the piece in his nationally syndicated column, noting that Nixon and Kissinger were now entering the "column-writing business." He wrote that if "there's one thing officials hate more than criticism from columnists in general, its public advice from their predecessors in office." He lambasted the piece as a failure on multiple levels. "Consider your first column. It breaks the first rule of a good column, which is brevity, and it breaks the second rule, which is modesty, and the third rule, which is generosity."

But his harshest criticism was directed toward the failure of the Nixon-Kissinger piece to acknowledge what the Reagan administration was trying to accomplish: "They are trying to break a stalemate that has gone on for more than a generation. Like the early steps toward the unification of Europe, they are concentrating on the attainable rather than on the desirable, and hoping to build confidence in slow verifiable stages. For the first time since the invention of the atom bomb, both sides are talking seriously about major cuts in the alarming stockpiles of nuclear weapons, and you dismiss this as worse than nothing."[2]

At the White House, talk turned to what should be done. McFarlane had resigned and the new national security advisor, Frank Carlucci, suggested that Reagan meet with Nixon to air out their differences and see if they couldn't get back on the same page—and the sooner the better. Reagan agreed. He had little use for Kissinger (he had openly mocked Kissinger's foreign policy during the 1976 Republican presidential primaries). So he had no interest in meeting with Nixon's co-author. But he still admired and respected the former president. The White House reached out to Nixon's office and a date was set. Nixon would meet with Reagan on April 27 at the White House.

Nixon arrived at the White House North Lawn entrance on the afternoon of the twenty-seventh and was taken by elevator up to the residential quarters. It must have brought back a flood of memories for the former president—it marked his first visit to his former living quarters since he had resigned from office thirteen years before.

Upon arriving upstairs, he was greeted by Carlucci and Chief of Staff Howard Baker. They took him inside the room where Reagan was waiting, dressed in a light brown suit. The two men shook hands and then sat down in two upholstered club chairs separated by an ottoman. Nixon, dressed in his usual blue suit, tried to break the tension with some humor. "I assume that the place isn't taped," he joked. Mild laughter greeted the remark. Nixon could tell the president's mood was not good. "I think I sensed a certain coolness on his part," he would say later. And he certainly could not have been surprised.

But the former president was not cowed by Reagan's "coolness" toward him. Nixon's post-presidential career as an elder statesman offering his expertise on foreign policy to current presidents had been leading up to this moment for years. Since *The Real War*, Nixon had been urging a more forceful posture with the Soviets than he had during the days of détente. He recognized the opportunity that Reagan had with Gorbachev and wanted the president to negotiate. Indeed, the very strategy of offering SDI technology to the Soviets came not originally from Reagan, but from Nixon.[3] But Nixon wanted Reagan to negotiate the right deal. And he feared that Reagan's advisors—particularly his old friend George Shultz, serving as Reagan's secretary of state—were pushing toward a deal that might be unacceptable. Hence, he had written the op-ed to get Reagan's attention.

And on that count, the op-ed had been a success. But it had done perhaps more than Nixon wanted it to do. Reagan didn't like being publicly criticized by a former president.

Now with Nixon sitting in front of him in the White House residence, Reagan made his own appeal to change Nixon's mind. Reagan said he believed that his position and Nixon's position weren't all that different; Reagan and Baker wondered if it would be possible for Nixon to tell his contacts inside the Soviet government that he was on board with the Reagan approach. Nixon flatly refused.

"I could see of course what he was driving at," Nixon later observed, "and pointed out that I didn't think it was a good idea." When Reagan continued to press him on the point, the former president again put his foot down. "I'm afraid we just don't agree on that point," he said.[4]

Nixon used the meeting to press his case with Reagan. Why was the president so willing to eliminate ballistic missiles and leave the Soviets with an advantage in conventional weapons? Reagan tried to reassure Nixon that when U.S. conventional forces were combined with the conventional forces of Western Europe, the Soviets were outnumbered. Reagan was unimpressed.

Nixon knew that to convince Reagan to rethink his position he would have to challenge the staff whose advice had helped Reagan form his position. And so he turned his aim on Shultz. "I did get in one shot at Shultz, which I thought was quite effective," he would write. "I introduced it by saying I didn't want anyone to get the idea that I had anything against him [Shultz]. I said he had been a great secretary of the treasury, a great secretary of labor, and a great director of OMB [the Office of Management and Budget], and that he did an outstanding job of negotiating with [AFL-CIO chairman George] Meany for a period. But I said that negotiating with Meany was much different from negotiating with Gorbachev."[5]

That shot may have seemed effective to Nixon, but it did little to change Reagan's mind. As the meeting ended, Reagan made little effort to hide his displeasure at the impasse between the two men. "I don't know whether Nancy was in the residence at the time," Nixon later observed, "but if she was, he did not suggest that she come in and say hello. My guess is that she is probably as teed off as Shultz is."

As Nixon returned home to Saddle River, he sensed that his relationship with Reagan had changed and would not be the same again. It had always been a complicated relationship, but in the first several years of the Reagan administration, Nixon had genuinely tried to help Reagan—while of course trying to help himself, as well. He had encouraged the president and given advice and counsel on the Soviet Union. But now the two men were clearly traveling down different paths. Reagan, sensing that Gorbachev represented a different kind of Soviet leader, believed the time had come to make major concessions. Nixon, still very much a Cold Warrior, doubted that Gorbachev was all that different in his ambitions from Brezhnev or even Krushchev.

As Nixon would write in a memo about his unhappy meeting with Reagan at the White House, the president seemed "far older, more tired, and less vigorous in person than in public." In the former president's view, Reagan "candidly, did not seem to be on top of the issues—certainly in no way as knowledgeable as Gorbachev, for example, which of course would not be surprising." Nixon now believed that there was "no way he [Reagan] can ever be allowed to participate in a private meeting with Gorbachev."[6]

How much this impression was a product of Reagan's rejection of Nixon's advice is hard to measure. Like many intellectuals, Nixon tended to think his ideas were the best ones. And when someone didn't agree with them, he could take it personally. After years in the wilderness following the Watergate scandal, he had enjoyed a special place of privilege in Reagan's world where he could offer ideas that were often accepted. Now, ironically, the father of détente was urging the conservative Reagan to be more aggressive with the Soviets.

From this point forward, if Nixon was going to exert any influence on any Reagan policy, it would most likely have to come through Reagan's staff. And even there, Nixon's influence was waning. One former staffer, in particular, who had lost his position was very much on Nixon's mind in these days—not out of any hope that he could still influence Reagan, but because his life was in danger.

———

While Reagan was working behind the scenes with Soviets in the spring and summer of 1987, he was also dealing with his own political crisis at home. The Iran-Contra scandal had now become hot enough that congressional hearings were being held. Marine lieutenant colonel Oliver North became the key figure in the investigation. As a staffer at the National Security Council, North had coordinated the efforts to funnel money to the Nicaraguan Contras. But who had given North the orders to do so? It became increasingly apparent that the orders had been given by Nixon's friend, Bud McFarlane.

McFarlane had resigned as national security advisor before the scandal broke. But once it became news, he knew he would be in the line of fire. At his home in suburban Virginia one morning in February, McFarlane took things into his own hands. He went to the medicine cabinet, took out twenty-five Valium pills, and then swallowed them all in an effort to commit suicide. He was revived at the hospital. McFarlane, still completely despondent as he recuperated, dreaded what awaited him—the congressional hearings and likely criminal prosecution. Still, he was cheered up by the cards and flowers that came into his hospital room. President Reagan even called and spoke with him on the phone. When McFarlane told the president that he had let him down, Reagan refused to accept it. "You didn't fail me at all," the president said to McFarlane. "It was a sensible goal to pursue and you shouldn't blame yourself because it didn't work."

But perhaps no visitor did as much to lift his spirits as his first visitor. Within hours of the story breaking that McFarlane had tried to kill himself and was at a Washington-area hospital, Richard Nixon arrived to greet his old friend.

Nixon directly addressed the depression that had led McFarlane to try to kill himself. "He urged me to remember that Churchill and de Gaulle had suffered their 'black dogs' and said that even though I would be portrayed by the media as a weak figure, I could overcome the setback of my suicide attempt," McFarlane would recall.

Revealingly, Nixon asked McFarlane about his faith. He wanted to know if he was praying and reading the Bible. "I said I was doing a lot of that," McFarlane remembered. "That's good," Nixon answered. "You need an anchor. Your strong faith will take you through this."[7]

As the two men talked, Nixon urged his friend to focus on his future. "From now on, don't look back," he said. "Get busy, go earn yourself some money. You've done the right things in the past, now look to your future. You can do it."

The words meant more to McFarlane than Nixon could have ever known. "Coming from him, I can't tell you what a tonic that encouragement was," McFarlane remembered.[8]

The words mattered to McFarlane because they were spoken from experience. Here was a man who had gone through the fires of the worst political crisis in American history and had survived. Now all these years later, here he was reflecting on his own journey back into the sunlight. He provided such powerful words of encouragement because he, too, had almost died in 1974—both literally and metaphorically. The advice he gave to his friend was borne of his own experience wrestling with his own darkness. The words were empowering because the words were true. Nixon, McFarlane remembered, "was unbelievably sympathetic" in the hospital visit. In reality, he was really being not sympathetic, but empathetic.

Ultimately, the Iran Contra scandal didn't become the second coming of Watergate. The president's advisors had kept Reagan out of it and Reagan made little attempt to help cover for his friends. Ultimately, McFarlane pled guilty to four counts of withholding information from Congress. All were misdemeanors. His sentence was two years' probation and a fine of twenty thousand dollars. Later, on Christmas Eve 1992, he was pardoned by President George H. W. Bush.

The year 1987 saw the Republican Party beginning to look beyond Reagan to the future. Vice President Bush was running for the 1988 GOP nomination and claiming the Reagan mantle. But others were considering running, as well. One who was interested in running and caught Nixon's attention was Kansas senator Robert J. Dole.

The two men had a relationship that went back to the Nixon presidency. Dole had served as Republican National Committee (RNC) chairman during the Watergate era and then had to face the Kansas voters as he sought reelection to the Senate in 1974. He survived. But it had been a harrowing experience. In 1987, the two were brought together again by a common friend. Robert Ellsworth, a Kansan who had served in the Nixon administration, suggested that Dole visit Nixon in his New York office to get advice as he pondered his next move.

"I went up to see Nixon I don't know how many times in '87," Dole would say, "to get some foreign policy ideas because he was always good. I still feel he had more at the tip of his fingers than all the rest of them put together, myself included. I don't think he was always right, but he had the knowledge and the information."

Nixon wasn't yet sold on Bush and was looking for a viable alternative. Could Dole be the one? After Dole won the Iowa Caucus in January 1988, Nixon publicly criticized Bush as having "insufficient drive." But when the Bush campaign, led by Lee Atwater, came storming back and all but wrapped up the nomination several weeks later on Super Tuesday, Nixon got on board and said the vice president had "really come into his own." Not that he had given up on Dole. Nixon called their mutual friend Ellsworth. "Tell him he must keep fighting," Nixon said to Ellsworth. Dole did, before eventually dropping out and endorsing Bush.[9]

Nixon still had reservations about the vice president. He told the media he found Bush to be a "weak individual on television," but that he would still likely win because of the strong economy. But if the economy turned south, Nixon warned, that would change everything. At that point the Democrats could nominate a "jackass" and still win.

Meanwhile, Nixon still thought Dole had a future. And Dole still had ambitions. Inside his desk in his Senate office, he maintained a collection of personal notes Nixon had written to him over the years.

One of them had come in November 1984, shortly after Dole's ascension to Senate majority leader. "As Disraeli would have put it," Nixon wrote, "you have now reached the top of the greasy pole in the Senate. The vote you received is a recognition of your superior brain power and your years of loyalty to the party in many tough battles."[10]

A more personal touch from Nixon had helped shape Dole's opinion of the man. When the two men first met years ago, Nixon had reached out with his left hand to shake Dole's non-injured hand. He continued this gesture every time he saw Dole. This small action had a big and lasting impact on Dole.

But as the 1988 election approached, Dole would have to wait. It would be Vice President George Bush who would run as the Republican nominee.

Nixon took time out in late 1987 to praise yet another potential political star. "I did not see the program, but Mrs. Nixon told me that you were great on The [Phil] Donahue Show," he wrote to New York developer Donald Trump on December 21. "As you can imagine, she is an expert on politics and predicts that whenever you decide to run for office you will be a winner!" The next month, Trump— famously susceptible to flattery—would fly Nixon on his private plane to a juvenile diabetes fundraiser in Houston where the two men talked extensively about politics.[11]

On January 9, 1988, Richard Nixon celebrated his seventy-fifth birthday. The occasion was made even more special because on that day he completed the manuscript for his latest book. *1999: Victory without War* would be published by Simon & Schuster later that year.

Nixon found great enjoyment in this season of his life. He regularly attended New York sporting events. He had long enjoyed a close relationship with Yankees owner George Steinbrenner and was sometimes seen at Yankees games. But Nixon always saw himself as an outsider, an underdog. And so he naturally grew quite fond of the New York Mets, often attending games in his friend Bob Abplanalp's box at Shea Stadium. He even became friends with some of the players. Several times he and Mets captain Keith Hernandez met for lunch at Rusty Staub's restaurant. And when pitcher Ron Darling was traded to the Expos, Nixon sent him a note celebrating his time as a Mets pitcher and lamenting that Darling had suffered from a "lack of support and too many no-decision games which should have ended up in the W column." He wished Darling well in Montreal with the exception of "when you pitch against the Mets."[12]

Nixon's family often joined him at the games. He took great joy in spending time with his grandkids. Family can warm the cold of any life and Nixon found particular pleasure in being so close to both of his daughters and all of his grandchildren. He quite enjoyed the role of family patriarch and loved spoiling his grandkids. Jennie Eisenhower, Alex Eisenhower, and Melanie Eisenhower lived with their parents, David and Julie, near Philadelphia. And Chris Cox lived in New York with his parents, Ed and Tricia. Nixon often told the story of the time former Bulgarian President Todor Zhivkov visited him in 1982. Zhivkov told him, "You are a very rich man. Having grandchildren is the greatest wealth a man can have."[13]

Still, Nixon's mind was restless, as always. He needed to be working. And the new developments in U.S.-Soviet relations were very much on his mind in early 1988. His latest book book centered on that topic and continued the evolution in Nixon's thinking on the Cold War.

"One of the more interesting developments on the American political stage over the past decade has been Richard Nixon's metamorphosis from execrated figure of the Watergate affair to experienced conservative statesman and commentator upon world affairs," began the review of *1999: Victory without War* in the *Washington Post*.[14]

Nixon was clearly still concerned about the Reagan negotiations with Gorbachev. His main take on the Soviet leader was not to underestimate him or what he was trying to achieve. Gorbachev, Nixon wrote, was motivated not by a desire to end Communism, but rather by a desire to "make the communist system work better." But the former president shrewdly predicted that Gorbachev would face challenges that had been unthinkable just a few years before. Nixon believed that "Eastern nationalism" was a real threat to the Soviet occupation of Eastern Europe. "Without genuine reform," he wrote, "a political earthquake in Eastern Europe is inevitable in the years before 1999." Nixon called for an effort to "Finlandize" the countries of Eastern Europe to create pressure on the Soviets.

In the meantime, he continued to push for a policy of standing firm against the Soviets. This included his long-held view that the Strategic Defense Initiative should be pursued and funded as leverage for negotiating for "massive reductions in not only Soviet nuclear forces but conventional forces."

As part of the promotion for the release of the book that April, Nixon agreed to an interview on the NBC News Sunday morning talk show *Meet the Press*. The questions inevitably turned to Nixon's past. And the former president offered some surprising insights.

His biggest regret? Bombing North Vietnam in 1972 rather than 1969. "I wanted to do it," he said. "I talked to Henry Kissinger about it, but we were stuck with the bombing halt that we had inherited from the Johnson administration, with Paris peace talks. I knew that, just like the cease-fire talks down here in Nicaragua, I didn't trust them at all. And they proved to be, of course, phony. But if we had done that then, I think we would have ended the war in Vietnam in 1969 rather than in 1973. That was my biggest mistake as president.'"

In response to questions about Watergate, Nixon again expressed contrition while asking that the whole context of the times be considered. "In 1972, we went to China," he said. "We went to Russia. We ended the Vietnam War effectively by the end of the year. Those were the big things. And here was this small thing, and we fouled it up beyond belief. It was a great mistake. It was wrong, as I've pointed out again and again." Nixon directly addressed his role and his regrets over it. "It was a small thing, the break-in, and break-ins have occurred previously in other campaigns, as well," he said. "At that point, we should have done something about it. We should have exposed it, found out who did it, rather than attempting to contain it, to cover it up. It was the cover-up that was wrong, and that was a very big thing; there's no question about it at all."[15]

————————

On December 8, 1987, just a few months before the publication of Nixon's new book, Ronald Reagan and Mikhail Gorbachev signed the Intermediate Range Nuclear Forces (INF) Treaty they had been negotiating. It essentially eliminated all nuclear and conventional missiles, as well as their launchers, with ranges of 500–1,000 kilometers (short-range) and 1,000–5,500 kilometers (intermediate-range). The treaty was a triumph for Reagan, although many in his conservative base criticized him at the time. George Will sneered at the president's performance in his syndicated column: "Four years ago, many people considered Reagan a keeper of the Cold War flame. Time flies."[16]

One of the sharpest critics at the time was Richard Nixon. For some time he had feared that Reagan would give away too much. He had pleaded with him in the *Los Angeles Times* op-ed and in person at the White House the previous April to focus more on the Soviet advantage in conventional weapons. But Reagan believed that

Gorbachev was a unique person representing a unique opportunity at a unique moment in time. Since the Strategic Defense Initiative had been left alone in the negotiations, Reagan felt like he had gained much more than he had given.

Nixon didn't agree. The patron saint of détente had now come full circle: he was more of a hardliner on confronting the Soviets than Reagan. Still, he measured his words with the president. Nixon wrote diplomatically to Reagan that "Rome was not built in a day and it takes more than three days to civilize Moscow."[17]

As the Senate prepared to ratify the treaty in 1988, Nixon continued his subtle critique in the form of promoting his book. "The beginning of the Gorbachev era does not represent the end of the rivalry between the two superpowers," read his words in the cover story in a March 1988 edition of the *New York Times Magazine*. "Rather, it represents the beginning of a dangerous, challenging new stage of the struggle." The article was excerpted from his book. "We must respect the Soviet Union as a strong and worthy adversary," Nixon urged. "Respect is important between friends; it is indispensable between potential enemies in the nuclear age. Gorbachev himself is a powerful reminder that we underestimate the Soviet Union at our peril. He is a highly intelligent, sophisticated man of the world and a great communicator—the antithesis of the common perception of a bearded Bolshevik intent on blowing up the world."[18]

Nixon's view of the treaty and of the Soviet Union was both wrong and right. He was wrong to think that Reagan had given away too much in the treaty; indeed, Reagan had been right all along about the advantage the U.S.—when combined with Western European countries—still held in conventional weapons. But Nixon was right about the relative weakness of the Soviet economy. In his book he predicted that the economies of Japan and China would race past the Soviet economy in the coming century. In fact he did not see the full implications of that insight or foresee how powerful a factor the weakened Soviet economy would be in the eventual demise of the Soviet Union.

On the whole, Nixon's advice to Reagan through the summits with Gorbachev undoubtedly led to a more effective American negotiating strategy. Using SDI as a negotiation tool and offering to share the technology with the Soviets helped to neutralize the issue and preserve the program for the U.S. It was an inspired piece of diplomacy. And once that objection had been neutralized, Gorbachev—painfully aware of his country's anemic economy—could do little but negotiate the best terms possible with Reagan. That those terms were more generous than Nixon advised does not mitigate his importance in helping Reagan get to that point.

Statecraft is almost always a team effort. Many people are involved at many different levels. Several people deserve credit for the 1987 INF Treaty. First among them is Ronald Reagan, who took on his own party to sign a treaty that many conservatives reviled. But Richard Nixon's role in providing advice and counsel merits credit, as well. He used a lifetime of experience and knowledge to advise Reagan. Just thirteen years before, he had been politically radioactive. Now he had helped achieve one of the most monumental foreign policy achievements of the twentieth century. From this point forward, no one needed to ask if Nixon was back. The facts spoke for themselves.

Chapter Seventeen

# The 1988 Election and the Bush Administration

*"People don't vote against peace and prosperity."*

"Governor Dukakis won the Democratic nomination without the advice of Mr. Nixon and I think he will win the election on November 8 without heeding Mr. Nixon's advice." That was the statement from Michael Dukakis's press secretary, Lorraine Voles. The occasion for her comment was a memo Nixon had written about the upcoming election that was sent to his friends and leaked to the press.

In "The Final Four Weeks: Predictions for November 8th" memo, Nixon handicapped the race between Republican nominee George Bush and Democratic nominee Michael Dukakis. He thought Dukakis had little chance of success. And he explained why.[1]

Nixon wrote that "it would take a genius" to squander the massive eighteen-point lead that Bush had at the time. "Jim Baker is smart," he quipped of the Bush campaign chairman, "but he is not that kind of a genius." To Nixon, the race came down to a thriving economy and relative tranquility in world affairs. "People don't vote against peace and prosperity," he wrote.[2]

At a tactical level, Nixon was critical of the Dukakis television ads. "Dukakis should file a malpractice suit against his ad agency," he wrote. "His ads look as if they have been produced by Roger Ailes"—who was doing ads for the Bush campaign.[3]

Bush went on to win a landslide victory over Dukakis that November. The Reagan Revolution would continue. And what would Nixon's relationship with the new White House be? No one seemed to know. Nixon had always had ambivalent feelings about the president-elect. But he certainly hoped to continue his role as outside counselor.

The former president immediately began conversations with James A. Baker, Bush's long-time friend who had been tapped to become the next secretary of state. Nixon respected Baker's intellect and realized how much the president-elect valued him. Baker, for his part, appreciated Nixon's insights on foreign policy. In early December, Baker arrived at Saddle River to talk things over with Nixon. The two men began with an hour-long conversation in the library, followed by another forty-five-minute discussion over lunch, and then concluded with more talks over coffee back in the library.

With his perfectly tailored suit and Texas accent, Baker cut a striking figure. And he was the consummate Washington insider. That George Bush's campaign manager in 1980 could end up as Ronald Reagan's chief of staff was a measure of his skill. And that he could do what almost no other Reagan staffer had been able to do—successfully manage the expectations and demands of Nancy Reagan—was proof of his talent as a diplomat. Nixon knew that Bush foreign policy decisions would start with Baker. So he went out of his way to ingratiate himself with the soon-to-be secretary of state.

After the two men discussed ideas on how to staff the State Department, talk turned toward negotiations with the Soviets. After the signing of the INF Treaty, the Reagan administration had proposed what would become known as the START Treaty (Strategic Arms Reduction Treaty) with the goal of making even further cuts in the nuclear stockpiles of both nations. Nixon was concerned about the talks and returned to much of the messaging he had used with Reagan on dealing with the Soviets in his discussion with Baker. Fearing that Baker had been "brainwashed by Shultz," Nixon went "chapter and verse" through his concerns about where the Reagan negotiations with Gorbachev had left the United States. Nixon even got in a personal plug, suggesting that for more detail Baker could "read our book."[4]

"Where we had our biggest disagreement was in regard to linking START with conventional weapons," Nixon would recall of his meeting with Baker. The Texan demurred, saying that if Bush insisted on an agreement on conventional weapons it would put the negotiations on nuclear weapons in jeopardy. Nixon left the meeting feeling like it was a lost cause. And he blamed the professional staffers at the State Department. "Here is one that the foreign service has won" he would later write, since they were "unalterably opposed to linkage."[5]

When the talk turned to Latin America, Nixon urged Baker to seize the opportunity, especially with Bush's "ties to Mexico," to create a new policy. He suggested continuing to stand strong against the Communist infiltration of Latin America and said that regardless of whether the Monroe Doctrine was still in effect, the U.S. could not tolerate Communist interference south of the border.

On the Middle East, Baker told Nixon he had never been to the region and asked for his advice. Nixon responded by recounting a story from his own trip to the Middle East not long after war there broke out in 1967. Upon his return, a friend asked him what the U.S.

should do in the Middle East. Nixon said he thought about the question for a long time and then replied, "Nothing." Baker listened to the story, but he seemed determined to try and do something. At that point, Nixon suggested that it was "in Israel's interest to make a deal now when they were strong rather than waiting until later when the strength of the Arabs would force them to do so."

The men also discussed what impact domestic issues would have on foreign affairs. Kissinger had already met with Bush and told Nixon that he had gotten the distinct impression that Bush wanted a deal with the Soviets to cover for the difficulties he would have domestically with the budget. When Nixon raised the point with Baker, the Texan responded that the pressure for Bush and Gorbachev to meet was going to be "unbearable."

That led to a discussion of Bush's predicament on the budget. He had promised not to raise taxes, but clearly that was an option now being considered. "I made the political point that he should not be concerned about Bush having to renege on his campaign promise," Nixon recalled. But Baker suggested it would be difficult to do. He said the "read my lips" pledge from the 1988 GOP convention speech was "a very powerful signal" and it would be "devastating" for Bush to back off it. Nixon mentioned that as president he had never called for raising taxes but that his successor, Gerald Ford, had. "Why in the hell did Ford do it?" he asked, knowing that Baker had been a senior advisor to Ford.[6]

Overall, Nixon left the meeting with Baker with cautious optimism. "This is a very bright man," he would recall. "He asks the right questions." He had carefully observed Baker's demeanor throughout the meeting. "He is also a very cold man," Nixon concluded, "which is not said in a condemning way but more in a respectful way." He did record that Baker had made one odd and revealing comment. He told Nixon that because "he had known Bush as a friend and advisor for thirty years or so he felt that he would have considerable influence." Nixon found this to be a "defensive comment to make." Only a person worried and trying to "reassure himself" would say such a thing.[7]

Baker was not alone in seeking out Nixon's advice. In the fall of 1988, a steady stream of visitors came to see Nixon and get his insights on events. In fact, Nixon had decided the time had come to conserve more time for advising, thinking, and writing and to spend less time on the commute to New York City each day. In September, he announced that he would close down his office in Manhattan and would begin working from New Jersey. "It occurred to him that if he could move the office to New Jersey," Chief of Staff John Taylor told the media, "it would allow him to have an office within walking distance of his house."

Nixon would not go without in his new office digs. "His new premises, roughly equivalent in space to his office in the Manhattan building, [is] in a two-story building built in an ornate Italianate style, with a copy of Michelangelo's *David* crowned by a Florentine chandelier, at the middle of a central rotunda," reported the *New York Times*. "The style was a bit luxurious for the former president's taste, Mr. Taylor said, but the GSA picked the site because it suited the agency's rental guidelines and security needs."[8]

Once settled into his new office, Nixon continued in his old routine. One exception was that nowadays Nixon often met in the morning with a political figure or intellectual to discuss foreign policy. "Perhaps he had a fear that if he stopped working, his mind would atrophy," Taylor recalled, "but the more time I spent with him the more I realized that here was an extraordinarily powerful and unorthodox intellect which simply had to exercise itself."

As had been his custom in the years since Watergate, Nixon's main form of intellectual exercise came from researching and writing books. In 1989, he began working on what would become his seventh book since leaving the White House. For this one, which would eventually be called *In the Arena*, Nixon focused inward. When Simon & Schuster announced the book later that year, the publisher quoted Nixon saying that it would be "the most personal book I have ever written."

But there were occasional signs that Nixon's fear of becoming out of shape mentally was not entirely unjustified. Like most people in their late seventies, he was slowing down a bit.

His editor at Simon & Schuster was Michael Korda, a well-established New York editor who had also edited Graham Greene and Joan Dideon. Korda attended one of Nixon's famous dinners at his home in 1989. Nixon began by offering everyone a daiquiri. "The recipe was said to be one of his more closely guarded secrets," Korda recalled and said that it was indeed very good. "The president's claim that he made the best daiquiri ever was the truth." But things went downhill from there. At dinner, Nixon offered one of his usual monologues on world events. But on this particular night Nixon began using the third person to describe himself. Korda found it odd but thought no more about it. Then later, after dinner, Nixon announced that he would provide a tour of the house. He seemed confused. "At one point, he opened a closet door, apparently thinking that it was the door to his study, then slammed it shut hastily, with a muttered oath," Korda recalled. When the former president did finally make his way to the study, he again reverted to the third person to announce: "This is where Nixon works." Korda left that night sensing that perhaps old age was catching up with Nixon.[9]

Still, Nixon forged ahead. And there was much in the news to keep his mind active. Most notably, events in China came to the forefront that June when the Chinese Army entered Tiananmen Square to crush an uprising of students who were protesting for freedom.

The images of the tanks rolling through the square shocked the world and roiled policymakers in Washington. Almost immediately Congressional leaders of both parties began demanding that the Bush administration impose sanctions on the Chinese government.

Sitting in his office in New Jersey, Nixon followed the news and saw the proposals coming out of Washington as overreactions. He believed his effort to open the door to China in 1972 had been a signature achievement that had made the world safer. He didn't want to see that achievement abandoned in an emotional reaction from Washington. For that matter, neither did the Bush White House. When President Bush suspended military aid to China but refused to impose any further sanctions, Nixon publicly supported him. "Those on the far right who oppose any relations with China will demand economic and diplomatic sanctions," he wrote in an op-ed for the *Los Angeles Times*. "So will the human rights lobby, which calls for punishing every regime that does not live up to our standards regardless of our interests or those of the millions living under those regimes, whom sanctions would hurt the most."

Instead, Nixon urged the U.S. to take the long view and consider any decision on China as part of the larger American foreign policy strategy. "Whatever happens in the future, it is imperative that Sino-American relations remain strong so the United States can help maintain the balance among China, Japan, and the Soviet Union." He also suggested that those in Washington who were outraged at the events in China were exhibiting naivety. "No one who knows China should be surprised when its leaders turn to violence to pursue their political goals," he wrote. "They have done far worse before Tiananmen Square."[10]

"The Chinese got along without the West for a quarter-century and they could do so again," Nixon told the media. "If we force them back into their angry isolation from the West, we risk prompting a potentially disastrous entente between the two great Communist powers."

But for Nixon, the U.S.-China relationship was personal. He quickly decided it wasn't enough to just write an op-ed suggesting a way forward. Perhaps no one had better relationships inside the Chinese government than he did. Why not take advantage of that? Why not try to bridge the gap with China one more time? Nixon decided the time had come to return to China.

Nixon didn't ask permission from the Bush White House, but he did let the president know he intended to go to China. In October, Nixon landed in China and began a whirlwind of events and meetings. When he met with Deng Xiaoping, he gave brutally honest advice. "I have watched Sino-U.S. relations closely for seventeen years," he said. "There has never been a worse crisis than now in those relations." Later at a banquet held in his honor, Nixon warned that another tragedy like Tiananmen Square "would be the death of a relationship and of policies that have served so well."[11]

On November 5, Nixon found himself back at the White House. In a lengthy discussion over dinner that included the president, the first lady, the vice president, the national security advisor, and the FBI director, Nixon gave an account of his trip.

The meeting had been set up in part because the Bush White House wanted to know firsthand how the Nixon trip to China had gone. But it was also in part because the president and his team weren't happy with Nixon's candor in China. White House spokesman Marlin Fitzwater suggested to reporters that the Bush administration did not like the tone of Nixon's comments.

For two hours, Nixon held court at the White House and described his meetings in China. When reporters found out about the meeting between Bush and Nixon two days later, Fitzwater responded to their questions tersely, saying that the president appreciated Nixon's report but that "our general policy has not changed."[12]

Back home in Saddle River, Nixon prepared a memo for congressional leaders about his trip. In it he said bluntly that there was little that could be done to find an agreement on Tiananmen Square. The difference in opinion, he wrote, "is totally unbridgeable." In fact, the Chinese had pushed back when Nixon raised the topic of Tiananmen. "They believe the American reaction was an unacceptable intrusion in their internal affairs," he wrote to the congressional leaders.

Nixon was trying to strike a balance on China. He understood the domestic political pressures on Congress to get tough on China. And so he had bluntly told the Chinese that another such tragedy could damage the relationship between the two countries. But he also knew what he had known since 1972—that China was not going away. And U.S. policy had to acknowledge China's growing power and importance. "China will provide a huge market for the advanced industrial countries," he wrote in his memo to congressional leaders. "Do we want to rule ourselves out and leave that potential market to the Japanese and the Europeans?"

In the end, the fever in Washington over China finally broke. Events in Europe soon interceded and changed the conversation. But once again Nixon had played a role in a foreign policy debate that would have lasting implications. His meetings in both China and Washington had helped calm passions on both sides. Who else could have spoken so bluntly to the Chinese but the man who had done so much to bring them into the modern world? And who else could have helped tone down the rhetoric in Washington except the elder statesman who had just used his personal clout with China to put them on notice that there must never be another Tiananmen?

And his policy prescriptions had largely been right. Nixon had sternly warned the Chinese to knock it off while also cautioning U.S.

lawmakers of both parties that they couldn't overreact, given China's growing size and importance in Asia. It was his last great contribution to American foreign policy. The U.S.-China relationship could easily have been destroyed in the aftermath of Tiananmen Square. In the end, the man who helped save it was the man who had helped start it in 1972.

———————

With his shuttle diplomacy to China and Washington concluded, Nixon returned to finishing the manuscript for his latest book. As had been previously announced, his book would be part memoir. The book was divided into chapters with simple titles like "Philosophy" or "Purpose" or "Struggle." And as he had done with previous books, Nixon carefully planned out a media push to promote its publication.

*Time* magazine showcased Nixon on its April 2, 1990, cover with the headline, "Nixon: In an emotional memoir, he describes the agony of his exile and his struggle for renewal." Inside, readers were presented with excerpts from the book, as well as an interview with the former president. It marked the sixty-seventh time Nixon had appeared on the magazine's cover.[13]

Though not as revealing as his many media critics wanted it to be, the book did offer new insights in Nixon's life and career. It was in this book that Nixon first hinted that Pat's stroke in 1976 had been caused in part by her reading *Final Days*—the Woodward and Bernstein account of the end of the Nixon presidency.

But as always, it was his take on world affairs that most readers were interested in reading. Nixon continued his journey back to the right on the Cold War. "In geopolitics," he wrote, "the game never ends. There is no point at which all sides cash in their chips." If Ronald Reagan had urged a policy of "trust, but verify," Nixon seemed to advocate for a policy of verify, but don't trust. He urged the U.S. to be wary of providing economic aid to the Soviets now that it was becoming clear that their economy was faltering. Instead, he urged the Soviet Union to end its domination of Eastern Europe and reduce its conventional weapons before the U.S. offered any economic help.

And he returned again to the first conversation he had had with Gorbachev on his Moscow trip just a few years before. In retelling the story, Nixon again stressed what had been a key principle of his during the Reagan years: the power of SDI as leverage with the Soviets. "Our most spirited discussion with Gorbachev involved the Strategic Defense Initiative," he wrote. "He said it was a myth that the Soviet Union opposed SDI because it feared the huge cost to the economy or because it could not keep up technologically. He was emphatic in declaring that the Soviet Union would be able to evade and overcome any SDI system that the U.S. might eventually deploy." Nixon described in detail how Gorbachev had tried to reframe the debate about SDI. "His major objection to SDI," he insisted, was that it would "inevitably lead to increased tensions between the Soviet Union and the U.S. and destroy any chance for a new, less confrontational relationship."[14]

Gorbachev's arguments, Nixon now claimed in his writing, left him unpersuaded. "He made these points vigorously and persuasively, but there is no doubt whatever in my mind that his major concern was and remains that the huge cost of competing with the U.S. in developing SDI would bankrupt the already strapped Soviet economy." The book also included Nixon's domestic policy prescriptions, which clearly indicated that he had become a man without a party. Perhaps no issue had brought more new voters into the GOP than Reagan's embrace of pro-life policies. Evangelicals who had voted for Carter in 1976 now proudly called themselves Republicans. Nixon wanted none of it. "In 1980, the Republican nominee for Senate in Colorado, Mary

Estill Buchanan, lost in a very close election," he wrote. "I was surprised when a Republican friend told me that he had not voted for her.
I asked why. He replied, 'She was wrong on abortion.' As a result, we
got six more years of Gary Hart, who was wrong on everything."[15]

Nixon also wrote in favor of the controversial idea of federal
assistance for catastrophic health care. President Reagan had supported and signed the bill in 1988. But Republicans repealed it when
costs skyrocketed. Still, Nixon wrote that while he opposed "com-
pulsory national health insurance, I have always supported federal
assistance for catastrophic health care. My strong feelings in this
respect are a direct result of losing two brothers to TB."

On welfare, Nixon struck a more conservative note. Essentially
calling for welfare reform, Nixon wrote that the "difficulty comes in
setting the level of support to the less fortunate. If set too low, it causes
unnecessary hardship. If set too high, it creates disincentives to achieving self-sufficiency and fosters dependency. Our objective should
therefore be a welfare system structured not to trap the poor in dependency but to enable them to escape poverty."[16]

Nixon had always been something of a domestic policy enigma.
The man reviled by the Left for campaigning on law and order was
the same man who as president extended affirmative action in federal
hiring and helped create the Environmental Protection Agency. In the
Reagan era, Nixon's domestic views were out of step with the direction of his party.

But as a president and as an elder statesman, Nixon had always
seen foreign policy as the first priority. And it was here that his views
were still widely regarded and valued by leaders in both parties. In
fact, when Gorbachev came later that year to Washington seeking
economic assistance, Nixon's warnings against providing such aid
almost certainly helped the Bush administration and Congress resist
the urge to help the Soviets.

Perhaps the most revealing moments in the book came when Nixon described how he had tried to find his way out of the wilderness he found himself in after Watergate:

> Those first years after resigning the presidency were profoundly difficult and painful. As I look back over those years in the wilderness, I would say that I was sustained by always bearing in mind 3 principles:
>
> 1. Put the past behind you. Analyze & understand the reasons for your defeat, but do not become obsessed with what was lost. Think instead about what is left to do.
> 2. Don't let your critics get to you. Remember that they win only if they divert you into fighting them rather than driving toward your goals.
> 3. Devote your time to a goal larger than yourself. Avoid the temptation of living simply for pleasure or striving only to leave a larger estate.[17]

Nixon then took the lesson of his own failure and tried to apply it directly to his audience. "While few people will experience a loss as devastating as resigning from the presidency," he wrote, "these principles remain valid for the defeats we all suffer, whether in business, in sports, or in personal life. The key is to live for something more important than your life. As Einstein said, 'Only a life lived for others is worth living.'"

On July 19, 1990, the dream of a presidential library became a reality at long last. The Richard Nixon Presidential Library and

Birthplace would be different from other presidential libraries because it still would not control the actual presidential records. But the twenty-five-million-dollar pink limestone facility situated next to the white frame kit house Nixon's father had built was a beautiful addition to the Yorba Linda community.

A crowd of fifty thousand people gathered on the grounds for the opening. Longtime Nixon advance specialist Ron Walker orchestrated an elaborate celebration with balloons, bands, dancers, and the dramatic release of two hundred white doves. Joining the festivities was Reverend Billy Graham, who led a prayer. Also included in the formal program were former presidents Ford and Reagan, as well as current president Bush. Bush went out of his way to praise Nixon and salute his achievements. "Richard Nixon helped change the course not only of America but of the entire world," he told the crowd. "Today, as the movement towards democracy sweeps our globe, you can take great personal pride that history will say of you: 'Here was a true architect of peace.'"[18]

In his own speech, Nixon waxed philosophical about his career. "Won some, lost some, all interesting," he told the crowd in quite an understatement. Then he pointed at the house behind him. The house, which his father had ordered from Sears and built with his own hands, still stood and looked in decent condition. But it was a modest, unassuming structure. Nixon told the crowd that it was "a long way from Yorba Linda to the White House." He added, "I believe in the American dream because I have seen it come true in my own life." As the ceremony ended, Nixon joined several guests inside the library for a lunch catered by Chasen's, one of Nixon's favorite restaurants. That night, Nixon joined another fifteen hundred friends at the Century Plaza Hotel up the road in Los Angeles for a celebratory dinner.

The press coverage of the day's events was, predictably, more critical. R. W. Apple noted in the *New York Times* that Watergate had never been mentioned during the entire ceremony. Nixon biographer Stephen Ambrose had told Apple that the building represented "more of a museum than a library" and denounced it. "He never, ever gives up," Ambrose said. "You see what Nixon wants you to see. So the cover-up continues."[19]

If Nixon ever read those comments, he never let on. He loved seeing the crowd and he reveled in being with so many of his old staffers, including Henry Kissinger, William Simon, and Rose Mary Woods. Ron Ziegler also attended and found himself emotionally moved by the celebration. "There were times when it would have been easy, in the days at San Clemente after the resignation, to walk into the ocean with a bottle of Chivas under your arm," he said. "But he didn't."[20]

In the coming years, Nixon would carefully watch events at his beloved library, which would be run by his trusted aide and friend John Taylor. He wanted the library to succeed. And he often called with suggestions. "I'm watching George Will speak at the Reagan Library on C-SPAN," he called and said to John Taylor one night. "Why I am not watching him at the Nixon Library?"[21]

But on the night of the grand opening of his library, Nixon could not have been happier. After the banquet in Los Angeles had concluded, Nixon turned to his longtime friend Ron Walker, who had put the day together. "I guess this is one of the happiest days of my life," he said.[22]

Chapter Eighteen

# The Last Mile

*"But now all I can do is offer advice."*

T hroughout 1989, the events unfolding in Eastern Europe
had commanded Nixon's attention. Proof that the Cold
War was ending came in November of that year when East
Germans began crossing through checkpoints at the Berlin Wall
and the Communists did not stop them. Freedom at last was coming to Eastern Europe. By 1990, the wall itself was torn down.

To Nixon, the demise of the wall and the looming collapse of
the Soviet Union were significant achievements. He had essentially
predicted the collapse. But it did not represent the end of the fight.
At a speech to the Boston World Affairs Council on April 12, 1990,
Nixon argued that even if Communism had failed, freedom had
not yet prevailed. He wanted the United States to be prepared to fill
the vacuum that would be created by the dissolution of the Iron
Curtain. The formerly Communist countries would need help making the transition into democratic states. In a play on Woodrow
Wilson's famous phrase, Nixon said that the time had come to make
the world "safe for freedom."[1]

That summer, Nixon hired a new research assistant. Monica Crowley had been studying at Colgate University when she wrote a letter to Nixon about his book *1999*. A few weeks later, she was shocked when Nixon wrote her back and asked her to come visit him. She did and the two hit it off immediately. Then in the summer of 1990, Nixon hired Crowley as his research assistant. On her first day in his office, he asked her to read a speech he would give in Boston about the end of the Cold War. The next day, she entered his office and was greeted by Nixon with a question: "What does Gorbachev really want?"

Crowley gave a thoughtful answer about how Gorbachev could not continue to try and strike a balance between the reformers like Boris Yeltsin (who had already quit the Communist Party) and the traditional Communists.

Nixon agreed. "No, he can't," he said. "He runs the risk of losing both sides if he continues this way." He added that the "train has left the station as far as the collapse of Communism is concerned."

Nixon then expressed his concern about what the Bush administration might do to help Gorbachev. "Unfortunately," he continued, "we have a major political problem on this score because the right will not raise any warning flags because they have to stand by Reagan, who, based on his performance during his last months in office, would go even further than Bush toward making a deal with Gorbachev."

Nixon's position was that the U.S. should continue to be cautious with the Soviet Union (including keeping defense spending high) while looking for ways to bolster the European countries. He suggested to Crowley that "rather than a Marshall Plan, what is needed is a Bush Plan, under which the nations of Western Europe and the United States would develop a coordinated program for credits, debt relief, technological assistance, and even aid to compensate for the years lost during the period they have been under Soviet domination."

Still, Nixon didn't rule out helping the Soviets under the right conditions. He believed the U.S. should help only if "Soviet foreign and defense policy is clearly defensive and not aggressive."[2]

Later that year as the Soviet Union teetered on the brink of collapse, Lithuania began seeking its independence. The small country not only had been controlled by the Soviets, but also had been a part of the Soviet Union. The Bush administration, not wanting to interfere directly in Soviet affairs, resisted calls to publicly support the independence movement.

"Has Bush lost his mind?" Nixon angrily asked Crowley one day in November. "Has he been asleep throughout the entire Cold War? Look at this: he isn't moving an inch on Lithuania. He just keeps letting his friend Gorbachev roll over the poor place." To Nixon, Bush didn't have to choose between supporting or opposing Lithuanian independence. He often painted in shades of grey when it came to the canvas of foreign policy, and he believed that there was a way for the Bush White House to neither support nor oppose the Lithuanian independence movement.

When Crowley pushed him to do more on the issue publicly, Nixon demurred. "I can't really go to Bush because he'll resend it—too close to Gorbachev to be objective," he said. "And I cannot and will not [go] to Baker."[3] The comment revealed that Nixon's opinion of the secretary of state had soured considerably. And it revealed that Nixon knew he no longer had the influence he once had in the Reagan administration.

Since his long meeting with Baker after the '88 election, Nixon had feared Bush's selection for secretary of state might not be up to the job. Now the fears had turned to reality in Nixon's mind.

"If Baker doesn't stop drooling over [Eduard] Shevardnadze," he told Crowley one day—referring to Baker's attempt to win over the Soviet foreign secretary—"I'm going to gag." Nixon had long believed that Baker—and to some extent Bush—put too much stock in personal diplomacy. "Smart leaders act on behalf of their national interest," he said, "personal relationship be damned." When Shevardnadze resigned on December 20, Nixon felt that Baker had been duped because Baker's strongest contact in the Soviet government was now gone.[4]

But Bush and Baker were about have an even bigger foreign policy challenge on their hands. And this one would prove to be the defining issue of the Bush administration.

---

When Iraqi tanks crossed over the Kuwaiti border on August 2, 1990, the world watched as Iraqi forces seized Kuwaiti oil reserves. Almost overnight, the world oil market was in turmoil. The question quickly became, what would the U.S. do in response?

"I should have seen this coming," Nixon remarked at the time of the invasion. Watching events from his office in New Jersey, he knew that no easy options or simple solutions existed for the Bush administration. Less than two years before, he had told Baker that there was not much that could be done in Israel. Now his realpolitik suggested a similar dearth of solutions on Iraq.

"Conflict has engulfed the Middle East for two thousand years," he said. "We can do some things at the margin, but nothing the United States can do will change that. It's up to the direct parties involved, not us."

Still, Nixon knew that the Bush administration would have to respond. He wondered what that response would be. "Never tell your enemy what you will do," he said to Crowley one day in August in his office, "and never tell him what you won't do."

Nixon clearly didn't have the same relationship with the Bush White House that he had enjoyed with the Reagan White House. Yet on September 5, President Bush called Nixon to seek his advice. Nixon promised a document with his specific recommendations.

He immediately set to work on outlining his ideas for Bush. In the final document, he called for removing Saddam Hussein from power or "at the very least, eliminating his war-making capabilities...." He also suggested avoiding any language about "trying to bring 'democracy' to Kuwait." To Nixon, this was a land grab and a power play by Hussein, and Bush should simply defend Kuwait's territorial integrity—nothing more and nothing less.

Nixon worried that the Bush-Baker diplomacy with Gorbachev could come into play in the Middle East. If Gorbachev offered to help in any way, Nixon urged Bush to decline the offer. He saw no reason to invite Gorbachev into the issue.

He also suggested that Bush take his time. He did not believe that a military attack before the midterm elections would help Republicans. "No advice could be more stupid," he wrote in reference to campaign consultants calling for action before November. He wrote that any military attack before the election would only produce a "marginal effect."[5] Crowley was deputized to hand deliver the memo to the White House.

The Persian Gulf War marked a change in Nixon. During the Reagan years, he had relished the chance to offer advice and be back in the game after years in exile. But the shine of those experiences had now grown dim. Nixon, now more than fifteen years removed from his resignation, no longer simply longed for influence.

"I did what I could when it was my time in there," he said wistfully, "but now all I can do is offer advice. If they take it, fine; if they don't, what can I do?"

The old Cold Warrior still wanted to be in the arena as momentous conflict was transpiring. And if his advice was ignored, he knew there was little else he could do but watch the events at home like everyone else. For a man with a keen and restless mind, it was perhaps the greatest punishment of all that he had to leave office before he finished his work on foreign policy and that he was relegated to simply offering advice.

Still, when Bush came out strong and ordered a military mobilization in the Persian Gulf, Nixon was pleased. As he prepared to send Bush a note praising his speech announcing the policy, Nixon told Crowley that he simply wanted to "buck the guy up. He needs some encouragement. He's surrounded by critics and people who don't want to step up to this. He needs to be reassured that he's doing the right thing."

During the ensuing weeks, Nixon's pleasure turned to frustration as Bush painstakingly tried to build international support for his action, including working to secure the passage of UN Resolution 678, which essentially blessed military action.

"What is the point of being number one if we don't use that power?" he railed to Crowley one day that fall in his office. "We simply have to do what it takes, criticism be damned. If we don't, who will?"

Again, the continuing evolution of Nixon's thinking on international affairs could be seen. As he had with Reagan on the Soviets, Nixon continued to move in a more hawkish direction. "If Bush falters even an inch on this," he said privately, "Hussein will dig in, and every goddamned dictator in the world will have a field day." The man who had wanted Woodrow Wilson's desk in the Oval Office during his presidency now dismissed the idea of the international community solving problems. "I've always believed that the United States should use the UN when necessary but not be used by it," he said. He found the UN resolution "helpful but really not necessary."[6]

When Bush offered later in November to send Secretary Baker to Baghdad in one last diplomatic gesture, Nixon was aghast.

"Diplomacy has its place, and this is not it," he raged in his office. "My God! What in hell is going on down there? Don't they know this will backfire right in their faces?"[7]

January 15, 1991, was the deadline that had been imposed on Iraq to withdraw from Kuwait. On January 6, Nixon—who still was concerned that Bush might opt for diplomacy at the last minute—published an op-ed in the *New York Times*. The article, which was called "Why," made the case for military action in the Middle East in direct, realpolitik terms. "Had we not intervened, an international outlaw would today control more than forty percent of the world's oil," he wrote. "We cannot allow Mr. Hussein to blackmail us and our allies into accepting his aggressive goals by giving him a choke-hold on our oil lifeline."[8]

Three days later, Nixon turned seventy-eight. But there was little time for celebrating. That day, Secretary Baker again attempted to find a diplomatic solution to prevent the outbreak of war. When his discussions with Iraqi Foreign Minister Tariq Aziz fell apart, Nixon's birthday mood brightened. "Baker may have wanted a deal," he said, "but I know that the White House didn't want one. How could they? Hell, if the Iraqis weren't negotiating in good faith, why should we?"[9]

When the U.S. launched its invasion on January 16, Nixon watched the news from New Jersey. The early air assaults were successful. It became clear that the vaunted Iraqi Republican Guard would be no match to the U.S. military. Back at home, President Bush's approval ratings began to skyrocket. Nixon worried that Bush would misread the numbers.

"I know Bush," he told Monica Crowley. "He and the others down there are riding high on this 85 percent and won't be open to suggestions."

Still, Nixon sent another memo to Bush on January 28 with just that—more suggestions on how to conclude the war and deal with its aftermath. His main point was that Bush should continue to attack aggressively until the Iraqis surrendered. Nixon referred to a conversation he had had with Lyndon Johnson in 1969. LBJ had complained to Nixon that he had received bad advice when he was encouraged to halt bombings in Vietnam. Johnson said he had been advised that "if I called a halt the North Vietnamese and Vietcong would stop shelling South Vietnamese cities. But nothing happened." Johnson, Nixon wrote to Bush, regretted his decision and lamented that every "one of the bombing halts was a mistake."[10]

While Nixon's opinion of Bush continued to improve, his view of Baker continued to decline. When Baker worked with the Soviets on a joint public statement demanding that the Iraqis back down, Nixon was outraged. "What the hell is Baker doing?" he asked. "Including the Soviets in this now is a major mistake." Later, when the White House distanced itself from the Baker statement, Nixon still raged against the secretary of state. "Bush should fire him over this," he said.

On February 23, Bush called Nixon and told him that the ground assault was about to begin in Iraq. Just a few days later, the Iraqis were ready to surrender. Nixon worried that Bush had ended the conflict too soon. He particularly worried that Hussein still had troops available to him. Indeed, not long after the conflict ended, Hussein used his remaining troops to attack the Kurds and the Shiite Muslims in Iraq.

Not long after the fighting stopped, President Bush called Nixon again and invited him to come meet with him at the White House. Nixon agreed. But still raging at Baker, he told Brent Scowcroft that his only request for the meeting was that "no State Department people" be in the room.

On April 22, Nixon met at the White House with the president and several senior staffers. The only State Department representative was Deputy Secretary of State Lawrence Eagleburger, whom Nixon actually liked. Baker was not present. Nixon spoke to the group for nearly two hours. He focused on the demise of the Soviet Union and the Soviets' attempts to stave off their now inevitable collapse. "I told them not one dollar of American aid should be sent to the Soviet Union until it demonstrates a real commitment to democratic reform," Nixon would recall.[11]

But he did not feel like he made the impact he had wanted to make in the meeting, and he was critical of the team Bush had assembled. "Reagan was very good in that he picked some excellent advisors," he said later. "I just don't see that with Bush."

The U.S. victory in the Persian Gulf War represented the high tide moment for the Bush administration. As Nixon had predicted, Bush's high poll numbers wouldn't last and he would soon find himself in a tough reelection battle. But the war itself had been successful.

Nixon had strong opinions about what the Bush administration was doing right and what it was doing wrong, but he took his case straight to the principals and urged his course of action.

Nixon's behavior during this time contrasted sharply with that of another former president. In the months following the Iraqi invasion, Jimmy Carter had been worried that the U.S. would engage in military action—something Carter opposed. But rather than work directly to influence the White House, Carter worked behind the scenes to influence the UN Security Council. Later on, Carter wrote to several Arab countries and urged them to "call publicly for a delay in the use of force," suggesting that they might "have to forego approval from the White House, but you will find the French, Soviets, and others fully supportive. Also, most Americans will welcome such a move."

Carter's efforts failed, and the U.S. succeeded in confronting Hussein. But for the former president from Georgia, it was not a profile in courage.

———

With the Persian Gulf War successfully winding down, Nixon's mind again turned to the Soviet Union. He prepared for another trip to Moscow in March of 1991. Now that the Soviet Union's collapse seemed inevitable, Nixon worried about how the dissolution would transpire. How would the Soviets handle the transition? To Nixon, figuring out that question required figuring out Gorbachev. So he set out to meet the Soviet leader yet again.

He arrived in Moscow and met with both Mikhail Gorbachev and rising political star Boris Yeltsin. Gorbachev struck Nixon as still very much on top of his game. He urged the Soviet leader not to try and execute a summit with the U.S. to shore up his position in the Soviet Union. "Even by our standards some summits do not help an American president at home, as I am well aware," he commented, reflecting on his own attempt in 1974 to stave off domestic political trouble by traveling overseas. After the meeting, he said that Gorbachev was "either the greatest actor in the world—and incidentally, I've often heard that my Soviet friends are great actors as well as great liars—or at least he gives the impression at this time of being a deeply committed man."[12]

But if Nixon was impressed with Gorbachev, he was awed by Yeltsin. He told Monica Crowley that the "difference between Gorbachev and Yeltsin is that Yeltsin stands for democratic principles. And he doesn't have the material resources to launch a dictatorship. If Russia has any future, Yeltsin is it."[13]

Nixon told Crowley that while he had been in the Soviet Union he had purposely chosen to visit the exact same market that he had visited when he had traveled to the Soviet Union in 1959. He noted that the people he met were perhaps better off financially in 1991 than they had been in 1959, but that they were "poorer in spirit." He sensed that people now realized that the Communist system "has just come to its end."[14]

On April 14, Nixon wrote for *Time* magazine that Yeltsin represented the future. He wrote that American policy should embrace the reformers in the Soviet Union. "Supporting reform is morally right," he wrote.

Again, Nixon was in the news and the White House took notice. On April 22, he met again at the White House with President Bush. From Nixon's perspective, the meeting did not go well. "They don't understand the potential or the energy of the reformers," he said of the president and his team. "The Russian people," he continued, "who have to stand in line two hours for bread, don't care if Gorbachev is tipping vodka glasses with Bush!"[15]

The Bush administration did appreciate the diplomatic opening that the collapse of Communism represented. But the administration also recognized the challenges, as well. President Bush wanted to move cautiously. Some twenty thousand nuclear weapons were still located in the region and Bush didn't want to make any sudden moves that could lead to a more unsafe world.

Nixon realized that his influence with the Bush administration was waning. So once again he turned to the media to ensure his voice was heard. In the June 2 *Washington Post*, he went public with the views he had expressed at the White House. He prescribed his own plan for U.S. policy toward the Soviet Union:

> Instead of promoting political and economic reform, premature Western assistance would ease the mounting pressure on Gorbachev to expand *perestroika* into a comprehensive dismantlement of the Soviet system. Since the Soviet Union only reforms when under pressure, a helping hand would hinder the cause of democracy. Although they are on the

ropes, the forces of reaction are not down and out. They will exploit Western aid to preserve the communist system, even if only in a modified form.

The West should therefore set three preconditions to any consideration of major economic aid to Moscow: Geopolitical accommodation: While relations have improved, important issues still divide the superpowers. Until Gorbachev resolves satisfactorily the date disputes in the Conventional Forces in Europe Treaty, signs a stabilizing and verifiable Strategic Arms Reduction Treaty, accepts a settlement giving genuine self-determination to the Afghan people, and cuts off aid to Third World client states like Cuba, aiding the Soviet economy would simply enhance Moscow's ability to challenge our interests. Market reforms: It would require a great leap of faith to offer the Soviet Union massive assistance in exchange for a verbal promise from Gorbachev that he will adopt more radical reforms. Some have touted the proposed one hundred billion dollar aid package as a "grand bargain." But a "grand con job" sounds like a more appropriate term.

Nixon concluded the op-ed essentially by calling for an election that he knew Yelstin would win:

A new revolution of free nations, free peoples, free ideas, and free markets has driven the communists from power in Eastern Europe and is now sweeping across the Soviet Union. Gorbachev's only long-term hope is to set aside the ideological and imperialist baggage of the Soviet past and lead this new revolution. To do so, he must establish his legitimacy by submitting his fate to a nationwide free election. By showing the same boldness in economic and political reform that he has demonstrated in his foreign policy reforms, he could save his nation and his place in history.[16]

Events soon got ahead of the analysis, as is often the case in foreign affairs. When the Soviet military briefly arrested Gorbachev that August, the rise of Yeltsin became inevitable.

The moment was not lost on Nixon. The great Cold Warrior who had debated Krushchev in Moscow in 1959, had gone on to create détente with Brezhnev as president, and then had urged Reagan to take a hard line in the negotiations that helped accelerate the Soviet demise had been a part of the Cold War from beginning to end.

"When Khrushchev said, 'Your grandchildren will live under Communism,'" Nixon, said referring to their 1959 debate, "and I said 'Your grandchildren will live in freedom,' I knew he was wrong, but I wasn't sure I was right. Now it turns out that I was."[17]

Chapter Nineteen

# The Greatest Honor

*"Everyone goes about God differently."*

he 1990s were off to a great start for Nixon. When historian Richard Norton Smith reviewed a biography of Nixon
in the *New York Times* and praised it for its objectivity,
Nixon joked to his friends that the paper of record usually had
something good to say about him once a decade. In this case, he
joked, "they decided to get it out of the way early."

Then in early 1992, Richard Nixon's tenth book, *Seize the
Moment: America's Challenge in a One-Superpower World*,
appeared in bookstores. In it the former president celebrated the
end of the long Cold War, but also gave stern warnings for the
U.S. in the coming years. In describing what American policy
toward Russia should look like, Nixon continued downplaying
Gorbachev, who, he pointed out, carried the "baggage of the
Communist past." The real key, Nixon wrote, was for the U.S.
to work alongside the countries newly freed from the Soviet bloc
and offer support as they sought to build democratic institutions
and free markets.

235

To promote the book, Nixon agreed to an interview with C-SPAN founder Brian Lamb on *Booknotes*. On February 2, 1992, Nixon, dressed in a dark grey suit with a striped blue tie, calmly explained why his proposed solutions represented the best way forward for the U.S. and the world.

In one of the most telling—and self-revealing—moments of the interview, Nixon talked about the differences between the two main figures in Russia. Gorbachev, Nixon told Lamb, had always been popular with the U.S. foreign policy establishment because of his "style," while Yeltsin had too often been disregarded as "boorish." Nixon recounted the story of an observer criticizing Yeltsin's table manners at a State Dinner at the White House.

"Well, let me tell you," Nixon said to Lamb, "Yeltsin may not know what fork to use at a State Dinner, but he has a very sharp mind." Nixon undoubtedly saw some of himself in Yelstin, who, in his view, offered more substance while Gorbachev focused more on style. Nixon, never known for having the style of Kennedy or Reagan, felt a kinship with Yeltsin.

That spring, the U.S. presidential election was well under way. A slew of candidates had emerged on the Democratic side, including a relatively obscure Arkansas governor named Bill Clinton. On the Republican side, euphoria over the Persian Gulf War had long given way to concern over a somewhat anemic economy. And Bush now faced an uprising on his right flank led by none other than Nixon's old staffer Pat Buchanan. Nixon still liked Buchanan and admired his fire. "Buchanan is a bulldog," he said, "he'll go after them." But he had no doubt that Bush would emerge victorious from the primaries, although a bit bloodied.[1]

Nixon worried about the emerging Democratic frontrunner, Bill Clinton. The charismatic Southern governor possessed shrewd political instincts. Clinton had decided early on that he couldn't win the election on foreign policy; more importantly, he had decided that voters weren't really interested in foreign policy. His campaign headquarters in Little Rock was decorated with a sign that the staffers could see every day reading, "It's the economy, stupid." Clinton ran a relentless campaign on domestic issues and vowed to be a "New Democrat" who would not tack to the left as Dukakis and Mondale had in the previous two presidential elections.

Bush also found himself challenged by a third-party candidate: Texas billionaire Ross Perot. In some ways, Perot's campaign provided a preview of Donald Trump's later success in presidential politics. Perot was an outsider with little discernible ideology who promised voters he would bring his business acumen to the job and get things done. Initially, he appealed strongly to voters and even led in some polls that spring.

But to Nixon, foreign policy still mattered most. And he worried that not only was President Bush not making it a central campaign issue, but that he wasn't making the right moves regarding Russia. In particular, Nixon worried that Yeltsin, who had taken over as president of Russia at the end of 1991, was not receiving the support he needed from the U.S. The former president decided to write yet another memo detailing his concerns. This one would go to his friends and to the press.

Nixon spent weeks working on the memo with his assistant, Monica Crowley. To her it represented an "exercise in defiance" because Nixon refused "to accept defeat" and was determined to have his voice heard.[2]

"The hot-button issue in the 1950's was 'Who lost China?'" Nixon wrote in the memo in March of that year that he called, "How the West Lost the Cold War." He offered a brutal assessment of what he saw as Washington's failed policy. "If Yeltsin goes down, the question 'Who lost Russia' will be an infinitely more devastating issue in the 1990's." The memo went on to say that the "stakes are high, and we are playing as if it were a penny-ante game."

Nixon sharply criticized the Bush administration's lackluster support of Yeltsin. "What has the United States and the West done so far to help Russia's first democratic, free-market oriented, non-expansionist government?" he asked. "We have provided credits for the purchase of agricultural products. We have held a photo-opportunity international conference of 57 foreign secretaries that was long on rhetoric but short on action." To Nixon, the Bush policy was "pathetically inadequate."

Ironically, some of the reasoning for Bush's reticence to do more for Russia came from Nixon's old friend Pat Buchanan. Although Bush clearly would prevail in the primaries, Buchanan was still hammering away his "America First" theme and denouncing the administration as too focused on matters beyond the U.S. border.[3]

As President Bush began a meeting with congressional Republicans at the White House on March 11, reporters asked him about the Nixon memo, which by now had appeared in the press. "I didn't take it as personally critical," the president said unconvincingly, "and I think he would reiterate that it wasn't."[4]

In a note he sent later to Nixon, Bush acknowledged reading the memo. But he struck a defensive tone and suggested that the U.S. was doing quite a bit to help the Russians and that it was the Europeans who "must open their markets more."[5]

Bill Clinton was quick to pounce on the news of the memo and essentially side with Nixon. "I think Baker and Bush have good instincts on what to do in the former Soviet republics," he told reporters, "but I think they've been a little too timid in doing it. I think they know they ought to be with the republics. They know they ought to be trying to dismantle nuclear weapons. They know they ought to be trying to help convert the currency, but I think they're just a little timid on it. I think they're afraid of looking like they're too preoc-cupied with foreign policy."[6]

Nixon followed up, taking advantage of the momentum from his memo. It had always been planned as the appetizer for the main course: a conference on Russia that the Nixon Library hosted at the Four Seasons Hotel in Washington on March 11. There, Nixon delivered a speech in which he cited Truman's policy of sending aid to help Greece and Turkey resist Communism during the first years of the Cold War. "We responded magnificently to the threat of war then," he told the audience, "Can we not respond to the promise of peace now?"[7]

President Bush was scheduled to deliver the keynote address that night at the conference's black tie banquet. Nixon had essentially boxed him in—how could the president not embrace some of the Nixon strategy at the event Nixon was hosting?

But if Nixon hoped Bush would accept his agenda on Russia, he was disappointed. Bush's speech nodded in Nixon's direction but didn't offer any substantive changes in course on Russia. Afterwards Nixon fumed to Crowley. "I gave him everything he needed," he complained, "including, incidentally, the political protection from *both* Buchanan and Clinton, and he didn't take the bait." But the media coverage of the event was largely positive. And within days, the Bush administration reconsidered. "Baker is going to claim the idea is his," Nixon joked when the news broke.[8]

For the Bush administration, the change represented a step for-ward. But for the Bush campaign, the damage had already been done. The Nixon memo and the subsequent conference created a devastating moment for the Bush campaign. Nixon's image had been successfully rehabilitated to the point that he was now widely regarded as one of the preeminent minds on foreign policy. And here he was sharply critiquing Bush on one of the former president's

The Elder Statesman (Nixon in 1992). (Maureen Keating)

strongest issues—foreign policy. That the Nixon memo was being praised by the Democratic candidate for president—whose wife had worked as a lawyer on the Nixon impeachment hearings—showed how respected and how important Nixon's voice had become again.

Nixon couldn't help but be impressed to see Clinton praise his memo. But he still had ambivalent feelings about the Arkansas governor. Much of it had to do with the candidate's wife, Hillary Clinton. Nixon found her too partisan and too left-wing, and he told reporters that "if the wife comes through as being too strong and too intelligent, it makes the husband look like a wimp."[9] The comment was not well-received in the Clinton campaign. Nixon also remained doubtful about the candidate's abilities on foreign policy.

That June, Nixon traveled to Moscow to meet with Yeltsin. The trip was timed so that Nixon could meet with the Russian before he traveled to the U.S. later that month to visit with President Bush. Nixon was determined to try and influence events. Afterward, Nixon tried to throw Bush some cover and put the onus on Congress to pass the aid legislation that Bush was proposing. "Congress should stop its foot-dragging and pass President Bush's Freedom Support Act, which provides for America's contribution to twenty-four billion dollars in Western aid," he urged in the *New York Times*. "Congress's approval of International Monetary Fund assistance will create an incentive for the Parliament to approve the Yeltsin reforms. If we link our aid to passage of those reforms, we will give President Yeltsin greater leverage in his battle."[10]

When Yeltsin arrived in Washington a week later, he agreed to another reduction in nuclear weapons with President Bush. But the economic aid package was still stuck in Congress. And with the presidential conventions fast approaching, the odds of Congress doing anything on Russia diminished with each passing day.

Indeed, the Bush-Yeltsin meeting provided the last high point of the Bush presidency. That summer and fall, voters told pollsters that they weren't much interested in foreign policy. And Bush proved no match for Clinton on domestic policy. The Arkansas governor operated like a smooth insurance salesman—he had policies for everyone at every stage of life. On Election Day in 1992, the American people chose William Jefferson Clinton as the forty-second president of the United States.

Nixon immediately wrote to the new president-elect to congratulate him. "The strongest steel must pass through the hottest fire," he wrote to Clinton. "In enduring that ordeal you have demonstrated that you have the character to lead not just America but the forces of peace and freedom in the world." When no response came, he assumed the Clintons were still bitter over his comments about Hillary during the campaign. Still, too much was at stake in world affairs. Clinton would be the next president and Nixon wanted to try to influence him.[11]

In a November 19 op-ed for the *New York Times,* Nixon once again returned to the theme of America's responsibility to support

Yeltsin's reforms. "If Mr. Yeltsin survives," he wrote, "and freedom and democracy succeed in Russia, we will live in a safer world." Still Nixon received no response from Clinton or anyone on the transition team.

In early 1993, President Clinton announced plans to meet Yeltsin. Nixon, who had just returned from another trip to Russia, was pleasantly surprised to see the new president taking an interest in Russia. "It's smart," he said privately. "Shows he's presidential. And at least he's thinking about the goddamned issue."[12]

Then, on March 2, an improbable chain of events began that would eventually lead Nixon into an advisory role with yet another president. Senator Dole called Nixon and said that Clinton had told him that he wanted to call Nixon to discuss Russia. Dole, knowing that the new president needed all the help he could get on foreign policy, encouraged the idea. Within hours, the phone at Nixon's home in Saddle River rang. The voice on the other end announced itself as calling for the White House and asked if Nixon could speak to the president. Nixon waited several minutes on hold before the operator came back on the line and asked if Clinton could call back. Just before ten o'clock that night, the phone rang again, and this time Clinton was on the line. The two men talked for forty minutes.

Clinton was particularly interested in Nixon's recent trip to Russia. Nixon told him that with Yeltsin, "what you see is what you get." Clinton concurred, but wondered if the Russian president could survive. Nixon seized on Clinton's comment to make the case that Yeltsin would survive only if the U.S. helped him out. Toward the end of the call, Nixon promised Clinton that any advice he would offer in the coming years would only be on foreign policy.

"It was the best conversation with a president I've had since I was president," Nixon said, clearly impressed with the new president. "This guy does a lot of thinking."

For Nixon, the moment was personally poignant. He was acutely aware that his advice to Reagan and Bush had been in private and that neither president had seemed eager to be seen with him in public. But here was a president from the opposition party reaching out on his own to seek his opinion. And Nixon knew that Clinton, as a Democrat, could provide him with that that extra bit of approval that would seal his comeback.[13]

Later, Nixon heard that Clinton told associates the phone call was "the best conversation" he had conducted with anyone since becoming president. And he told a colleague that Nixon's post-election letter had touched him.

Soon, the Nixon-Clinton courtship was ready to go to the next level—a personal meeting. On March 8, Nixon arrived at the White House and met with Clinton. When Nixon appeared inside the White House, he was greeted by several Clinton associates, including First Lady Hillary Clinton. Then President Clinton took him aside for a private talk.

"The meeting at the White House was the best I have had since I was president," Clinton would say. The two men talked about Russia at length. And Nixon sensed the president was becoming more engaged on foreign policy. But beyond the substance of the meeting, the symbolism of it meant a great deal to Nixon. "I think that Clinton showed real guts by having me there," he told Crowley back in his office in New Jersey. "And I think we could work together on the Russian thing," he added.[14]

On March 24, Clinton again called Nixon. With Yeltsin now feuding with his own parliament, Clinton had chosen to stand by Yeltsin and sought reassurance from Nixon that he was doing the right thing. Nixon affirmed the president's decision, telling Clinton that it was "a risk to support Yeltsin, but if he goes down without U.S. support, it will be far worse."

The two men spoke again on April 26, after Yeltsin had triumphed in a referendum. After the two leaders commiserated about the media's lack of attention to the Yeltsin victory, the talk turned to Bosnia. At the end, almost in passing, Clinton casually referenced a topic near and dear to Nixon—China. The move was not lost on Nixon.

"Clinton is very clever," he said. "By mentioning China at the end of the conversation, he leaves you tantalized, waiting for the next call."

His place in history was very much on Nixon's mind in these days. He was doing his part and writing books. Still, he worried about the biographies being written about him. Historians like Stephen Ambrose, who wrote three books about Nixon, took a critical view of the Nixon era.

Nixon had long complained about historians being "liberals" or "cut-and-paste" biographers. When he was approached by Tory member of Parliament Jonathan Aitken about a sympathetic biography, Nixon not only agreed to be interviewed but became the virtual ghost editor of the book. He sent Aitken scores of previously unseen documents and diary entries. Aitken sent back entire chapters for Nixon to review and edit.

"Thank you very much for answering my questions with such speed and with such a wealth of fascinating information," Aitken wrote after Nixon had provided detailed answers to a series of questions. Nixon also encouraged former aides to meet with Aitken. And once the manuscript was completed, Nixon and his staff began trying to get the book published. Alas, it proved to be a tough sale.[15]

"Your foreknowledge of the chimes of political correctness at W. W. Norton proved all too prescient," Aitken wrote to Nixon's chief of staff, John Taylor, after yet another rejection from a publisher in New York. "For the fourth time in the curious progress of *Nixon: A Life* around the publishing houses of New York, the book was turned down by a publishing board (who had not read it) after a recommendation from a senior editor who had read it!"[16]

Nixon had feared that a book favorable to him could not win a contract in New York. So he planned accordingly. Having the book published was more important to Nixon than who published it. He urged Aitken to pitch his book to Regnery, the conservative publishing house in Washington. Aitken did so and found success.

In October 1993, Aitken wrote to Nixon that "all is well at Regnery. I have signed a contract with them and they plan to publish in April or May of next year."[17]

Still, the main books that Nixon hoped would shape his legacy were the ones he was writing. In the spring of 1993, he began working on yet another one. Tentatively called *Beyond Peace,* the new book would tackle the end of the Cold War and address what America should focus on next. Nixon clearly hoped he had more time and believed that he could use his new relationship with Clinton to impact world affairs.

But time waits for no one. And for Nixon, it was dusk. Earlier that year he had turned eighty. "Don't look at the past, look to the future," he said that day, "because if you do you may live long enough to enjoy it." He was joined at his home in Saddle River for a birthday celebration featuring a cake with eight candles—one for each decade of his life. A conference line was established so that Nixon could hear well-wishers at his Presidential Library in Yorba Linda sing "Happy Birthday." Nixon enjoyed the celebration. "I hated the idea of becoming 80 years of age until I thought of the alternative," he joked.[18]

But even as Nixon's annual doctor visits showed him to be in reasonably good health, the same could not be said for his wife. Most of Pat's days were spent at home. She called the Nixon house the "Eagle's Nest" and she rarely ventured outside of it. She had fought emphysema for years and struggled to breathe. On April 25, she was taken to the New York Hospital and it soon became apparent that cancer would take her life within weeks. Nixon tried to be strong for his daughters, who were virtually inconsolable. Meanwhile, his old friend John Connally passed away in Texas—another blow to Nixon's psyche. Nixon insisted on flying to Texas for the funeral. Afterwards he met with the family and told them Connally's greatest legacy was his children. Back home in New Jersey, he appeared worn out from the stress of the travel and the funeral.

On June 21, the Nixons should have been celebrating their fifty-third wedding anniversary. Instead, Pat was entering the last stretch of her life's journey. She had suffered from lung cancer for some time. It had grown worse over the previous few months. Then on June 22, she passed away. Just before she did, Nixon sat by her bed and told her, "Your family love you, the country loves you, and people all over the world love you." A few days later at the funeral on the grounds of the Nixon Library, a lifetime of putting on a brave face finally came to an end for Nixon. He cried openly during the funeral.[19]

Afterward, the former president hosted a reception inside the Nixon Library. Nixon spoke to the crowd, which included friends as well as former adversaries. George McGovern stayed until the very end. When asked why he came, the former Nixon opponent said simply, "You can't keep campaigning forever."

As the crowd at the reception listened to Nixon, they soon were moved to tears, as well. Nixon spoke of his love for Pat and of their shared love for their family and their grandchildren. As he looked at his grandchildren in the crowd, he told the story of the time granddaughter Jennie Eisenhower had asked Pat what she wanted to be called. Pat responded that "Grandmother" would be too formal a name and that "Grandma" sounded too old. Instead, she had told her granddaughter to simply call her "Ma."

The story was charming enough. But Nixon then surprised his audience by continuing in a way that transformed it from amusing to poignant. He said that Jennie had also wondered what to call him.

"You can call me anything," he said, "because I've been called everything."

Among those visibly moved by the words were Senator Bob Dole, and even McGovern, who wiped tears away with a handkerchief.[20]

Pat's death took a toll on Nixon. His own health had already begun to deteriorate. He suffered from a bad back, which made it painful for him to bend over. Still he labored on. He had always worried that if his work stopped then his mind would stop, too. And so he carried on in the fall of 1993, finishing the manuscript for *Beyond Peace*. Then another blow came when he learned that Haldeman had died; then in December, his friend Norman Vincent Peale passed away. In early 1994, Nixon wrote a sympathetic note to Bill Clinton when the president's mother, Virginia Kelley, died from cancer. On January 9, 1994, Nixon reached his eighty-first birthday.

In February, Nixon visited a cardiologist after he felt a throbbing sensation in his head. The doctor warned him that he could be on the road to a stroke. Still, the doctor cleared him for travel. Nixon was scheduled to journey again to Russia. Continuing his mission of trying to support the young republics that were emerging in the aftermath of the Cold War, he met with Ukrainian president Leonid Kravchuk and became the first American to address the State Duma of the Russian Federation. Yeltsin was enraged that Nixon hadn't come to see him first and attacked the former president publicly. Then he refused to meet with Nixon. Upon his return, Nixon wrote

another op-ed for the *New York Times* in which he essentially called
for America to cultivate young leaders besides Yeltsin. "But America
should also pay close attention to the new generation of Russian
leaders—many of whom I met," he wrote, "such as Grigory Yavlin-
sky, an impressive, young economist; Sergei Shakhray, the analyti-
cally minded minister of nationalities; and the formidable economics
minister, Alexander Shokhin." Nixon threw shade on Yeltsin, saying
that he was "still a political heavyweight" but no longer "a super-
man."[21] Privately, he told Monica Crowley that Yelstin was in very
bad shape politically.

Nixon sent President Clinton a report on the trip. "He'll need a
foreign policy victory since this Whitewater stuff is dominating the
news," said the former president, in reference to the first major scandal of the Clinton administration.[22] But there would be no more
conversations between Nixon and Clinton.

On April 16, Nixon attended the wedding of the daughter of his
friend Bob Abplanalp. Sitting in the church caused Nixon to reflect
on his own faith.

"Everyone goes about God differently," he said afterward. "If
there were a good preacher or minister, I'd go," he said regarding his
lack of regular attendance at church. "Besides, when I go, it's like a
show. Everyone is watching me rather than listening to the important
things being said from the pulpit."[23]

On April 18, Nixon was at home where he had been working on
an upcoming speech. At around five forty-five in the evening, he
appeared on the deck of his house with a glass of water in his hand.
Suddenly, the glass fell to the ground. He made his way into the kitchen
where his cook, Heidi Retter, was making dinner. She saw that something was wrong, helped him onto a nearby couch, and called 911.

Nixon had suffered a massive stroke—so powerful a stroke
that he could no longer speak or see. He was rushed to New York

Hospital–Cornell Medical Center. Doctors discovered "prominent brain swelling," and two days later he went into a coma. New York mayor Rudy Giuliani and Reverend Billy Graham were among those who rushed to the hospital, along with Nixon's distraught family.

Nixon's condition soon deteriorated. And after a long journey filled with many comebacks during his eighty years, Nixon's body could no longer mount a rally. At 9:08 p.m. on April 22, 1994, four days after the initial stroke and surrounded by daughters Julie and Tricia, he died.

The news struck a chord with the American people. The Presidential Library in Yorba Linda was flooded with flowers. And even old enemies praised him in the media. "His historic visits to China and the Soviet Union paved the way," Jimmy Carter said, "to the normalization of relations between our countries, and to the SALT II accords we signed with the Soviets."

But no one said more and did more in the immediate aftermath of Nixon's passing than President Clinton. To him, Nixon was "a statesman who sought to build a lasting structure of peace." Clinton declared a national day of mourning. "No less than a month before his passing," Clinton said, adding in a personal note, "he was still in touch with me about the great issues of the day." Clinton then surprised many in Washington by announcing that he would attend Nixon's funeral.

---

On April 27, 1994, light blue skies accented by grey clouds covered the Nixon Library as mourners gathered for the funeral ceremony on the grounds of the facility. In the previous days, forty-two thousand people had walked through the Nixon Library to see Nixon's coffin. Now many of them had returned for the funeral.

Nixon had helped choreograph his entire life; it was no surprise
that he helped choreograph the final scene. The stage was built right
in front of the house his father had built. This meant that as the
various speakers addressed the audience, the striking image of Nixon's
humble roots would provide the backdrop.

Nixon had also played a role in deciding who would eulogize him.
He selected California senator Pete Wilson, who was in a tough reelection bid but had presidential aspirations, and Senate Republican leader
Bob Dole, who also had ambitions for another run for president. The
funeral, televised live nationally, would give both men a platform from
which the American people could see them speak. Nixon had found
a way to help his party, even in death.

It was Dole who really rose to the occasion. With the Fords, the
Carters, the Reagans, and the Bushes sitting in the front row, Dole
delivered perhaps the greatest speech of his life. Written mostly by his
longtime friend Richard Norton Smith (whom Nixon greatly admired
for his biographies), Dole's speech began with a striking declaration:
"I believe the second half of the twentieth century will be known as
the Age of Nixon."

He then went into a rhythmic speech where he would describe
some aspect of Nixon's hardscrabble upbringing and end it with
the line, "How American." At the end, Dole, unable to control his
emotions, fought his way through the final lines. "May God bless
Richard Nixon," he said in a quaking voice. "May God bless the
United States."

It was a masterful performance by the Kansan. But it was soon
eclipsed by another eulogy, this one given by the forty-second president of the United States. If Nixon's twenty-year efforts at redemption
needed a final seal of approval, it came that day from the presence
and words of Bill Clinton. When planning his own funeral, Nixon
had conceived the idea of Clinton delivering a eulogy.

Clinton spoke of the great impact of Nixon's life after Watergate. "Remarkably, he wrote nine of his ten books after he left the presidency," he told the crowd, "working his way back into the arena he so loved by writing and thinking and engaging us in his dialogue. For the past year, even in the final weeks of his life, he gave me his wise counsel, especially with regard to Russia."

Clinton declared himself amazed at Nixon's mind. "One thing in particular left a profound impression on me," he said. "Though this man was in his ninth decade, he had an incredibly sharp and vigorous and rigorous mind. As a public man, he always seemed to believe the greatest sin was remaining passive in the face of challenges, and he never stopped living by that creed. He gave of himself with intelligence and energy and devotion to duty, and his entire country owes him a debt of gratitude for that service."

Clinton handled Watergate with grace. "Oh, yes, he knew great controversy amid defeat as well as victory," he said. "He made mistakes, and they, like his accomplishments, are a part of his life and record. But the enduring lesson of Richard Nixon is that he never gave up being part of the action and passion of his times. He said many times that unless a person has a goal, a new mountain to climb, his spirit will die." Clinton paused, then added, "Well, based on our last phone conversation and the letter he wrote me just a month ago, I can say that his spirit was very much alive to the very end."

But perhaps the most profound moment of Clinton's eulogy came when he spoke of Nixon's life as a whole. "Today is a day for his family, his friends, and his nation to remember President Nixon's life in totality. To them let us say, 'May the day of judging President Nixon on anything less than his entire life and career come to a close.'"

It was an extraordinary moment. Bill Clinton had begun his political life protesting the Nixon administration and the Vietnam War; his wife had worked to impeach Nixon for Watergate. And yet here was Clinton saying that any accurate historical account of Nixon must not begin and end with Watergate.

The moment was almost too much for some longtime Nixon observers. Providing on-air commentary for ABC News, historian Stephen Ambrose, who had spent years writing about and criticizing Nixon, could hardly believe what he was witnessing. "I think every American over 30 years old is astonished at this outpouring of affection and emotion for Richard Nixon," he said on air. "And thinking back to the summer of 1974, I just don't understand how it happened."

Ambrose continued on in his bewilderment. "No one could have predicted it," he said of Nixon's comeback, "except for one person. And I think he saw it. I think that he landed in California after the resignation and he devoted himself to this moment, making this moment happen. And he's done it." Ambrose, clearly unsettled by Nixon's accomplishment, added, "He became not just an elder statesman—to everyone's amazement but his, he's our beloved elder statesman."

Nixon was buried later that day on the grounds of his presidential library, next to Pat. The inscription on his tombstone contains a simple phrase that he chose as his epitaph: "The greatest honor history can bestow is the title of peacemaker."

# Afterword

**"I**never saw anything like it," Stephen Ambrose said in late 2001, years after Nixon's death and funeral. "It was the most amazing thing I ever witnessed in politics."[1]

Ambrose still couldn't fathom what had transpired in the last twenty years of Nixon's life. A man who had been left for dead politically (and almost died literally) had become an essential thinker and advisor on American foreign policy. What began with his return to the White House during the Carter years evolved into a more regular role as an advisor to Reagan, transformed into a position as something of a policy critic and public agitator during the Bush years, and ended with Nixon enjoying perhaps his closest relationship with any president—William Jefferson Clinton, of all people. What he might have made of that relationship had he lived through the Clinton presidency can only be imagined. Even Clinton himself had suggested that he would have continued to rely on Nixon's advice.

Clinton had been right in his eulogy—Nixon's entire life deserves to be remembered. And while his ascent to power and use of power as president have been extensively written about, his fall from power and its aftermath also deserve attention. In the last twenty years of his life without the trappings of power, Richard Nixon exercised influence in a way few former presidents have—before or since.

For everyone, life is about overcoming obstacles. And Nixon certainly endured his share of challenges in his twilight years. His health declined, he struggled for years to make money, and he faced the constant torment of the memories of his resignation. Yet through it all he found a new life and a renewed purpose. Without the presidency, he had to rely on his greatest gift—his mind. He wrote nine books, dozens of articles, and gave countless speeches in an attempt to influence foreign policy. The record shows he succeeded beyond what even he probably could have imagined.

He helped guide Reagan toward historic agreements that led to the end of the Cold War. He provided an important public nudge to Bush during the uncertain days following the collapse of Communism. He helped prevent an international crisis—Tiananmen Square—from destroying U.S.-China relations. And he helped Clinton find a policy that would support the reformers in Russia and in former Communist Eastern European countries. Nixon, sensing the end was nearing, had specifically asked that Clinton deliver one of the eulogies at his funeral. He knew that Clinton was perfectly suited to provide the final bit of redemption on his long road back. Throughout this time, Nixon was right and wrong at various points. He was mostly right in his advice to Reagan, although he perhaps worried too much about the impact of Soviet conventional warfare. With Bush he was right to suggest supporting Yeltsin. And with Clinton, he correctly urged the president to look beyond Yeltsin to the next generation. All in all, not a bad scorecard for the elder statesman.

Though no one has ever written of the entire Nixon post-presidency, many have taken exception to Nixon's constant campaign to make his voice heard during this time. Some have accused him of having a secret plan. That is certainly not reflected in the evidence, nor in the memories of those who were around him in those days. What emerged from the abyss after Watergate was an organic effort by a restless mind. His presidency might have ended, but Nixon's mind was still very much alive and he wanted to help shape policy in Washington.

In the end, Nixon prevailed because he refused to fail. He could not and would not let Watergate be the end of him. He set out on a course to be something and to do something with the rest of his life. Like a ship at sea amid stormy waters and stiff winds, he followed his compass and found his way back into the harbor. And once he was safely there, people wanted to hear what the old captain had to say. Presidents listened to him, foreign leaders respected him, and more and more average Americans began to forgive him.

"He didn't just survive in those last years," Ambrose said. "He thrived. He became important again. He became acceptable again. He almost became indispensable. Just incredible."[2]

After the fall, Richard Nixon endured for twenty impactful years that helped shape the course of events for his country and for himself.

# Selected Bibliography

The research in this book primarily came from the Nixon post-presidential files at the Richard Nixon Library in Yorba Linda, California, and from interviews with Nixon's aides and members of his family. In addition, the following books also provided helpful insight into Nixon's later years.

Aitken, Jonathan. *Nixon: A Life*. Washington, D.C.: Regnery, 1993.

Ambrose, Stephen. *Nixon: The Education of a Politician 1913–1962*. New York: Simon & Schuster, 1979.

_____. *Nixon: The Triumph of a Politician 1962–1972*. New York: Simon & Schuster, 1989.

_____. *Nixon: Ruin and Recovery 1973–1990*. New York: Simon & Schuster, 1991.

_____. *Nixon: The Triumph of a Politician 1962–1972*. New York: Simon & Schuster, 1989.

Anson, Robert Sam. *Exile: The Unquiet Oblivion of Richard M. Nixon*. New York: Simon & Schuster, 1984.

Black, Conrad. *Richard Nixon: A Life in Full*. New York: Public Affairs, 2007.

Buchanan, Patrick J. *Right from the Beginning*. Washington, D.C.: Regnery, 1990.

Crowley, Monica. *Nixon in Winter: The Final Revelations*. New York: I.B. Tauris, 1998.

_____. *Nixon Off the Record*. New York: I.B. Tauris, 1995.

Dallek, Robert. *Nixon and Kissinger: Partners in Power*. New York: HarperCollins, 2007.

Dean, John. *Blind Ambition: The White House Years*. New York: Simon & Schuster, 1975.

Haldeman, H. R. *The Haldeman Diaries: Inside the Nixon White House*. New York: Putnam, 1994.

Hoff, Joan. *Nixon Reconsidered*. New York: Harper Collins, 1994.

Eisenhower, Julie Nixon. *Pat Nixon: The Untold Story*. New York: Simon & Schuster, 1983.

Ehrlichman, John. *Witness to Power: The Nixon Years*. New York, Simon & Schuster, 1982.

Lungren, John C. *Healing Richard Nixon: A Doctor's Memoir*. Lexington, Kentucky: University Press of Kentucky, 2003.

MacMillan, Margaret. *Nixon and Mao: The Week That Changed the World*. New York: Random House, 2007.

Morris, Roger. *Richard Milhous Nixon: The Rise of an American Politician*. New York, Henry Holt, 1990.

Nixon, Richard. *1999: Victory Without War*. New York: Simon & Schuster, 1988.

_____. *Beyond Peace*. New York: Random House, 1994.

_____. *In the Arena: A Memoir of Victory, Defeat and Renewal*. New York: Simon & Schuster, 1990.

_____. *Leaders*. New York: Random House, 1982.

_____. *No More Vietnams*. New York: Avon, 1985.

_____. *Real Peace*. New York: Little, Brown, 1983.

_____. *The Real War*. New York: Warner Books, 1980.

_____. *RN: The Memoirs of Richard Nixon*. New York: Simon & Schuster, 1978.

_____. *Seize the Moment: America's Challenge in a One-Superpower World*. New York: Simon & Schuster, 1992.

Perlstein, Rick. *Nixonland: The Rise of a President and the Fracturing of America*. New York: Scribner, 2009.

Reeves, Richard. *President Nixon: Alone in the White House*. New York: Simon & Schuster, 2001.

Reston, James Jr. *The Conviction of Richard Nixon: The Untold Story of the Frost/Nixon Interviews*. New York: Harmony Books, 2007.

Safire, William. *Before the Fall: An Inside View of the Pre-Watergate White House*. New York: Random House, 1977.

Small, Melvin. *The Presidency of Richard Nixon*. Lawrence, Kansas: University of Kansas Press, 1999.

Strober, Gerald S. and Deborah Hart Strober. *Nixon: An Oral History of His Presidency*. New York: HarperCollins, 1994.

Thompson, Jake H. *Bob Dole: The Republicans' Man for All Seasons*. New York: Donald I. Fine, 1994.

White, Theodore. *Breach of Faith: The Fall of Richard Nixon*. New York: Antebellum, 1975.

Wicker, Tom. *One of Us: Richard Nixon and the American Dream*. New York: Random House, 1991.

Wills, Garry. *Nixon Agonistes: The Crisis of the Self-Made Man*. New York: Houghton Mifflin, 1969.

Woodward, Bob and Carl Bernstein. *The Final Days*. New York: Simon & Schuster, 1975.

# ACKNOWLEDGMENTS

Years ago, as a young White House staffer, I had the fortune of hosting David McCullough as he prepared to give senior Bush White House staffers a preview of his book on John Adams. Before the briefing, I made small talk with McCullough in my little office in what was then known as the Old Executive Office Building (later renamed the Eisenhower Executive Office Building). McCullough took great (and undue) notice of me and asked what I wanted to do when I left the White House. When I told him that I might like to write history, he gave me two pieces of advice.

"It does no injury to history to make it readable," he told me in what I would later learn was an axiom he often used. Second, he said when writing a biography to remember that one of the biggest myths in the world is "the myth of the self-made man."

Years later, I can still recall both pieces of advice; years later, I still marvel at their wisdom.

This book bears my name, but many hands were involved in the researching, editing, and thinking that went into it. One of the greatest ironies—for a biography of Nixon—is that perhaps no one did more to help me shape this story than a Harvard professor.

While I was completing a graduate degree at Harvard, this book started as my thesis. My advisor, June Erlick, spent months helping me refine my research and my writing and get closer to the heart of the story to be told. Thanks to her guidance, the thesis eventually won a Dean's Prize for Outstanding Thesis—something that would have amused Nixon, given his disdain for Harvard and other elite colleges. June's own biography of journalist Irma Flaquer was known to me well before I arrived in her classroom at Harvard. I'm grateful that she spent so much time helping me on this project. She is a great writer, but she's an even better friend.

Richard Norton Smith provided invaluable assistance throughout with his own insights into Nixon. Richard is not only the best historian in America, but he also knew Nixon. Plus, he's been a wonderful friend to me for nearly twenty-five years.

The story of the journey to tell this story deserves to be told, as well. When I first began thinking of turning the thesis into a book, I immediately spoke with Eric Jackson. He took a chance on me when he served as president of World Ahead Publishing and published my first book, *Ike's Final Battle: The Road to Little Rock and the Challenge of Equality*. At the time I pitched this new book to him, his publishing house was being sold and a new direction was being taken in the books it chose to publish. Diplomacy being one of his many gifts, Eric politely suggested a book about Richard Nixon might not be a good fit. Still, his advice and guidance over the years have been invaluable to me. And I am indebted to him for all he has done for me.

At that point, I hired Mike Hamilburg to shop the book around the New York publishing world. Mike, a legend as a literacy agent, sadly died two years ago. But in the time that we were together he did incredible work on my behalf. Richard Nixon remains a controversial subject in publishing. And there were many closed doors as we made the rounds pitching the book. Still, Mike forged ahead. The first offer came in 2012 from Skyhorse (a member of the Simon & Schuster family that published so many of Nixon's own books). Though we eventually passed on the offer, it was proof that a market did exist for an objective look at Nixon's final years. Then with the help of long-time friend Ken Mehlman, we reached an agreement with Regnery Publishing in 2013. And there are no words to express how grateful I am to the entire Regnery team. They believed in me and believed in this project from the beginning. Marji Ross, Harry Crocker, Elizabeth Kantor, Timothy Meads, and Alex Novak supported me throughout the process and were more than patient as I was continually delayed in turning in the manuscript.

I'd also like to thank the extraordinary team at the Richard Nixon Foundation and the Richard Nixon Library and Museum. I arrived at the Nixon Library not long after the two separate institutions—the library where the documents resided and the foundation which ran the museum and the exhibits—were finally merged. The media reported great tension between the two sides of the Nixon operation. But I never experienced any of it. The post-presidency papers are housed inside the library's archives—though no other researcher had the access to them that I did. Still, I experienced no challenges in getting the documents I needed. The Nixon Foundation was vitally helpful to me, especially former executive directors Ron Walker and Sandy Quinn. And of course, Fred Fielding, one of my colleagues from the Eisenhower Institute, proved indispensable as always in his role as Nixon Foundation Board chairman. I'm also grateful to the archivists at the Nixon Library with whom I worked on this book: Tim Naftali, Greg Cummings, Pamela Eisenberg, Mike Ellzey, Mellissa Heddon, Ida Kelley, Meghan Lee-Parker, Ryan Pettigrew, and Jason Schultz.

The license for the photograph of the exterior of the Richard Nixon Research Library (https://commons.wikimedia.org/wiki/File:Nixon_Presidential_Library_%26_Museum_(30873118546).jpg ) can be viewed at https://creativecommons.org/licenses/by/2.0/legalcode. The license for the photograph of the interior of the Nixon Library (https://commons.wikimedia.org/wiki/File:Nixon_Presidential_Library_%26_Museum_(30792944352).jpg) can be found at https://creativecommons.org/licenses/by/2.0/legalcode. The license for the photograph of the reflecting pool on the grounds of the Library (https://commons.wikimedia.org/wiki/File:Nixon_Presidential_Library_%26_Museum_(30873118236).jpg) can be found at https://creativecommons.org/

licenses/by/2.0/legalcode. The license for the photograph of Nixon's birthplace (https://commons.wikimedia.org/wiki/File:Nixon_Presidential_Library_%26_Museum_(30274784204).jpg) can be found at https://creativecommons.org/licenses/by/2.0/legalcode.

Of course, this project about the Nixon post-presidency could not have happened without the cooperation of the Nixon family. I'm grateful to Ed and Tricia Cox, David and Julie Eisenhower, and to Chris Cox, who first suggested to me that no one had written a complete history of his grandfather's post-presidency.

Closer to home, a number of friends and family helped get me to the finish line. I'd like to thank Jerry and Sue Pipes, Kerry and Beth Pipes, Ella Pipes, Nina Pipes, Bruce and Chanda Harville, Nick and Trisha Troutz, Grayson Troutz, Hunter Troutz, Guinn and Elsie Arrington, Joe and Karen Arrington, Tommy and Judy Pipes, Robert and Julie Camacho, Micaela Camacho, Greg and Stacey Losher, Corey and Lisa Stone, Drew and Triniti Hall, Ken Mehlman, Troy and Meredith Okruylik, Brannon and Meredith Latimer, Doug and Ruth Denman, Chris and Emily Trigger, Ty and Natalie Smith, Tom and Betsy Price, Glen and Brenda Whitley, Devan Allen, Scott Corley, Kay Granger, Roger and Patty Williams, Colby and Jennifer Hale, Chris and Kari Freeland, Robert and Tricia Earley, Archie and Olivia Manning, Jay and Katie Danzi, the Ruben Zapata family, Robert Boulware, Brent and Leslie Stephens, Todd and Wendy Collinsworth, Justin and Yvette Wardlaw, Ronnie and Darbie Brown, Steve and Stacy Hamilton, Joel Glenn, Robert and Brenna Head, George P. and Amanda Bush, Don and Susan Evans, Scott and Michelle Marlow, Mike Rushing, Alexis Groesch, Rita Eatherly, Dow Finsterwald, Conor Reeves, Brian Schorsten, Taylor Tivis, Mike Schultz, Jeff Hunter, Bryson Miles, Paul Muse, Casey Shane, Tim Fleet, Michael P. Shannon, Joe and Salome Regan, Bryan and Mary Beth Cox, Cade Harris, Blaine Bull, James Taylor, Tucker Eskew, Matthew Dowd,

David Cooke, Jay Chapa, Bob Riley, Charles Daniels, TJ Patterson, Betsy and Tom Price, Carlos Flores, Sal Espino, Kelly Allen Gray, Gyna Bivens, Dennis Shingleton, Zim Zimmerman, Danny Scarth, Brian Byrd, Cary Moon, Randle Harwood, Susan Alanis, Jungus Jordan, Ann Zadeh, Chris and Sally Gavras, Jeff Hooper, Greg Blaies, Grant Blaies, Wes Hightower, Jimmy and Adrienne Garza, Paula Bledsoe, Mel Hailey, Roy Brooks, Marc and Tonya Veasey, Danny Jensen, J.R. Hernandez, Karina Erickson, GK Maenius, Chris Perkins, Ash Wright, Steve and Lisa Hotchkiss, Steve and Camille Pinkos, J.D. Johnson, Gary Fickes, Ryan Lindsey, Andy Nguyen, Casey and Chavon Taylor, David and Scooter Cox, Scott Hamilton, Shawn Michael, Jordan White, Jeremy Fudge, Lynden Melmed, Robert Caballero, Constance Pegushin, David Berry, Derek Stanley, John McConnell, Matthew Scully, Eric Schmutz, Betsy Holahan, Karyl Ford, Barrett and Jennifer Fischer, Bo and Hillary Parker, Jarod and Beth Cox, Derran and Sharon Lackey, Kim Gill, Alyse Chung, Justin Furnace, Archie and Olivia Manning, Brad Cunningham, Dick Lowe, Hunter Enis, David and Mattie Parker, Tom and Amanda Stallings, Marcus and Jamie Mainord, Brent Barrow, Gary and Sylvia McCaleb, Bryan and Dana McCaleb, Dak and Robyn Hatfield, Craig Smith, Allison Ball Swope, Matt and Mandy Orlie, Matt and Christy Tyson, Matt and Vivian Campbell, Albon Head, Brian and Jeanette Davis, John and Laura Barclay, T.J. and Corbin Wilson, Mark and Kim Jacoby, James and Ann Bankes, Bryan and Sandy Mitchell, Chris and Tristyn Anagnostis, Kelby and Sharon Pope, Matt and Shelly Kacsmaryk, Brookley Valencia, Stewart and Joby Young, Brian and Courtney Tulbert, Connie Smith, Dana McKenzie, Doug Mocek, Jimmy and Paige Biggs, Chandler Merritt, Tim Hood, Dorothea Wolfson, Gary Blake, Justin and Courtney Holt, Jeffrey and Kelly Blavatt, Brian and Vicki Tinsley, Kirk and Kristen Saarloos, Laura and Jack Goleman, Seth and Lana Peugh, Bill and Danna West, Jason and

Samantha Skaggs, Mike and Patsy Thomas, Tory and Kelley Vieth, and Mike and Jan Flynn.

And of course, I am grateful for my family for allowing me to at times live what Stephen Ambrose called "a monk's life." The months and years spent researching and writing this represented times that I couldn't always be with them. But they never failed to show me grace through it all. I'm especially grateful to my wife, Lacie, for being by my side, encouraging me in the project, and helping to run the household while I was away. And I'm thankful for our kids: Lincoln, Crosby, and Betsy. They, too, helped make this book possible. And it's especially rewarding now that they are school-aged kids and have taken an interest in their dad's work.

Most of all, I'm thankful to a loving and graceful God who guides me every day. He has blessed me beyond what I could have ever imagined. And long ago he gave me an innate interest in redemption. This to me is the story behind every story—the seed that leads to the flowering of life. How ordinary humans struggle to overcome extraordinary setbacks is the universal story. In a spiritual sense, no one succeeds this side of Heaven. But there is work to be done every day by everyone to try and make amends for our failings. This is a universal story because redemption is a universal struggle. This fascination with redemption led me to write about Dwight Eisenhower and civil rights twelve years ago; it also led me to write about Richard Nixon and the aftermath of Watergate. I pray that the reading of this story will bless others as much as the research and writing of it blessed me.

# Notes

## Chapter One: The Beginning of the End
1. Nixon post-presidential papers.
2. Ibid.

## Chapter Two: In Exile
1. Nixon post-presidential papers.
2. Ibid.
3. Ibid.
4. Jonathan Aitken, *Nixon: A Life* (Washington: Regnery, 1993), 523.
5. Robert Sam Anson, *Exile: The Unquiet Oblivion of Richard Nixon* (New York: Simon & Schuster, 1984), 20.
6. Nixon post-presidential papers.
7. Anson, *Exile*, 23.
8. Ibid., 21.
9. Ibid., 22.
10. Nixon post-presidential papers.
11. Stephen Ambrose, *Nixon: Ruin and Recovery 1972–1990* (New York: Simon & Schuster), 447.
12. Author interview of Ed Cox, August 1, 2009.
13. Anson, *Exile*, 22.

## Chapter Three: The Pardon
1. Jonathan Aitken, *Nixon: A Life* (Washington: Regnery, 1993), 529.
2. Ibid., 529.
3. Author interview of Ken Khachigian, April 3, 2011.
4. Stephen Ambrose, *Nixon: Ruin and Recovery 1972–1990* (New York: Simon & Schuster), 458.
5. Nixon post-presidential papers.
6. Ambrose, *Nixon: Ruin and Recovery*, 460.

7.   Anson, *Exile*, 60.
8.   Nixon post-presidential papers.

Chapter Four: A Near-Death Experience
1.   Nixon post-presidential papers.
2.   Ibid.
3.   John C. Lungren, *Healing Richard Nixon: A Doctor's Memoir* (Lexington, Kentucky: University Press of Kentucky, 2003), 16.
4.   Ibid., 19.
5.   Robert Sam Anson, *Exile: The Unquiet Oblivion of Richard Nixon* (New York: Simon & Schuster, 1984), 62.
6.   Stephen Ambrose, *Nixon: Ruin and Recovery 1972–1990* (New York: Simon & Schuster), 466–67.
7.   Anson, *Exile: The Unquiet Oblivion of Richard Nixon*, 67–68.
8.   Ambrose, *Nixon: Ruin and Recovery*, 466.
9.   Lungren, *Healing Richard Nixon*, 21.
10.  Ibid., 26–27.
11.  Ibid., 32–33.
12.  Ibid., 36–37.
13.  Ibid., 85.
14.  Ibid., 87–88.
15.  Nixon post-presidential papers.
16.  Ambrose, *Nixon: Ruin and Recovery*, 473.
17.  Nixon post-presidential papers.
18.  Ibid.

Chapter Five: The Memoirs
1.   Nixon post-presidential papers.
2.   Ibid.
3.   Ibid.
4.   Author interview of Ken Khachigian, April 3, 2011.
5.   Ibid.
6.   Author interview of Loie Gaunt, May 13, 2011.

7. Robert Sam Anson, *Exile: The Unquiet Oblivion of Richard Nixon* (New York: Simon & Schuster, 1984), 89–90.
8. Nixon post-presidential papers.
9. Anson, *Exile*, 116–17.
10. Author interview of Loie Gaunt, April 5, 2011.
11. Author interview of Ken Khachigian.
12. Nixon post-presidential papers.
13. Ibid.
14. Anson, *Exile*, 180.
15. Nixon post-presidential papers.
16. Author interview of Hugh Hewitt, July 9, 2019.
17. Nixon post-presidential papers.
18. Stephen Ambrose, *Nixon: Ruin and Recovery 1972–1990* (New York: Simon & Schuster), 489.
19. William F. Buckley, "Opening Up Détente," *National Review*, March 19, 1976.
20. Nixon post-presidential papers.
21. Ibid.
22. Author interview of Ken Khachigian.
23. Julie Nixon Eisenhower, *Pat Nixon: The Untold Story* (New York, Simon and Schuster, 1983), 448.
24. Ibid., 450.
25. Ibid., 453.
26. Nixon post-presidential papers.
27. Ambrose, *Nixon: Ruin and Recovery*, 501.

## Chapter Six: Interviews and Apologies

1. Nixon post-presidential papers.
2. Robert Sam Anson, *Exile: The Unquiet Oblivion of Richard Nixon* (New York: Simon & Schuster, 1984), 114.
3. Ibid., 151.
4. Jonathan Aitken, *Nixon: A Life* (Washington, Regnery 1993), 540.

5.  Author interview of Ken Khachigian, April 3, 2011.

6.  Anson, *Exile*, 154.

7.  James Reston Jr., *The Conviction of Richard Nixon: The Untold Story of the Frost/Nixon Interviews*, (New York, Harmony Books, 2007), 111.

8.  Ibid., 106.

9.  Ibid., 132–33.

10. Author interview of Ken Khachigian.

11. Ibid.

12. Anson, *Exile*, 175–76.

13. Ibid., 176.

14. Author interview of Ken Khachigian.


Chapter Seven: The First Steps Back

1.  Nixon post-presidential papers.

2.  Ibid.

3.  Ibid.

4.  Author interview of Ed Cox, August 1, 2009.

5.  Nixon post-presidential papers.

6.  Richard Nixon, *In the Arena: A Memoir of Victory, Defeat and Renewal* (New York, Simon and Schuster 1990), 45.

7.  Robert Sam Anson, *Exile: The Unquiet Oblivion of Richard Nixon* (New York: Simon & Schuster, 1984), 191.

8.  Ibid., 188.

9.  "Nixon Welcomed to Kentucky by a Cheering Crowd," *New York Times*, July 2, 1978.

10. Ibid.

11. "Nixon's Nemesis: Political Prankster Dick Tuck Dead at 94," *Tucson Sentinel*, May 29, 2018.

12. Nixon post-presidential papers.

13. Anson, *Exile: The Unquiet Oblivion of Richard Nixon*, 197.

14. Jonathan Aitken, *Nixon: A Life* (Washington, Regnery 1993), 544.

15. Ibid., 546.
16. Ibid., 547.
17. Ibid.
18. Ibid., 552.
19. Stephen Ambrose, *Nixon: Ruin and Recovery 1972–1990* (New York: Simon & Schuster), 522.
20. William F. Buckley, *National Review*, December 22, 1978.
21. Nixon post-presidential papers.

Chapter Eight: The Move to New York
1. Author interview of Hugh Hewitt, July 9, 2011.
2. Ibid.
3. Conrad Black, *Richard Nixon: A Life in Full* (New York, PublicAffairs 2007), 1,021.
4. Stephen Ambrose, *Nixon: Ruin and Recovery 1972–1990* (New York: Simon & Schuster), 525.
5. Ibid., 526.
6. Ibid., 526.
7. Nixon post-presidential papers.
8. Ibid.
9. Author interview of Loie Gaunt, April 5, 2011.
10. Author interview of Ken Khachigian, April 3, 2011.
11. "The Ex-President's Men Reunite at San Clemente," *New York Times*, September 4, 1979.
12. Nixon post-presidential papers.

Chapter Nine: The 1980 Election
1. Author interview of Ken Khachigian, April 3, 2011.
2. "Nixon and Walters," *Washington Post*, May 9, 1980.
3. Author interview of Ken Khachigian.
4. Author interview of Ed Cox, August 1, 2009.
5. Author interview of Robert Odle, November 10, 2008.
6. *Washington Post*, July 28, 1980.

7. Richard M. Nixon, letter to the editor, *New York Times*, July 17, 1980.

8. "Why Nixon Believes We Are Losing the Race on Land, on Sea and in the Air," *Parade*, October 5, 1980.

9. Nixon post-presidential papers.

10. Ibid.

11. Ibid.

12. Ibid.

13. Ibid.

14. Ibid.

15. Robert Sam Anson, *Exile: The Unquiet Oblivion of Richard Nixon* (New York: Simon & Schuster, 1984), 238.

## Chapter Ten: Advisor to the President

1. Nixon post-presidential papers.

2. Ibid.

3. Ibid.

4. Ibid.

5. Ibid.

6. Ibid.

7. Ibid.

8. Ibid.

9. Ibid.

10. Robert Sam Anson, *Exile: The Unquiet Oblivion of Richard Nixon* (New York: Simon & Schuster, 1984), 252.

11. Nixon post-presidential papers.

12. Ibid.

## Chapter Eleven: A Home for the Nixon Library

1. *New York Times*, April 27, 1975, https://www.nytimes.com/1975/04/27/archives/nixon-library-plan-hailed-at-usc.html.

2. Bill Peterson, "Nixon Library Proposal Stirs Ruckus at Duke," *Washington Post*, August 31, 1981, https://www.washingtonpost.com/archive/politics/1981/08/31/nixon-library-proposal-stirs-ruckus-at-duke/547961ee-8ea1-4464-bb2c-16dce23a85a3/?utm_term=.d605acde0252.

3. Ibid.

4. Judith Cummings, "San Clemente Eager for Nixon Library," *New York Times*, May 28, 1983, https://www.nytimes.com/1983/05/28/us/san-clemente-eager-for-nixon-library.html.

5. Mariann Hansen, "San Clemente Closes Book with Finger-Pointing," *Los Angeles Times*, November 29, 1987, https://www.latimes.com/archives/la-xpm-1987-11-29-me-25421-story.html

6. Ibid.

## Chapter Twelve: Navigating the Turbulence

1. Richard Nixon, *Leaders* (New York, Random House 1982), 8.

2. Telford Taylor, "A President on His Peers," *New York Times*, October 31, 1982, http://movies2.nytimes.com/books/98/06/14/specials/nixon-leaders.html.

3. Nixon post-presidential papers.

4. Ibid.

5. Ibid.

## Chapter Thirteen: The Evil Empire

1. Anthony Lewis, "Abroad at Home; Onward, Christian Soldiers," *New York Times*, March 10, 1983, https://www.nytimes.com/1983/03/10/opinion/abroad-at-home-onward-christian-soldiers.html.

2. Nixon post-presidential papers.

3. Ibid.

4. Jonathan Aitken, *Nixon: A Life* (Washington: Regnery, 1993), 556.

5. Nixon post-presidential papers.

## Chapter Fourteen: The 1984 Election

1. Morley Safer, CBS, April 8, 1984.
2. Nixon post-presidential papers.
3. Ibid.
4. *New York Times*, May 10, 1984, https://www.nytimes.com/1984/05/10/us/nixon-wins-applause-from-newspaper-editors.html.
5. Jonathan Friendly, "Nixon Wins Applause from Newspaper Editors," *New York Times*, July 26, 1984, https://www.nytimes.com/1984/07/26/us/nixon-returns-for-kitchen-debate.html.
6. John Herbers, "After Decade, Nixon Is Gaining Favor," *New York Times*, August 5, 1984.
7. Nixon post-presidential papers.
8. Ibid.
9. Ibid.
10. Ibid.
11. Ibid.

## Chapter Fifteen: The Sage of Saddle River

1. "He's Back: The Rehabilitation of Richard Nixon," *Newsweek*, May 1986.
2. "Lunch Visit by Nixon Thrills a Burger King," *New York Times*, April 4, 1986, https://www.nytimes.com/1986/04/04/nyregion/lunch-visit-by-nixon-thrills-a-burger-king.html.
3. Gary Lee, "Nixon Meets with Gorbachev," *Washington Post*, July 19, 1986. https://www.washingtonpost.com/archive/politics/1986/07/19/nixon-meets-with-gorbachev/4ddd28e0-f1e4-4164-9008-76e09a342e60/?utm_term=.c6278735dae4.
4. Nixon post-presidential papers.
5. Ibid.
6. Ibid.
7. Ibid.
8. Ibid.

9. Bill Peterson, "Nixon: This Isn't a Watergate," *Washington Post*, December 10, 1986, https://www.washingtonpost.com/archive/ politics/1986/12/10/nixon-this-isnt-a-watergate/db343ba0-2f74- 4b86-b11e-b83b0fcfb6df/?utm_term=.3936da9455e7.

10. Nixon post-presidential papers.

11. Linda Kay, "Nixon on Hayes: 'Not an Ordinary Man,'" *Chicago Tribune*, March 18, 1987, https://www.chicagotribune.com/news/ ct-xpm-1987-03-18-8701210563-story.html

## Chapter Sixteen: The Public Critic

1. Richard M. Nixon and Henry Kissinger, "To Withdraw Missiles, We Must Add Conditions," *Los Angeles Times*, April 26, 1987.

2. James Reston, "Washington; Nixon and Kissinger," New York Times, April 29, 1987, https://www.nytimes.com/1987/04/29/ opinion/washington-nixon-and-kissinger.html?mtrref=www. google.com&gwh=E0DC7E4A53EAA69BE372B9C264B44DBE &gwt.

3. Nixon post-presidential papers.

4. Ibid.

5. Ibid.

6. Ibid.

7. Jonathan Aitken, *Nixon: A Life* (Washington: Regnery, 1993), 556.

8. Ibid., 556.

9. Jake H. Thompson, *Bob Dole: The Republicans' Man For All Seasons* (New York, Donald I. Fine, 1994), 223.

10. Nixon post-presidential papers.

11. Ibid.

12. Ibid.

13. Aitken, *Nixon*, 565.

14. Paul Kennedy, "Richard Nixon's Vision of the Future," *Washington Post*, April 17, 1988, https://www.washingtonpost. com/archive/entertainment/books/1988/04/17/

richard-nixons-vision-of-the-future/cd99c040-2781-40c1-bd00-
c40608fd9511/?utm_term=.2da478b75343.

15. David Johnston, "Nixon's Big Regret: Bombing Delay," *New York Times*, April 11, 1988, https://www.nytimes.
com/1988/04/11/us/nixon-s-big-regret-bombing-delay.
html?mtrref=www.google.com&gwh=4804A5DC85C24A0CEF
0E288D949196E6&gwt=pay.

16. George Will, "*Détente*, Reagan-Style," *Washington Post*, May 26, 1988, https://www.washingtonpost.com/archive/
opinions/1988/05/26/detente-reagan-style/144d71e1-cf2c-4b82-
aa67-c599fab804b1/?utm_term=.fb6e93327d38.

17. Nixon post-presidential papers.

18. Richard Nixon, "Dealing with Gorbachev," *New York Times Magazine*, March 1988, https://www.nytimes.com/1988/03/13/
magazine/dealing-with-gorbachev.html?mtrref=www.google.com
&gwh=8A86D9AC885B6115D5BA997641A6B6EA&gwt=pay.

Chapter Seventeen: The 1988 Election and the Bush
Administration

1. Nixon post-presidential papers.

2. Ibid.

3. Ibid.

4. Ibid.

5. Ibid.

6. Ibid.

7. Ibid.

8. Celestine Bohlen, "Commuter Nixon Pulling Out of Manhattan," *New York Times*, September 22, 1988, https://www.nytimes.
com/1988/09/22/nyregion/commuter-nixon-pulling-out-of-
manhattan.html.

9. Michael Korda, "Nixon, Mine Host," *New Yorker*, May 1994, https://www.newyorker.com/magazine/1994/05/09/nixon-mine-
host.

10. Richard M. Nixon, "China Policy: Revulsion Real, Reprisal Wrong," *Los Angeles Times*, June 25, 1989, https://www.latimes.com/archives/la-xpm-1989-06-25-op-6087-story.html.

11. Nixon post-presidential papers.

12. Andrew Rosenthal, "Nixon Tells of China at White House Dinner," *New York Times*, November 7, 1989, https://www.nytimes.com/1989/11/07/world/nixon-tells-of-china-at-white-house-dinner.html.

13. John F. Stacks and Strobe Talbott, "Interview with Richard Nixon. Paying the Price," *Time*, April 2, 1990, http://content.time.com/time/subscriber/article/0,33009,969732-1,00.html

14. Richard Nixon, *In the Arena: A Memoir of Victory, Defeat and Renewal*, (New York, Simon & Schuster 1990), 72.

15. Ibid., 336.

16. Ibid., 354.

17. Ibid., 42–43.

18. Nixon post-presidential papers.

19. R. W. Apple, "Another Nixon Summit, at His Library," *New York Times*, July 20, 1990, https://www.nytimes.com/1990/07/20/us/another-nixon-summit-at-his-library.html.

20. Ibid.

21. Author interview of Richard Norton Smith, September 20, 2010.

22. Jonathan Aitken, *Nixon: A Life* (Regnery, 1993), 569.

Chapter Eighteen: The Last Mile
1. Nixon post-presidential papers.

2. Monica Crowley, *Nixon in Winter: The Final Revelations* (New York: I.B. Tauris, 1998), 16–17.

3. Ibid., 22.

4. Ibid., 25–26.

5. Ibid., 221–22.

6. Ibid., 224.

7. Ibid., 229.

8. Richard M. Nixon, "Why," *New York Times*, January 6, 1991, https://archive.nytimes.com/www.nytimes.com/ref/opinion/15opclassic.html?_r=3&scp=6&sq=richard%2520kind&st=cse.
9. Crowley, *Nixon in Winter*, 224.
10. Ibid., 237.
11. Ibid., 244.
12. Nixon post-presidential papers.
13. Crowley, *Nixon in Winter*, 43.
14. Ibid., 44.
15. Ibid., 14.
16. Richard M. Nixon, "Gorbachev's Crisis—and America's Opportunity," *Washington Post*, June 2, 1991.
17. Crowley, *Nixon in Winter*, 66.

Chapter Nineteen: The Greatest Honor
1. Monica Crowley, *Nixon in Winter: The Final Revelations* (New York: I.B. Tauris, 1998), 275.
2. Ibid., 68.
3. Nixon post-presidential papers.
4. Thomas L. Friedman, "Nixon's 'Save Russia' Memo: Bush Feels the Sting," *New York Times*, March 11, 1992, https://www.nytimes.com/1992/03/11/world/nixon-s-save-russia-memo-bush-feels-the-sting.html?mtrref=www.google.com&gwh=B473589692C42E88712DCEC39C5A9D67&gwt=pay.
5. Nixon post-presidential papers.
6. Ibid.
7. Crowley, *Nixon in Winter*, 83.
8. Ibid., 86–87.
9. R. W. Apple Jr. "For Clinton and Nixon, a Rarefied Bond," *New York Times*, April 25, 1994, https://www.nytimes.com/1994/04/25/us/for-clinton-and-nixon-a-rarefied-bond.html?mtrref=www.google.com&gwh=866E856F05F1C6A3FEAFC1C9FECDC614&gwt=pay.

10. Nixon post-presidential papers.
11. Nixon post-presidential papers.
12. Crowley, *Nixon in Winter*, 127.
13. Ibid., 128–29.
14. Ibid., 131.
15. Nixon post-presidential papers.
16. Ibid.
17. Ibid.
18. *New York Times*, January 10, 1993, https://www.nytimes. com/1993/01/10/us/nixon-is-80-and-elvis-joins-party. html?mtrref=www.google.com&gwh=7FC9D46D565215B4BB8F 879709499F96&gwt=pay.
19. Crowley, *Nixon in Winter*, 393.
20. Author interview of Richard Norton Smith, September 20, 2010.
21. Nixon post-presidential papers.
22. Crowley, *Nixon in Winter*, 154.
23. Ibid., 401.

Afterword
1. Author interview of Stephen Ambrose, November 2, 2001.
2. Ibid.

# INDEX